A CINCH—
Amazing Works
from the
Columbia Review

A CINCH

Published for the Columbia Review *at*

—*Amazing Works*
from the Columbia Review
Edited by
Leslie Gottesman,
Hilton Obenzinger,
and Alan Senauke

Columbia University Press : New York
and London : 1969

Introduction

In the beginning you go to school, and we edit the *Columbia Review*. Did you know what these amazing works were going to do to you? You shall knuckle under. Almost unknown, almost unavailable, the *Columbia Review* is on the moon. For the last ten years it has been the only magazine to do this. It's the truth. Up your brains!

The "May-I-touch-your-pants,-Mr-Pound?" editors of the 1950s got phased out by people like Ron Padgett and Jon Cott. R. P.'s poems were strange gash huckleberry. This was the start, the new language antagonizing the klunkhead academics. One, *Review* business manager Bob Kolodny, brought the spring 1963 galleys to Dean Calvin Lee of student activities. This is not funny. Lee flipped over all the references to shit; too many non-Columbia writers, too.

Lee stopped publication. Editors Cott and Mitchell Hall resigned, mimeographed the offending issue, peddled it on campus at 25¢ a copy, it sold out. Kolodny meanwhile, with a staff of sheep, published a cleaned up "official" issue. But the magazine fell out of their hands again when Phillip Lopate swept in as editor, 1963-1964.

Lopate reminded deans that the charter granted by Columbia to *Review* says hello, the editors can be anyone and print anything. The deans turned cheddar-orange, having violated their own kaka, you bet. Genuinely remorseful, they lavished money on the *Review* (see—before—they were giving us *less* money each year), and Lopate could afford to publish giant issues. The giant magazine headed down the road to the present.

That year's freshman writers had a sensational magazine to

coast on. Most of them took the sparkplug writing class, C1015x-
C1016y, of Professor Kenneth Koch, the Charles Atlas of writing
teachers.

Students joined Koch in the outer spaces of humor, where they
still are, as you will see in this book.

The madcap adventurousness of this writing comes from Koch.

The sober professionalism of these same works is a standard
Koch stresses.

The eclecticism of these stories and poems was inspired by
Koch's teaching.

The many Spanish words you will find in these works stem
from Koch.

Kenneth Koch is an indescribable white light.

Among his students that first year were Aaron Fogel, a nervous
genius from Queens; football player Mitchell Sisskind from Chicago; and Arnold Eggers, a spooky pre-med playwright.

Fogel's writing first appeared in Lopate's Big Issue (128 pages),
along with a Joe Brainard-Ted Berrigan cartoon, Lopate's "The
Disciple," poems by Charles Stein, Alan Feldman, and Padgett,
and a section from Padgett's endless novel, *Furtive Days.*

Sisskind and Eggers began publishing in the *Review* when
Feldman became editor the following year. Sisskind's story, "The
Dawn of a New Day," was sent from Chicago and turned the
editors' minds around and around. At this time Sisskind was
being mistreated by the draft and by Columbia deans who had
asked him to leave the college despite his teachers' enthusiastic
recommendations that he stay.

Feldman was an efficient editor who wrote about home. *The
Household,* his book of poems, was published in 1966 by Columbia Review Press, a satellite enterprise he set up.

Feldman's issues introduced Leslie Gottesman's poems, Eugene
Schwartz's stories about college romance, and David Shapiro's
poems.

Freshman Shapiro was a new gunslinger in town. *January,* his first book of poems, was already in the presses at Holt, Rinehart and Winston. A vociferous esthete, he hysterically ripped up staff meetings. But Shapiro's poetry is fine, tender, choked with beauty and interesting ideas, and exerted a strong influence on younger poets like David Lehman.

Aaron Fogel, the next *Review* editor, decided to make his spring issue *"in-sane!"* It opened with poems by Gottesman, including the monumental, totally abstract "Gas Days of Pompeii," and closed with Schwartz's "Superboy at Sarah Lawrence." Mozart Keith Cohen's "You Froze the Light and Flew" and Johnny Stanton's "Hi!", his first story for *Review,* were in between.

Stanton showed up one night at a *Columbia Review* meeting with his son Sean; since then his stories are in every issue. Known as The Knifefighter, Stanton was an on-and-off student who finally quit, disgusted with teachers and deans who are fascists.

Fogel printed few of his own works in the *Review,* but he was a high-powered guy, and his editing was merciless and spiritual, spiritual and to the point.

Bruce Kawin, the next editor, encouraged many of the younger writers whom Fogel had first attracted to the magazoon. But Kawin failed to gain the respect among writers that Fogel had commanded. His issues were slender, but the writing was good or better. In were Shapiro's elegy to his grandfather "for Chagy" and his "Elegy to Sports," and chapters from Johnny Stanton's novel about Indians *Mangled Hands,* and Mitchell Sisskind's astonishing poems.

Making first appearances in Kawin's issues were Alan Senauke, Hilton Obenzinger, David Lehman, David Anderson, and Larry Wieder. And Wieder is Senauke's stepbrother once removed. Story writer David Anderson is soft-spoken or weird.

Leslie Gottesman emerged as 1967-1968 editor, the third from the class of 1967. But he was editor in 1967-1968 because he left school in February 1966 and returned the following September. Actually graduating, unnoticed by the deans, in February 1968, Gottesman nevertheless stayed on as editor for the spring semester, though no longer a student.

His issues presented fiction by cynic Paul Spike, a sociable free-lance journalist, and by locomotive Charles Lindholm from Denver. Dick Gallup's perfect poems also appeared.

That year Gottesman and Sisskind founded the Poem Team, *Review* writers giving, giving poem readings at high-class girls' colleges. At Vassar, in the Aula, as poets met girls who comforted them after a terrible auto accident connected with the reading, Mitchell Sisskind re-met his future wife.

Co-editors Hilton Obenzinger and Alan Senauke, who succeeded Gottesman, led the Poem Team to a night reading at Sarah Lawrence College. David Anderson read there in a trance, Stanton was drunk, he was jumping up and down, he was shouting at the table. The audience blemished. "And Darkness and Decay and the Red Death held illimitable dominion over all."

Janet Benderman, a mimeographed handout initiated by editor Feldman in 1965, got resurrected by Obenzinger and Senauke and Gottesman. *Benderman* stood for life death north south. Offbeat poetry, essays on radical thinking, and character assassinations offended some teachers and students but pleased hundreds. And *J. B.* inspired other papers, for instance, the infamous *Double-Suck.*

Equally resurrected was the Columbia Review Press, which published Senauke's bland epic, *Kansas Days.*

Now Lopate and Padgett published in *Review* again. Britt Wilkie, a meticulous visionary and dresser, did the covers and collages for the Obenzinger-Senauke issues.

Ex-monk Tom Veitch, a Columbia dropout of years back, contributed to *Review* for the first time. His stories you are nobody home. Chris Peterson and Ira Stollak were new writers that year;

maestros were Anderson and Stanton, Lehman, Spike. Spike, Paul Spike became editor in September 1969.

Who lives?

Now Leslie Gottesman will not see you again.

Editor Obenzinger is troubled and on the road. Alan Senauke is working on his car.

Wild birds on the roof call insistently. It's dawn, and we just want to thank a few people: Harry Segessman and Kenneth Koch, mostly; Carl Hovde, Phillip Lopate, George Stade, Edward Tayler, John Unterecker.

Leslie Gottesman
Hilton Obenzinger
Alan Senauke

Shady, New York
June, 1969

Contents

RON PADGETT

Cointreau

This Cointreau
spring in honey
browning once
upon the blue
glass image eyes
as I did were
they green or
gray? O let me breeze
your meadowlarks

Now as summer
and the twelve
years that you have
Provence coming round
the corner in a towel
the smell of soap
and peppermint

Often in the meadow
larks an orange
skirt comes plaid
over the brown and
olive barks of
afternoon

And you have much become
umbrellas tilting on the morning
veranda in yellow
balloons sometimes your thighs

May, 1962

In the billowing wind
Of that cleanest cambric,
O soft chrysanthemum,
May Lady, "Call me evil!
Call me temptress!"
Your dark proclivities
Despite your protestations
Come, sighly forth:
O touch-spot
Of the hottest stone
Devoured, the mouth,
The muliebrous mouth,
O mouth! O mouth!

The Crayon

Called to
but never turning
corners of the cobble
stones as cold as lips
the tail of her
last imagining in
the park, she speaks
a while with blue bears
and colorbooks lift
her chin up turns
her back many days,

public school and
the smell of hallways,
how when so young
and so fair she
raised her hand
to answer, but
received no chalk
upon her dress as
if congratulations
the baby blue and
what idylls she
kept in the single
room, scattered
by his measured
method of dissimulation
she turns again
back to his, back
to what is hers, she
fondly coos
the blue letters

Dad

My lass shall not dissuade me. I am bold.
Searing thy heart, which I will leap so airy,
Unhooked for joy in that I bonus must,
And in their shelves their hide lies buried dead.

And rig "pill" benches in thy sooty shield
Is but the beaming raiment of my art,

My hand folded and put away like combed hair
Turf, flying to us in the Dream Monsoons.

Who will reek of us when we are gone?
How lunch stores raze and splurge thy loot his muse
Where I may snot deluge nor be unglued;
How can I then be colder than thy wart?

My lass shall not dissuade me, though I fold
And peel and dry the sooty raiment of my hair.

Two Sonnets

I. For Ted Berrigan

"Drop dead" was the password to our Balloon U.S.
In these days when everyone does it I get "nervous"
Seeing "them" with the fatal drop of pus
Which looks so inconspicuous
As to excite no attention on a train or bus.
But O the vile thing that made that curse
"Drop dead" for the Balloon U.S. is a fiend villainous!

You've never seen a child of three with groin in truss?
The handiwork of Gus!
You've never seen the result of the aged who make a fuss
Upon being denied entrance to the Balloon U.S.?
You'll be racked with pity but sickened by disgust!
But Gus shall be undone by us, by Zeus!

II. For Dick Gallup

O State, the State State!
Land of the finest fishing bait!
Land where I did celebrate
The art of being celibate.

Land where the human pate
Is always tan as a date!
Land where folks don't chew, but masticate!
This is the land where late

I left, where learned to roller skate!
Where the air is filled with aromatic slate
And where I blushed through my first date,
Where 'tis foul to speak such words as ".......".

But O I think 'twas my dark fate
To leave you, State, the State State!

Plans

It was something to be passed on so
You continue this trend of being more like birds.
But still, taking it down off the wall, you felt
That you were going to go back there
Where you lost your head, where your mother's quiet
Slipped onto the postcard, under the white
Beach chairs, the umbrellas and the hot water.
But that could only happen when you take emotional risks
As if one's feelings were some sort of polished bobsled.
Then opposites become the same, cigarette smoke, etc.
So I suppose this means
Everything it's supposed to, though

You, for instance, meant something else when you went
In the water for the last time.
"But now the angry motors grit their teeth overhead."
That, again, was not what I meant
To you when you say "scotch tape body."
I still love you even though "you" keep turning
In, asking me to read to you, never listening
To the note I left on my desk
And forgot to give you. Sometimes they call us
Up and "emotional disturbance," love or hate,
I like them all. Give me some of that.

That day there were cranes on the roof,
Dinner was ending and there were sighs for the experience.

The Four Flying and Singing Assassins

Today that girl has one face saying 36 things at once
With her exploding teeth
But why does there have to be a particular number of cigarettes
In her mouth? as if rhetoric
Somehow depended on the kind of tapestry one is standing in
     front of

Chester the King stood on the pale yellow veranda
Of his summer palace, watching himself smoke
And thinking up interesting lies

Then back in the city palace he sits down at his desk
For a long afternoon of history in the making

In his art museum six dwarfs are standing before a blot of orange
They have custom-made pencils and small pink tablets
What they really want to do is stand before the red gash

When it is time for night to come after a cigarette
He is going to decide which of the 36 faces
To save from the electric chair

Furtive Days

(An Excerpt from a Novel of the Same Name)

(NOTE: *This section of the novel follows a brief digression on the
part of the author, in which he chastises himself for having thus
far in his narrative pleased and amused the reader without giving
moral instruction at the same time. Though the following excerpt
is self-contained, perhaps the reader should know that Mr. Flange
Barstow is the father of Tibby Barstow; the remaining characters
are friends of Mr. Barstow.)*

Now to resume our story.

We left our band of characters shuddering in horror beneath a
crevice in the wind-swept and icy Andes, where they found themselves stranded, guideless, without food or protection against the
elements, in fact, naked. Even in such an extreme and perilous
situation, the lust that forever lurks within the depths of man's
soul awakens and stretches its whelp-scarred limbs. The five
naked men stared at the beautiful figure of Tibby Barstow, whose
14 years on earth had served to make her a replica of some nymph
of old. Sensing the seething eyes of her five male companions
burning into her warm and succulent flesh at ten places, she withdrew further into the crevice. Edgar was the first to act. He removed a rope from his pouch. Manipulating it in a series of deft
motions, he fashioned a sort of halter, which he placed around the
neck, under the arms and about the legs of the frightened girl.
No longer able to withstand the terrible pressure of lust, Roscoe
began to shape the snow into a crude, but human figure. Lard,
Flange and Keeka began gnawing into the stark rock which
jutted over the group. In six days the five men had completed

their bestial engine. Having eaten their way 48 miles into the stone, a large area was consecrated to the performance of the act. The Palace, as they called it, was filled with hundreds of figures chiseled out of ice and snow, and at the feet of these figures there were strewn literally tons of mumu flowers. The entire ceiling of the palace was covered by a series of ropes, pulleys, and like devices. In the center of the Palace a huge bonfire was kept roaring day and night, and over which hung a mammoth black cauldron into which the five men had urinated during the construction of the Palace. The walls were tastefully decorated with reproductions of the old masters, while about the door facings the utmost care had been lavished on the construction of rectangular cages, which Keeka filled with gnashing cobras. Leading from these cages were deep furrows in the floor of the Palace, each furrow passing under a snow figure, and eventually leading up to the central fire and cauldron. Likewise, the complex network of ropes and pulleys were joined together six feet over the bubbling muck; these were held together by a single hair, delicately plucked from the pampered body of the still-virgin Tibby. One inch from the hair was the nose of a snub-nose .45 caliber pistol, loaded and cocked, and supported by a sculptured figure of Count Mony Vibescu. The arm and finger of the right arm were moveable, having been hinged on the otherwise immobile figure. Directly behind the arm was a wire box, which contained a mongoose, while directly over the door of the cage hung a huge moona crusher, a variety of the hox snake found only in Batavia. The mongoose sprang continually at the door of its cage in a feverish attempt to sink its slavering teeth into the body of the moona. The door of the cage was of the sliding type, and could only be opened by a wire which was connected to it and which led upward toward a small pulley, over it, and down again to a platinum stake which was driven into the rock through the mumu flowers which seemed to foam up about the legs of the quivering and nigh-hysterical girl who lay amongst

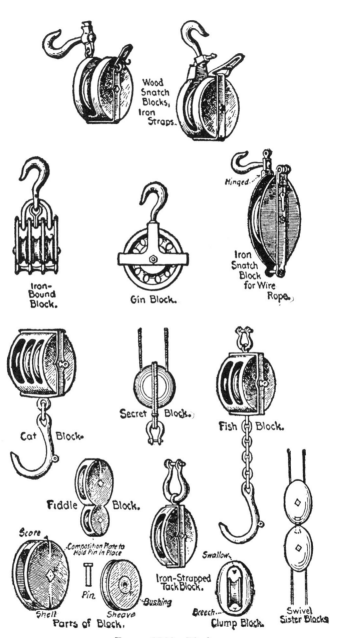

Wood Snatch Blocks, Iron Straps.

Iron-Bound Block.

Gin Block.

Hinged.

Iron Snatch Block for Wire Rope.

Cat Block.

Secret Block.

Fish Block.

Fiddle Block.

Composition Plate to Hold Pin in Place

Score

Pin.

Shell

Sheave

Bushing

Parts of Block.

Iron-Strapped Tack Block.

Swallow.

Breech.

Clump Block.

Swivel Sister Blocks

FIGURE 15-10.—Blocks.

them, bound by silver threads and Christmas seals. The wire which controlled the cage door was of a special type: it had been treated with motor oil and mica powder, so that the slightest drop of moisture would cause it to contract in the manner of wet rawhide, but at a rate and extent thirty times that of the latter material. Keeka had learned much in the Indian Wars. Over the treated wire there was suspended a tiny, almost invisible vial of the universal solvent, the target of a bee-bee rifle which was lodged and welded into the rock directly over Tibby's head. The delicate trigger of the rifle was made of loadstone, so that the presence of a magnetic or magnetized material within a radius of 4″ would cause the trigger to be activated. In fact, our party of men had, on the other side of the Palace across from Tibby, placed a magnet, which was held in place by a captive ant at the top of a long and well-polished sliding board, the end of which came 3½ inches from the rifle's trigger. The method of binding the ant is interesting, in fact, quite clever. Flange had snared the creature in the middle of the night as the tiny beast had dared to saunter over our hero's barrel chest. Flange had been startled out of his dream-shot sleep by the intrusion of this microscopic denizen of the lower animal world, but had quickly regained his use of reason and proceeded to encage the ant between his (Flange's) contact lenses. Thus the doomed critter was forced to spend the rest of its days as a captive in a plastic ball which lay at the foot of the horseshoe magnet. As we have seen earlier, Flange was not lacking in some bit of sympathy and warmth of heart; he was, after all, a good father. His largesse of heart had prompted him to provide the ant with a means of escape: he had placed in the plastic ball a cryptogram, which, if correctly solved, would give the ant its freedom. Flange had provided a little bell atop the ball, which the ant could ring if and when he reached a solution to the following verbal puzzle:

Munt fipp anok zooi klg dhey ubakkkdioo
dioowpdjr fh t fffkl fuheu chioos nousih
cnxiso ghg dkiu ee tuifnbhgi mm i gudhi
amsiughoe pooiriot mk mk mk kjdry uiioas

Realizing the difficulty of the puzzle, Flange had gone to the ends
of his pity by giving the ant the following clues:

1. that the cryptogram was a quotation, in fact, a quotation of a
   poem by a sixteenth century red haired poet whose left leg bore
   a scarlet C;
2. that the puzzle could be solved with less expenditure of energy
   if the puzzler stand on his (or her) head;
3. that a solution could be reached more quickly if the words
   "Nearer My God To Thee" were repeated day and night;
4. that a solution would be realized as valid if the puzzler used a
   fountain pen rather than a pencil, chalk, crayon, oil paint, or
   any other writing medium;
5. that there were three possible solutions.

Thus the ant set himself to work, the prize being his own life as
well as the chastity of the captive maiden. Did he reach a solution,
and thus effect a triumph of the forces of good over those of evil?
Imagine yourself, dear reader, as the ant. Would you have the
perseverance to work on through snow, hail, wind, sleet, tar and
onions at such high stakes? In fact, the Muse dictates that I, a
mere tool, allow you to be the ant: the consequences for your own
life, as well as the life of the terrified ant and the hapless maid, are
enormous. You must solve the puzzle. You must!

JONATHAN COTT

A Night

We went back to the Saugatuck bridge.
I felt the pleasure through my teeth.
The green lights glimmered in the river.
Green, the glass was emerald fever.

The house was lit while the heated moths
Beat the wire screens to enter.
Lights, after the sunshower,
Spread mist over all the doors.

So sweet! Magnolias
Blossomed as if your body
Rose from the grass after mowing.
Crazy brook, where my wish drifts, floating!

We left the beach at six o'clock.
Everything silences—a girl lifeguard
Clutching her white tower; the shocking
Breeze snapping the aged women's playing cards.

When the rain broke the night apart
And the leaves shivered in the dark,
I stole the sight of your streaming hair
Whose beauty dies, soft as a sheet's tear.

A Fever

I write these lines, a headache in my chest,
My feet above my eyes, the guns are drawn.
The Mae Wests float about my head. The best
I do sinks like a sun without a dawn,

But I have lights. O, everywhere the lights
Are cold! They spread out through my stomach, dine
On metals of my sleep which tries to fight
Itself. My dreams are beating up my mind!

I lie? I'll kill the grass before they see,
And then I'll run to you to feel my head
So you will let me go away and be
A sleep within itself without sick lead

To weigh my dreams down with complexity
When all I want to feel is wordless free!

The Disciple

When Diego's family moved from Valencia to the small village of Montoro, the young man made no effort to conceal his bitterness. Glancing with a hostile stare at every detail which affronted him, he wandered continually through the dull narrow streets of the town in the hope of finding some escape or diversion. Like many other sixteenth-century settlements that lay at the foot of the Sierra Morena, Montoro was a sprawling clutter of low, grey-brown houses protected by the church. On the outskirts of the village, corn fields, sugar-beet fields and vineyards were spread out in every direction. In his native home of Valencia Diego had also been dissatisfied with the provincial surroundings, but at least he was able to console himself there with flower markets and orange groves; here, despite its vineyards, the countryside looked so arid and scorched that he found himself yearning for the sight of a green meadow.

Diego's contempt for the town and his refusal to make the expected gestures of a newcomer quickly earned him the hatred of his neighbors. The children made fun of him when he strolled through the streets, but Diego's only reaction was to limit the number and distance of his walks and spend most of the time sulking defiantly in his bedroom. This threw his parents into a terrible panic; but they knew that no matter what decision they reached from their midnight conferences in bed, he had already grown stronger than they, and was beyond their power to control.

It was during an unbearably hot evening at the dinner table, roughly three weeks after he had arrived in Montoro, that Diego's suspicions were aroused by a peculiar silence and gravity which usually preceded one of his father's discourses. The wine merchant waited until the servant had cleared away the dishes and left the room before resting his elbows heavily on the table, pausing in an attitude which clearly announced his intention to speak.

"May I please leave the room?" Diego cut in maliciously.

"Your mother and I would like to talk to you." Bartolomé Rojas was a tremendously fat, pious individual, who had passed on some of his fatness to Diego, but none of his faith in God. His face, which had become red and bloated from years of wine tasting, was covered with a narrow bald skull on one end and several layers of quivering chins on the other. Yet despite his repulsive appearance he was well-liked by the townspeople, and in the space of a few weeks had already gained the reputation of a jolly soul.

"I'm not in the mood for a scolding. This wine gives me a headache."

"Please, Diego. Listen to what your father has to say." His mother, Angelita, was an enormous woman who had spread out so relentlessly after the birth of her son that no further traces were left of her once-delicate figure.

"Son, you are no longer a little boy. You are eighteen years old."

"I am well aware of that fact."

"Then why do you never act like an eighteen-year-old?" his father shouted, losing patience. This outburst shamed Diego into a temporary silence, during which Señor Rojas took the opportunity to regain his composure. "Your mother and I have been discussing your future. We have both decided that no matter how many sacrifices are involved, we will be able to send you to the university."

"But I don't want to go to the university," Diego said quietly.

"And why not?"

"Because I don't care to become a priest."

"I realize that, Diego. Much as I had wanted you to enter the cloth, I would be the first to admit that your temperament isn't suited for such a profession. However, there are other things to study at the university. You might go into medicine. . . ."

"No."

"Then what about law? We know that you like to argue—I'm sure you would find it a very amusing career."

"Absolutely not!"

"You see?" cried Señora Rojas. "I told you he would act this way."

"Angelita. Let me handle this. Diego," he said in a wheedling voice, addressing his son as one would speak to a little child, "try to be reasonable. I know that you can be reasonable; I have seen it on many occasions. You can be more intelligent than anyone around here, when you put your mind to it."

"I don't want to be a student of theology, or law, or medicine. Studying doesn't interest me."

"Then you will have to become a soldier!" Bartolomé Rojas uttered his decision with terrible finality, and Señora Rojas sat back complacently. Diego, however, was completely unmoved, and played disinterestedly with a lock of his curly hair.

"You're not in the least bit interested in my future, either of you. You're just trying to get rid of me."

"How can you say that?" his mother cried in an offended voice.

"Then why didn't Papa ask me to go into business with him?"

Señor Rojas looked disconcertedly at his wife.

"But Diego," said his mother, "ever since you were ten years old you told us that you hated your father's business."

"Maybe I've changed my mind now."

"Angelita, forget it. He's just trying to make fools of us."

"You *are* fools," exploded Diego. "I was just trying to force you into telling the truth. Admit it—I'm in your way here. I'm spoiling your business. You just want to get rid of me so that you can make more money."

"That's right!" Señor Rojas stood up in anger, knocking over the chair. "You're in the way here! Either you lounge around all day in your bedclothes, or you walk around town with insulting airs. Don't you see what it does to my trade when you irritate the farmers? I *need* those people, Diego. I need their trust and their friendship. Otherwise I might just as well move back to Valencia."

"Why *don't* we go back to Valencia? I can't understand why we ever came to this dungheap."

"You know very well why we came here," said his father. "In Valencia I am only one of a hundred wine merchants. In Montoro, I am a wealthy businessman, respected by the other leaders of commerce. . . ."

"Leaders of commerce! A bunch of filthy Marranos that the Inquisition hasn't had a chance to burn yet."

"Marranos, eh? Why you little snot nose! Do you think I'd have anything to do with Marranos? You call Señor Gemirez a Marrano?"

"I apologize for my error," said Diego. "A bunch of filthy Marranos *and* a crooked old miser whose dirty little ass you lick—"

"Is that the way you talk to your father?" She was about to slap him with the back of her massive hand when he plunged under the table and scrambled to the other side.

"It's no use. I don't know how to talk to him any more," said Bartolomé Rojas. "He's always listened to you, Angelita. . . ."

"Oh, it's me he listens to! I'm sorry, I don't know how to talk to him any better than you do."

"Then, since neither of you knows how to talk to me," said Diego, "I think I'll leave the room." They stared at him in perplexity as he stood up to leave.

"Listen, Diego," said Señor Rojas, placing his hand paternally on the young man's shoulder, "Your mother and I don't know what's wrong, but we want to help you."

"Nothing's wrong," Diego snarled impatiently.

"Son! Who will you be able to talk to? You have no friends

here. You refuse to make friends with the young men in the village. You don't even seem interested in girls. Why won't you at
least go to the priest, and talk to him?"

"You want me to go to confession?"

"Please, Diego, just do this one thing for me. The priest here is
a very religious man. People come from hundreds of miles just to
ask his advice. I know that he can help you. Go to him, confess to
him, open up your soul. Maybe he will be able to lead you back
to God."

"I doubt it."

"But will you go to him?"

"If it pleases me."

Diego pondered the matter for several days. Since there was no
other diversion in Montoro, he knew that he would eventually
pay a visit to the church; but he found himself unable to decide
on the particular character and pose to assume in his conversation
with the priest. Each new element of information about the holy
man led him into greater uncertainty. Fray Tomas de Hojeda had
entered the clergy at a relatively late period in life (his thirty-sec-
ond year); he had been assigned the position at Montoro after a
voluntary period of consoling the sick in the beggar's district at
Valladolid; in his twenty years of priesthood to the village no one
had ever heard him say an impious word or lascivious expression,
despite his irritable temper; he performed the rites and religious
duties with great zeal and humility; the report of his saintly character spread throughout the countryside, and it was even rumored
that the Inquisitors of Cordoba had invited him to serve on the
tribunal, which he mysteriously refused; sometimes the watchman
of the town, wandering into the church late at night, saw him
gazing in silent contemplation at the figure of Our Lord on the
crucifix, or studying old manuscripts by the yellow light of the
altar candles. All these reports Bartolomé Rojas had gathered in
his discussions with the people of the town, and had passed on to

his son in an effort to excite the young man's curiosity. Diego at last came to a decision: he vowed to make his appearance as a jeering cynic. He would give Fray Tomas a full account of his sins, perhaps making up a few, and when the doddering old man began to lecture him on his immoral conduct he would laugh in his face.

Walking up the flight of chipped steps leading to the archway, Diego felt the sun beating directly on his forehead. "At least there will be shade inside," he thought to himself. A statue of the Virgin and Child occupied the central axis of the doorway, with figures of saints and apostles resting in the niches of the facade. Diego, pausing to collect himself, shook off an oncoming headache and entered the nave with a nonchalant expression.

No one was in the church. Diego shuffled down the aisle, feeling his customary irritation at houses of worship: he knew that by their very appearance they were supposed to inspire some divine emotion, but they always failed to arouse him. What was it about churches that gave people a sensation of religious awe? The height and size of the building were important, but they alone could not explain the atmosphere of mystery. Diego examined in turn the altar, the crucifix, the hanging relics, the candles, the rose window, the benches, the floor, the pillars, and concluded that nothing other than lack of movement accounted for the pervading impression of spirituality. Outside, there was the constant motion of commerce, drinking, lovemaking; but within the church, even during services, everything was still.

"Then it's all a hoax," he thought to himself. The echoes of his footsteps on the hard stone floor were the only distinct sounds to be heard in the building. "Fray Tomas! Fray Tomas!" he called out, seized by an attack of giddiness. Above his head he could hear footsteps descending a flight of stairs, then turning to one side and climbing down another staircase, which seemed to be located to the left of the altar. Within a few seconds the priest approached Diego.

"Did you call me?"

"I—" Diego could say nothing for several moments. He stood there marvelling at the physical appearance of the man.

"You have come to confess?" Diego nodded. "Step this way." They entered a small room off of the staircase. Fray Tomas gestured to Diego to sit on one side of the booth, before entering the other side and parting the curtain.

"Father, I have come to confess."

"First I must know who you are," the priest cut in sternly.

"Excuse me. My name is Diego Rojas. My family moved here only a month ago."

"Oh, yes. Rojas. Your father came to confession last week, and your mother has also been in to see me. . . . It is unfortunate that you haven't taken the opportunity of visiting our church sooner," observed the priest. "But go on, I didn't mean to interrupt."

"Father, I have sinned," began Diego. "I have quarreled with my father and mother. . . . I have viciously insulted my father. . . . I have refused to do any work. . . . I have stolen money and wine from my parents. . . ." Each time he remembered another sin, Fray Tomas shook his head with a mournful sadness that made Diego want to hide his face, yet a certain dissatisfied expression in the priest seemed to indicate that he still expected more. "I have been guilty of gluttony. . . . I have sworn out loud. . . . I have blasphemed against God. . . . I have lied to my parents. . . . I have neglected my prayers. . . .

"Father, please forgive me," Diego broke off, throwing himself down on his knees. "For I am evil."

"You have more to confess, my child," the priest answered calmly.

Diego thought for awhile. "There is something else. I seem to despise everyone, not only my parents, but the townspeople also. I feel as if I am different from everyone around me."

"Different? In what way?" asked the priest, obviously interested.

"It's hard to explain. They seem to be absorbed in hundreds of tasks that don't have the slightest interest for me. They all pretend to be so kind and honest, but really, Fray Tomas, they're nothing but hypocrites. And when I try to show them what liars they are, they act as if I were crazy."

"Go on."

"There's something else I must tell you. I don't believe in God anymore. I've lost my faith!" Diego fell silent, lowering his eyes from shame.

"You say that you lost your faith. Tell me the truth now . . . did you ever actually believe in God?" The young man shook his head dismally. "No, not even that," he sobbed.

"So . . . you never believed in God," Fray Tomas said reproachfully. He waited until Diego had dried his eyes. "Have you finished your confession?" Diego nodded. "I think perhaps you have more to tell me. Are you sure that you have confessed everything?" the priest asked in an encouraging tone. Diego wanted more than anything else to please him.

"Father, I am guilty of still another grave sin. I have slept with a prostitute and committed fornication."

"You slept with a woman. And did you enjoy it?"

"It was all right," Diego said indifferently.

"Describe it to me." As the priest leaned forward Diego felt his stomach fluttering so nervously that he was unable to offer an explanation. The priest waited patiently for a minute, then admonished him in a voice which was at the same time stern and charitable. "My boy, I can see that you have barely entered your manhood, and that you are shy about your lack of experience. No doubt you even wanted to impress me with this small boast, to prove that you had reached maturity. However, I must warn you that I will not admit lies under confession. And until you have decided to give up these little games and acknowledge your errors in the correct spirit of humility, I cannot continue as your spiritual advisor."

In his bedroom, Diego wondered at the mistaken image he had formed of the priest before their first encounter. Instead of an old, wizened, kindly cleric with white hair and a stooped back, Fray Tomas presented the opposite appearance. He could not have been older than fifty-five. His dark brown hair hung down in plaits and mingled with his pointed beard. His back was straight, his limbs powerful, his shoulders broad, his physical structure tall and lean. As for kindliness—he did seem quite warm and encouraging at times, but there were other moments when he could not have been more forbidding. Through fasting, Fray Tomas had lost every particle of wasted flesh and retained only what was essential: the skin of his face had been pulled tight around the formation of his skull, leaving his features with a fixed expression of severity. His eyes especially bore the marks of a torturous ascetic discipline: they were scarred with an intensity of suffering which can only be found in one who has struggled a lifetime to communicate with God. Altogether, Diego was exhilarated with having discovered such a man.

The next day he rushed to the church, begged the priest's pardon, and offered his services. Fray Tomas seemed reluctant at first, but he finally decided to take the confused young man under his care and provide him with spiritual guidance. Diego quickly made himself useful by cleaning the church, supplementing the holy man's wine and taking care of other minor details. Within a few weeks he had shaken off his lethargy and had saturated himself in the details of his new surroundings.

Of all the changes that had rapidly taken place in the young man, the most remarkable was his enthusiastic devotion to the rituals and tenets of the Catholic Church. Under the wise tutelage of Fray Tomas, Diego acquired a sincere veneration for the Virgin Mary, God the Father and the Holy Ghost, but above all for Christ himself. Never before had the story of the Son of God, coming down from Heaven to walk among men, seized Diego's imagination with such lucid intensity. Each evening, after the last worshiper had left the church, Diego knelt beside the clergyman in prayer—a habit which provoked in Fray Tomas a mild irritation. His parents, however, were overjoyed with the new vocation their son had adopted. Diego had become a familiar sight to the churchgoers; the people of the town began to treat him with a certain degree of respect, if only because of his close proximity to the holy man. His position was made official one day when Fray Tomas gave him an old choir robe, signifying to everyone that Diego had been appointed the priest's assistant.

Spending his days in the unalterable calm of the church, Diego let a full year pass rapidly by him. He had managed to make himself so entirely indispensable that the priest was no longer conscious of the services or the conveniences which he depended on his assistant to provide. Yet Diego remained unsatisfied, for he could never come close enough to Fray Tomas. No matter how he tried to approach, the priest always held him off, refusing to emerge from behind the protection of mystery. In his bedroom he would sit up and imagine the presence of Fray Tomas. The image frequently blurred, and he watched his master coming into focus, then out of focus; then closer, then farther away. The vision would end with his whole world being filled by Fray Tomas, like a huge ghost spreading out into the contours of his room.

It was at this same time that the Inquisitional tribunal of Cordoba announced it would intensify its efforts in nearby Montoro. The townspeople, who had almost forgotten the existence of this ecclesiastical court (which, in the preceding years, had concentrated on other villages in the district), were possessed of an immediate and hideous terror. Those Conversos who had relapsed into the observance of Jewish rituals began to hide their articles with a frantic haste; the Old Christians, who had nothing to conceal, still feared that the tribunal's widening search would implicate them in some area of guilt. No one felt secure in his innocence, since the mere denunciation by a fellow villager was considered sufficient evidence for imprisonment and torture.

Within a few weeks after the announcement had been made, the judges of the tribunal entered the city. The faces of the townspeople who had been watching the slow procession from the front of the church began to twitch uneasily. One of the judges stopped his horse, dismounted, and calmly made his way through the seated spectators to the door of the church, where he attached a proclamation. Then, since the jail was too small and there were no nearby castles, the judge rode on to the mansion of old Gemirez, who had offered them his spacious lodgings. The apparatus of the Inquisition could thus be set up in the home of the wealthiest and most venerated citizen of Montoro.

The notice had declared the establishment of a Term of Grace— a period of fifteen days during which the citizens could voluntarily confess all signs of heresy in themselves and in others. They were urged to have no reluctance in informing on their closest relatives, since a full confession would grant them immunity from execution or life imprisonment, while the punishment for leaving out this information was invariably severe. The people of Montoro rushed forward in a panic to denounce each other. Every merchant or laborer spied on his neighbors for evidence of the guilty actions that had been listed on the Edict of Grace: "If they observe the Sabbath, putting on clean or festive clothes, arranging and cleaning their houses on Friday afternoon; if they do not eat pork, hare, rabbit, strangled birds, eels or other scaleless fish; if they clean their meat, cutting away from it all fat and grease; if the dying turn towards the wall. . . ." Unfortunately, at the end of the fifteen days almost all of the confessions were declared imperfect on the grounds of having omitted details, and the information derived from them was used not only against those who had been accused, but also against the informers. Bartolomé Rojas, being an upright, pious man and a friend of Señor Gemirez, managed to escape arraignment, but several of his competitors were thrown into prison.

Among the hundreds of witnesses who passed before the tribunal was a dignified landowner of untarnished reputation, Alonso de Espina. He had been summoned to testify in the trial of his mother, Beatriz, who had passed away of old age nearly twenty years before. Her conviction of heresy was a foregone conclusion since the defendant, being tried in absentia, was not in a position to vindicate herself. As in all such trials of the deceased, the inherited property was confiscated and turned over to the treasury of the Inquisition. The son, finding himself suddenly penniless, was forced to march in the procession of the auto-da-fé in the humiliating penitential garments of sackcloth and hairshirt. After standing all afternoon in the sun and listening to a long recital of the sentences, he watched his mother's disinterred bones piled on the same fire that had been used to consume the body of a Marrano. This had the effect of hurling Espina, a deeply religious Christian, into a state of mental derangement. He immediately disappeared into the hills, taking with him only a box of money and a few trusted servants. From this vantage point he made several raids on the town, arbitrarily slitting the throats of sheep and peasants without any apparent plan. Wherever possible he started fires, and in the course of several attacks he succeeded in burning his own farm down to the ground. Espina rode with several assistants, but it was never made clear whether they were his own servants or a collection of bandits.

On the night of his capture, he had been trying to destroy a flock of sheep belonging to Señor Gemirez when a troop of soldiers surrounded him. His companions, seeing the soldiers approaching, rode off without a word and Espina was taken alone. For over a month the townspeople of Montoro had alternated their terror between the Inquisition and the gang of renegades; now that one of the forces had been brought under control, they felt free to abuse Espina with a doubled venom. As he rode into his former village slumped over and tied to his seat, Espina had the satisfaction of knowing that he was the most hated man in the entire province. Such was their horror of him that they might have torn his body apart in the middle of the street, had not an escort of soldiers been there to protect him.

But it was in this situation, as in so many previous instances, that the good priest stepped forward and showed the true character of his saintliness. Calming the crowd and bidding them go home, he convinced them by his own example that there was nothing to gain in hating such a man. His sermons in church gave them the courage to forgive Espina (or at least to control their loathing of him), and to bear the misfortunes which had been inflicted on them by the Inquisition. But even more remarkable were his daily visits to the jail, in which he would pray with the prisoners in an effort to console them. Espina, who had been isolated from the others because of his wildness and locked in a private room, seemed of particular interest to Fray Tomas; each afternoon, after visiting the other prisoners, the priest asked to be admitted to the crazy man's cell. There, in the almost total darkness of private confinement, he would question Espina in minute detail about the nature of his crimes, thus extracting a complete confession from him. As to the motives behind the criminal acts, Fray Tomas interrogated him thoroughly and diligently but could learn nothing except for Espina's conviction that he had seen "visions" of the Holy Ghost. These visions had shown him what he would be expected to do. In vain did the priest continue to

examine him in an effort to discover the real motives; Espina
went to the stake believing that he had followed the dictates of
the Holy Ghost.

That evening Diego was cleaning one of the inner chapels when
Fray Tomas approached him with a strange look of determination.

"You frighten me," said the assistant, taken by surprise. "Did
you just come from the auto-da-fé?"

"Yes. They burned him alive," Fray Tomas muttered angrily.

"But surely you didn't expect them to do otherwise." Diego sat
down on a bench and made room for the priest, hoping to draw
his master into a discussion. "After all the terrible crimes he committed, it seems clear that he was possessed by Satan."

"On the contrary," answered Fray Tomas with a strange smile.
"It was the Holy Ghost who possessed him."

"I don't mean to disagree, but do you really believe that ridiculous story? In that case, anyone can go off and do as terrible
things as Espina did by claiming that it was an angel who inspired
him."

"And what exactly did Espina do that was so terrible?"

Diego looked questioningly at the priest, trying to decide if Fray
Tomas was perhaps playing a game with him. "Why, how can
you say that? Didn't he slaughter whole families indiscriminately?
Didn't he bleed to death some of the finest sheep and oxen in the
countryside? Didn't he steal from his neighbors, and burn their
fields and houses to the ground? I doubt whether there has ever
been a man as evil as Alonso de Espina in the whole history of
Montoro!"

"I have done worse," Fray Tomas said calmly.

Diego's tongue was paralyzed for several seconds, but his curiosity finally spurred him forward. "How? How, worse?" he
prompted indignantly. "How is it possible?" The priest examined
him intently.

"If I told you of the terrible acts I have committed, would you

believe me, I wonder? Would anyone in this town believe me? . . .
You, Diego," he exclaimed sarcastically, "You will be the first to
know." The priest shut the door cautiously, then returned to his
listener.

"Now, let me see . . . where shall I begin? Before I came to
Montoro I had practiced every form of depravity," said the priest,
leaning back casually and searching his memory for a full record
of his diverse career. "I was a thief for several years, robbing and
assaulting travelers along the road to Seville. After I left the gang
of bandits I operated on my own as a pickpocket. From there I
drifted to Santillana del Mar, where I procured for a group of
aristocrats. I also entertained them as the buffoon, and I taught
them several little tricks which they practiced after dark. They
had a particular appetite for torturing animals. When I had so
thoroughly corrupted them that they no longer possessed any
interests other than quarreling, drinking and making love among
themselves, I left Valladolid. Oh yes . . . I should also mention
that I had been an informer for the tribunal in Seville. Then at
Valladolid I became a hired murderer—in the space of three years
I had strangled or stabbed fourteen men. Although this wasn't the
first time I had killed someone . . . before running away from
home I had strangled my cousin when she had threatened to
confess our love-making. I have also been a swindler, a rapist, a
forger, a smuggler, a prostitute . . . everything, in fact, that I
could conceive of as within the province of evil. The greatest
achievement of my career was the famous Ritual Murder of the
child of Saragossa, which caused several hundred Marranos to be
burned at the stake. In that killing I proceeded exactly according
to tradition, kidnapping an unbaptized infant, thrusting a needle
into his skull as Jews and witches are reputed to do, then drinking
his blood and nailing him to a crucifix. When they found the
body two of the local tradesmen were tortured and made to confess, and the whole crime was attributed to the vengeance of the

Marrano community." Fray Tomas's features broke into a reminiscent smile at the memory of this adventure, and Diego did not know whether to be more startled by the incredible confession he had just received, or by the slightly bored, casual manner in which the priest had delivered it.

"But how could you have done these things? It seems unbelievable!"

"If I tell you the reason perhaps you will think I am delirious, and yet there was a time when I believed in it more firmly than you now believe in the sacraments. You see, when I was a young man, about your age, I also felt nothing but contempt for the people around me. Their lives were shallow and futile; they all seemed to be waiting for the time when they would no longer have to work like oxen. My parents were field laborers—the kind of peasants who pride themselves in their honesty and devotion to their master. They might have been starving, but they would never think of stealing from others, because the Church preached against it. When I had grown old enough to reflect on the conditions of life around me, I realized that the priest held all the townspeople in a form of slavery. They were unable to satisfy their actual desires because of their fear of eternal damnation, and the civil authorities enforced the rule of the priest by punishing nonbelievers. It seemed to me that the strongest appetites of human nature had been suppressed by the laws of morality. What other explanation could account for the sluggishness and dissatisfaction of my native town than the general absence of evil? They were all good people, but even their goodness was a form of mediocrity, since it had not been tested by a powerful contact with sin. Yet, many of them seriously considered themselves terrible evildoers, and repented their petty offenses with ludicrous extremes of remorse. I vowed that I would devote my life to becoming a truly great sinner," Fray Tomas exclaimed in a tone of self-mockery. "I would spend my days in a constant state of excitement and adventure, yielding to every temptation that passed before me. I desired my cousin, and I slept with her. When she threatened to betray me, I strangled her in bed.

"This plan of action led me to experience in the next fifteen years every pleasure that can be discovered, including the most agreeable of all sensations—that seizure of ecstasy which pounds at the brain and fills the body with quivering agitation just as one is about to do the most horrifying acts. I have felt it only rarely in my life, and only at those moments when I myself withdrew in revulsion at my own destructiveness. Yet each successive return to this new mode of evil would only dull my excitement, and eventually I would abandon it for a new occupation. So I moved up the ladder of evil—from a thief, the crudest means of sinning, to an informer, from an informer to a pimp; from a pimp to a smuggler; from a smuggler to a rapist; from a rapist to a hired assassin; from a killer to a ritual murderer—always seeking some pure form of evil which would free me absolutely from the limitations of ordinary existence. I have searched for this perfect evil all my life, but I have not been able to find it."

A disturbing whirring sensation had penetrated Diego's brain; he was unable to absorb more than half of what his master had been saying. He lifted his head and saw the priest studying him for a reaction, but the only two emotions which occurred to him at the moment were a terrible craving for food and a desire to be as far away from Fray Tomas as possible.

"If it is true that you have done all these things—and it must be so, since you have no reason to lie," observed Diego, "what difference does it make? Since that period of evil you have devoted all of your energies to repentence. Why, you know yourself that the lives of the saints were often blemished by youthful sins, but they were able to redeem themselves through humility and an overwhelming faith in God. And Father, although I know this will offend your modesty, am I not stating the obvious by pointing

out that you yourself are one of these saints? The pilgrims who
journey to you from hundreds of miles away just to receive your
blessing, the flocks of worshipers who attend your sermons, even
the scoffers and the unbelievers—all these people revere you as a
holy emissary of God who has been sent to give them courage and
faith. Believe me, master, you have nothing to be ashamed of;
there is really no reason to torment yourself with these old
memories."

"I see you have not been listening to me very carefully, or you
would have gathered that I have not in the least abandoned my
original plan."

"But. . . . I don't understand," stammered Diego, reeling with
fright, "you don't still do those things, do you? I mean, the—the
stealing and the ritual murder?" Fray Tomas assured him with a
nod of the head.

"Those cloying old habits can no longer give me any satisfaction; I have exhausted their possibilities utterly. No, when I joined
the priesthood I was determined to move into a higher province
of evil, the spiritual realm. I had not the slightest belief in any
dogma of religion; it was all a farce, a theatrical show put on for
imbeciles. What could be more perverse than for Tomas de
Hojeda, the most implacable atheist, to join the clergy and administer the sacraments? Why, every time I conducted a Mass it
would be the most extreme form of blasphemy! In my twenty
years here I have contaminated the village with the worst kind of
poison—it saps their strength, cradles them to sleep and prevents
them from winning even a particle of freedom. Tell me, is there a
more virtuous or well-behaved town in all of Spain—disregarding
the bandit Espina who was executed this afternoon?"

"So you have been lying all these years," exclaimed Diego with
wonder. "Everything you said—in the sermons, in the confession
booth, in your talks with me—I can't believe it! . . . How can I be
sure that you're not lying right now, in order to test me?"

"Whether you believe me or not, it's true nevertheless."

"But . . . your whole life has been devoted to evil. Then you
must at least believe in Satan—"

"In him least of all! My experience has shown me that nothing
is more elusive or difficult to attain than evil. How many times
have I wished for a Devil to tempt me into greater acts of depravity? But he has never shown his face, and I have been forced
to rely on my own inventiveness. If there was a Satan, he would
surely have directed me to a more perfect evil by this time. Instead
I sit for years in this damp old church, torturing my brains for the
solution! Understand me, I realized from my previous experience
that I would soon become bored with chanting prayers and de-
livering sermons. I admit that it still amuses me slightly, but it
was not for this amusement that I became a priest: no, it was to
put myself into the right position, so that when I finally did receive my inspiration I would be able to carry it out. It seems only
logical that one should appear the saintliest of men if one intends
to be the most wicked. I studied the writings of the Church fathers
for a possible suggestion; I read tracts on demonology inscribed
by crazy old monks: I consulted secret manuscripts on sorcery and
the occult. Spiritual evil—how many times have I almost lost
hope, or even considered the whole idea a delusion brought on by
madness! Even now I torture myself with annoying questions:
'Why should evil be the means to freedom or to happiness? How
can one even know what is evil when it keeps eluding one's grasp
and turning into something else? Granted that the best means of
judging evil is by adapting the ethics of society—yet what if one
believes secretly that their code itself is evil? Then evil is constantly transforming itself into good, and good into evil—one may
never discover a pure example of evil!' Many times I have become
dizzy by the attempt to unravel these questions: I have even suffered terrifying despair. And yet, if evil is not the answer—then

what else could be? There is no other possibility. I must persist in
my course, no matter how many doubts obstruct me."

Diego went home and fell asleep in a sweat. When the sun
awakened him, he did not immediately prepare for work but remained in bed to consider what the priest had told him. The fever
of the previous night was past, and in the morning clarity it
seemed to him that much of what Fray Tomas had said was extremely sensible. Had it not been, in fact, the very answer which
explained the confusion of his whole existence? He too had felt
estranged from his neighbors like Fray Tomas, and had longed
for a way to satisfy his deep craving for action. What a noble life
his master had led; how full of adventure! As for his own life, it
had been nothing more than a succession of desires stifled by the
dictates of his parents. Everything seemed so clear to Diego, especially that shabby dumbshow of religion which he had brainlessly
accepted. The young man could have cracked his head open for
being so gullible.

He knew that he lacked the heroism to perform great actions;
even the prospect of entering the army had plunged him into
gloom. "How," asked Diego, "am I to acquire this courage? I
cannot remain a physical coward all my life—I must *do* something." He decided to learn by emulating his master. For the next
two months he followed the priest everywhere, coaxing him into
long discussions in which the priest would expound on his philo-
sophical views; listening for hours to his exciting stories and anec-
dotes; absorbing his figures of speech and gestures; even growing
a mustache in imitation of Fray Tomas' bearded features. This
last duplication provoked a burst of mockery from Fray Tomas.
Diego realized occasionally that the priest had begun to treat him
in an increasingly contemptuous manner, and this discovery
caused him moments of unspeakable sadness; yet he was more
than compensated for it by the friendship of Fray Tomas, who
had opened himself up and confided in him to a degree that

Diego had previously thought impossible. The wish of several months past had finally been answered, for his master was floating steadily and relentlessly nearer.

"Do you know what I admire most about your performance here?" said Diego to the priest as they were idly looking through a collection of old manuscripts. "Your self-control. What marvelous skill—to be able to fool them completely without ever dropping your guard for a second!"

"You like it, eh?" declared Fray Tomas with a self-satisfied air. "I think it's quite good myself. Now watch this—I would like to introduce you to the venerable Saint Tomas de Hojeda." His features changed from a malicious expression to a grave, mystical one, full of tragic emotion.

"Very good, very good," laughed Diego appreciatively, and the actor's features relapsed into a smile.

"And those sermons! I've never heard anything better in my life than the one you gave last week. Especially right near the end of it . . . you know what I mean, the part about lechery."

" 'Oh, how much bitterness of spirit, and how many heartaches' " quoted Fray Tomas, " 'there are in what we hear and see each day, in obscene acts of lechery! To think of losing the glory of God for a fleeting moment of unrestrained appetite, vile, filthy and horrible! Oh, how miserable and infamous is he, who for a brief carnal pleasure forfeits enduring bliss and condemns himself to the pains of hell!' "

Diego applauded loudly, then made the sign of the cross. "And they trust you, Father—it's wonderful to see them filing out of their church with those pious expressions on their faces. They would do anything for you. They would put their lives in your hands."

"Yes, I know it. I have been playing with the idea of telling them the truth, just to see how they would react."

Diego was tremendously upset at this suggestion. "No, you

mustn't tell them. You mustn't tell anyone but me. Promise me, Tomas—"

"Why should I? It seems like a perfectly charming idea. After all, you yourself admit that I have made these people believe in me as their most stable pillar. They all regard me as the living example of true faith and morality. What could possibly be more evil than if the saint were suddenly to reveal himself as an imposter and a libertine?"

"But . . . it would be suicide! They would burn you at the stake before you could utter another word."

"Would that really matter so much to you?" the priest asked ironically.

"Tomas!" cried Diego, squeezing his master's hand. "I love you!"

The priest blushed furiously and tried to extricate his fingers.

"I love you! I love you! Tomas, do you understand?" whispered Diego, brushing away his tears and trying to kiss Fray Tomas on the mouth. "I've loved you all this time. All this time I have wanted to sleep with you. Please, Tomas—" The priest shoved Diego away and jumped to his feet.

"What's the matter with you?" he shouted.

"Tomas . . . Tomas," Diego blurted on his knees.

"Get up! Stop groveling there! So this is what it's come to," said Fray Tomas, pacing angrily. "I might have known—telling a little girl like you. What could have made you do such a thing? I told you I was through with carnal pleasure!"

"Master . . . do you find me unattractive?" Diego asked simply.

"It would make no difference if you were the most beautiful man in Spain. But since you ask me, I have taken as lovers some of the strongest and finest-looking noblemen of Santillana del Mar, while you are nothing but a fat, greasy, weak-chested son of a wine merchant!"

"Tomas—don't be mean to me like this," whined Diego.

"You're only afraid to admit it. Why else would you have told me your secret?"

"Why? Would you really like to know? It was only as an experiment! I was playing a game on you. I wanted to control you, to make you run around in circles. How could I possibly love a thing like you? Why, you're nothing but a leech! You steal my ideas and then claim them as your own. . . . You're my little puppy dog who follows me everywhere I go."

"Then let me love you as a puppy dog!" implored Diego, crouching down on his legs like a mutt and licking his master's hands. "Awrr . . . Aarruff . . . ruff . . . awrrrr," he yelped, throwing himself with complete abandon into the spectacle. A stab of fear turned the priest's face completely white as he looked down at his snarling, malevolent puppy.

"Have you gone mad?" cried Fray Tomas in a trembling voice, disengaging himself from the kneeling lover. "Don't you have any pride?" Diego looked up quizzically. "I order you, right now, to stop this nonsense. Leave the church this instant!—and perhaps you'd better not come back." Diego stood up and left the room without saying a word; he was unable to look back at Fray Tomas.

The days which followed were the most miserable that Diego had ever suffered. He sulked in his room like a beaten cur and refused to come out, except for meals. Señor Rojas tried every threat and allurement to discover the reason for his son's unhappiness, but Diego would tell him nothing. The air in his room was suspended in a dense, burning mass; he would have liked to contract a fever, but even this release was denied him. The first day he pushed all thoughts of the incident from his mind, and lay inert, watching the heavy shadows gather in his room. On the second day, after some of his numbness had disappeared, Diego opened himself to the pain.

A thousand times, he stabbed himself with the memory of Fray

Tomas standing over him as he barked and slobbered like a clown. Each time he covered his eyes with horror, then broke into an involuntary giggle. He recreated every word of the conversation and returned each time with a certain amount of pleasure to the priest's attacks on him.

"But it's horrible!" Diego would remind himself with a shudder and groan aloud. He could do nothing then but bite his fingers in order to relieve the unbearable mental agony. The appalling humiliation which the priest had inflicted on him, the disaster of losing his position at the church, and worse than that, the absolute rejection of his love—all these shames had stirred in Diego the conviction that he would have to do something. The priest himself had demanded of him, "Don't you have any pride?" On the third day, he pondered a course of action which would salvage his honor.

"Perhaps I should kill him!" he thought agitatedly, and the idea gripped him like a sudden cramp. Diego's hatred of the priest had been festering for three long days, and he rejoiced at the prospect of his master's destruction. Yet this prospect became less attractive when he considered Fray Tomas' tremendous strength and his own acknowledged cowardice. He realized that he would have to devise a scheme in which the priest would be taken unaware; since they no longer trusted each other, Fray Tomas would never accept a glass of wine or a basket of cakes from his hand. Diego was most afraid of an assault in which the priest could free himself and turn on his attacker: for this reason, he rejected the possibilities of strangling Fray Tomas or suffocating him in his sleep with a pillow. The idea of setting fire to his master's chamber was similarly discounted because the priest might be awakened by the flames and manage to escape. The easiest and most dependable method was to plunge a dagger into his flesh when the holy man's back was turned.

Here Diego's thoughts entered another channel. He recalled

Fray Tomas' threat to expose himself before the congregation; the young man, after reviving the scene in his mind, saw that his master had only been joking and had no intention of sacrificing his life for a whim. "Supposing, however, that I myself were to go to the Inquisition and tell them about his crimes. Of course they wouldn't believe me at first; they would want evidence; but I know enough details to convince a score of tribunals. They would only have to trace his past life back to Valladolid or Seville or Santillana del Mar and examine the people who knew him. They would be certain to gain enough testimony for a death sentence. No doubt they would be more hasty in the case of an ordinary sinner, but for a saint like him!—there's no telling what they might uncover. And even if they can't find any witnesses, he certainly won't be able to keep silent under torture. And I'll be able to avoid the risks of committing a murder or getting caught." This idea intrigued him immensely. He began to compose the speech he would set before the tribunal: it was filled with expressions of moral indignation at the monstrousness of Fray Tomas's crimes—expressions which he had learned from the priest's own sermons. In the process of composition, Diego began to see the justice of his observations and recoiled from the evil career of his master with a strong moral revulsion. "I would be doing a truly worthwhile service for my countrymen if only I could rid them of this inhuman monster."

Another day passed by, and Diego became hesitant about the prospect of informing. The Inquisition had evoked in him such terrors and visions of torture chambers that he feared even the slightest contact with the judges. What was to prevent them from seizing him after he had given information and implicating him in the older man's crimes? If they chose to test Diego, he knew that he would confess to every heresy imaginable after a few minutes on the rack. There seemed no solution to the problem, yet he still remained as determined as before to act. Diego resolved finally to enter the Church late at night and stab Fray Tomas from behind. If his courage failed him at the last second, he would go to the Inquisition at Señor Gemirez' house the following day and inform on the village priest.

In the fifth night of his self-imprisonment, Diego slipped out of his house and gained undetected the outer nave of the church. He crouched soundlessly below the level of the benches, gradually edging along the right aisle until he had reached the transept. Fray Tomas' room lay just behind the inner chapel. He caught his breath, then tip-toed across the hard marble floor and paused before the entrance of his chamber. Diego's limbs quivered with agitation, and the tremor in his knees shook so vehemently that he was forced to clutch onto the wall. He nudged the door gently, leaving it open barely a finger's width, just enough to look inside; the priest was not in bed. Diego returned with a mixture of disappointment and relief to the altar of the church; he was just about to leave when he heard the muted sounds of voices issuing from the direction of the left transept. "That's strange," thought Diego. "He must be receiving someone's confession. Who would be troubling the priest for confession at this time of night?"

Diego crept across the front of the church; when he had reached the passageway, he darted into a recess of the confessional. There he hid in the shadows.

"But you haven't been to confession in almost a month!"

"Please, Fray Tomas, don't make me do so much penance," a child's voice was pleading. "I had to stay with my grandpa."

"Come, come. Don't lie to me like that."

"No, really—I had to stay with him! Grandpa's probably worried right now that I'm not in bed."

"Nonsense. Just tell him you went to confession. I'm sure he'll be very proud of you."

"And should I tell him also that you asked me to come here?"

asked the child innocently, but with a certain malicious cunning in his voice.

"There's no need to say that much," answered Fray Tomas suavely. "After all, you wouldn't want to get me into trouble, would you?" Diego slid his thumb nervously across the blade of the dagger.

"Well, then I won't tell my grandpapa if you don't give me any penance," said the child firmly, forcing the priest to laugh.

"Tell me, Raphael, how did you feel when your father died?"

"I can't remember. It was so long ago."

"Come on, my boy, don't play games with me. Your confession was much too short this week. I'll let you get away with that part, but I'm warning you that you'd better answer all my questions now...."

"All right. What was it you asked me?"

"How you felt when your father died."

"I didn't recognize him when they laid him in the box. He always used to scream at me. But I like grandpa much better."

"Better than your father?"

"Yes ... because he doesn't yell at me and he gives me lots of little things."

"Things? What do you mean, things?"

"Oh ... you know! Colored beads, and a dog, and pieces of chocolate."

"Would you like me to give you a present?"

"What kind of present?" the child asked suspiciously.

"Tell me, what would you like more than anything in the world?" Raphael was silent for a minute.

"A horse."

"Would you like me to give you a diamond?"

"Yes, a diamond!"

"I have one upstairs. Would you like to see it?" The child agreed enthusiastically, and Diego, from the corner of the room, heard Fray Tomas stand up and leave the confession booth. He gripped his knife resolutely.

"We just have to go up this long flight of stairs and then we'll be there. Watch your step now, Raphael." Diego edged along the wall to follow them.

"Ah, there you are, Diego," said the priest, turning at the passageway and watching with keen interest as the young man tried to hide his dagger. "I thought I heard something. Don't tell me you've been hiding here all this time!" The assistant came forward with a shame-faced, apologetic expression. "Diego, I want you to meet Señor Gemirez' little grandson, Raphael." Raphael ran behind Fray Tomas' robe, but for the first time Diego managed to get a look at him. He saw a well-proportioned little boy of about eight or nine years old, with a thick mass of curly black hair, dark intelligent eyes, and a soiled but fashionable outfit of playclothes.

"Why, what's the matter, Raphael? Don't tell me you're afraid of him." The little boy clutched onto Fray Tomas' leg for protection. "Ah, now I remember. You once confessed to me that you used to throw rocks at him. Is that it?" Ralphael nodded slowly. "Well, let's have no more quarreling between you. Come on, boys, I want you both to shake hands." Diego stepped forward and extended his hand, which the child clasped mistrustfully.

"I don't want to go up there with him," cried Raphael, pulling his hand away.

"You see, Diego? Even little Raphael knows that you've been mean, and he doesn't want to have anything to do with you. You're a wicked boy, Diego," the priest scolded him mockingly, then turned toward the other. "Don't worry, Raphael, I'll protect you. But really, you have nothing to worry about; Diego wouldn't hurt anyone—would you, Diego?" They began to ascend the narrow flight, Fray Tomas lighting the way. Diego saw his master leaping up the staircase with such joyful energy that the two younger men were rapidly left behind. The candle held by the priest painted his cheekbones with a fiery vermilion and threw a mass of dark and light patterns onto the wall. From below, Diego could see on one of these light patches the shadow of Fray Tomas' pointed beard cutting it sharply; he held onto the railing and tried to catch up with his master. Never had he seen Fray Tomas so playful, so exultant, so bursting with energy! Raphael was trying to elbow Diego aside and beat him to the top, but they both reached Fray Tomas at the same instant.

"This way, boys. The diamond I promised you is stuck in a big silver cross. Diego also hasn't seen it yet, because it was locked up all these years in a room that nobody uses any more." They followed the priest along a narrow passageway, barely lit by Fray Tomas' candle, until they came to a dust-laden wooden door.

"Wait for my signal," whispered Fray Tomas to his assistant. "Now you will see something interesting." He turned to open the door, and only then did Diego notice that his master's face was wrenched into an expression of utter futility.

"But that's not a silver cross," exclaimed Raphael once they were inside the room. "It's a wooden one."

"Your dagger!" whispered Fray Tomas urgently.

"What?" said Diego, startled out of his speechlessness.

"Your dagger! The one you hid in your vest!" Diego mechanically reached for his dagger and handed it over to the priest.

"No!" screamed Raphael, running for the door. He was sprawled unconscious by a sudden blow of the older man's fist. Fray Tomas lifted him onto the table, clearing away some of the rubbish which spilled into every corner of the room. From the wall he removed the large wooden cross, which was only a juncture of two crude planks nailed together. Diego stared motionless like a cataleptic, hypnotized by the priest's methodical preparations. His master was searching for a piece of rope and some nails; after he had found these at the foot of the closet he laid the nails on the table and began tying the child's arms and legs to the wooden planks. Raphael was groaning uneasily and stirring out of his drowsiness.

"In order to prevent him from crying out, I must first kill him with the dagger," Fray Tomas explained to his assistant. Each time Fray Tomas lifted the stained knife, he plunged it into a different part of the victim's body: his throat, his stomach, his thighs, his groin, his forehead, his nipples, his eyes. When he had finished, blood ran from the body of Raphael like the juices from a succulent roast. In the center of the torso, just below the navel, Fray Tomas had paused to cut out a round chunk of flesh which he chewed absorbedly and swallowed.

Diego's head was whirling endlessly, and as he gazed at his master to see what he would do next, all the blood drained from his face and he collapsed onto the floor.

"What are you doing!" Fray Tomas growled, abandoning the table and lifting his assistant to his feet. As soon as Diego opened his eyes, he saw the child and fell into a swoon, but the priest supported him with a heavy grip.

"Come over here. Sit down." Fray Tomas dropped him into a wooden chair, and Diego let his head fall heavily on the table. The priest started nailing Raphael's body to the cross with the edge of a stone; he worked slowly and with difficulty because of the smallness of the child's limbs. When Diego lifted up his head, he saw the priest stripping away Raphael's blood-soaked outfit of playclothes and tossing them on the floor.

"Oh, so you've finally come out of it!" exclaimed Fray Tomas. He leaned down and placed his mouth on the child's chest, where his tongue glided slowly over the wounds and licked up the fluid. Diego could not bear to listen to the smacking noises the priest's lips made as he slurped the blood into his gullet and swallowed it down.

"Your turn," commanded the priest. Diego shook his head

dumbly. "Come on, drink the blood," Fray Tomas ordered, pushing Diego's face directly into the gore. The young man struggled at first, then began to lick eagerly at the lacerated flesh. When he brought his face up it was smeared with blood.

"You see, Diego? I told you you would find it interesting." Fray Tomas patted him on the back, but the young man could no longer tolerate the dizziness which had followed drinking the blood; he staggered to a corner of the room and vomited profusely. Each time he regurgitated Diego thought that his stomach would collapse rather than endure another spasm, yet the soupy mixture kept spewing out from his mouth. After several minutes of throwing up, Diego stretched out weakly on a pile of rubbish. He wondered how much longer the ritual would last; the priest had been whipping himself into rages of enthusiasm for almost an hour, yet he still was unable to transcend the mood of despair that had taken possession of him.

"What was he doing now?" wondered Diego. Fray Tomas had thrown off his clothes and stood naked, exposing a large erection which Diego stared at with uncontrollable fascination. He mounted the boy and plunged his body repeatedly onto the mangled form, gripping the sides of the cross with every sinew of his strength. Diego saw him tightening and loosening his legs by turns, rhythmically jutting his buttocks into the air and rolling his fervid eyes in agony. The moment of satisfaction came, and the blood of the young boy mingled with his lover's semen. Fray Tomas relaxed, breathed heavily for a minute, then dismounted.

"Stand up, Diego. You have to clean up that vomit and scrape the knife," said Fray Tomas, putting on his robe. "Stay here while I get a bucket of water. Old Gemirez is sure to be missing his grandson by now, which means he will organize a searching party in the morning. As soon as I come back we'll have to remove the body." Diego kneeled down with a rag and began wiping up the floor.

Mindlessly Discoloring He Ponders

Mindlessly discoloring he ponders
The bored yellow cognition shoes
On his feet walking by

He does not offer to run his taste
To happy signs of other shoes
Colored black or tan or brown

He'd rather paint his shoes
Like a French disease
And not wake up
To walking in the rain

For he minds it less
To scuff his shoes
Than to let the paint run off
Them although it pleases children

And at night he can't be missed
When he takes a deep green
Breath in his freshly painted shoes

His Name Was Stanley

Danger in your arms
Leaky faucets in the barns
The fen atop the broken hill
Hang nails in the dawn
Dirt
He flicked the switch
A new electric brush

Run to Earth

Your feet are curled up in my heart.
Does that infer that it is cold?
Outside, it is. Going or coming
From the movies. And we sit
On our lives as if it might go
Off. Spooky freeways link us.
O, I guess it's smoky coming up
Like this in cloudy skies. So
Far away in the hard night.
The juice. Hang up that phone
And give us what we want. What
I want. The dreams we have
Are here and now.

Maturity

When you sit at home in a chair
And think about God in heaven
You are probably thinking about something else
It's one of the unfortunate things
That can happen to you in the modern world

That is to say
The time reverts to dusk
And I slack my pace recalling
In my dumb way what Katie Schneeman said
Yesterday which was "Hello" I think

And I'm still shocked when the Seasons
Change
              we've seen that before
My eyes say
The same thing happens!

...ESCAPED FROM THE STATE PEN, JAIL, OR PRISON WHICH IS SOMEHOW ONLY 100 YARDS FROM MIDDLEVILLE." BANG! BANG!" (KILLS 2 GUARDS WITH HIS BARE GUN.!!) RUN! RUN! HE RUNED INTO MIDDLEVILLE BLEEDING BLEEDING BLOOD, BLEEDING-HOUNDS CHASING HIM WITH MEAN GUARDS. MEAN MEAN GUARDS. **ETC.**

MEANWHILE

HE WANTS TO (TEE-HEE) RAPE ME. I THINK I'M GONNA LIKE HIM!! I TEND TO DO THAT, YOU KNOW!

NOTE: IN ARABIA THERE IS NO BILDUNGSROMAN, AND NO SIGN OF CHANGE FOR OVER 1 YEAR!

IT'S CLEAR FRESH PERSONAL FRAGRANCE FLOATS TO ME, PREVADING ALL THE ROOM...

TEE HEE
.1.2.3. GIGGLE GIGGLE
4!.. SNAP
POP!!

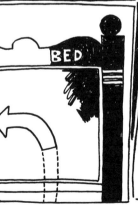

BED

.... NANCY, HAVING GIVEN VENT TO HER EMOTIONS, FELT RATHER LIGHT-HEADED. HER LIPS GROPED FOR EACH OTHER IN THE DARK. "STOP THAT" SAID HER TONGUE, "OR I'LL GIVE YOU A GOOD LICKING!" SHE DID.

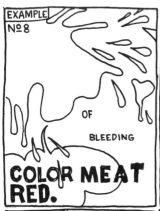

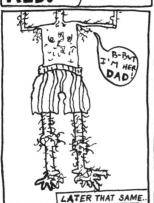

CHARLES STEIN

The Breaking of the House

The chairs fly in wild cartoon—

Donald's anger
                and the kids inside
wreck the room to keep him   out

some story of it
                the circular doorway abused by hurtling furniture
                in the plastic light
                of that anger

                        Donald's voice/itself—

damned pig of a bird hogs the air
we breathe   to make such squawking
clatter

                Donald Duck
                shut out of your
                house by your family   always
                smarter than you are—

                Idiot—Get inside!
                Break your own house.
                Tell everyone
                what to do.

Poem

Hard rain and hat sale.
Patterns, pattering, patter of
the problem: too many cars
on the road. road
too small.
too many folks
got cars
are parked
they make the road
small
too many folks
move in the rain. there are
too many folks.

Eat
the pigeons
out of the trees—

will ease the tension.

feed the pigeons.
rats breed.
it rains too often.
all the laws are bad.

ALAN FELDMAN

Canada

Susan, when I think of how we nearly went to Canada
It's as if we really went to Canada.
Taking our bicycles over jetties in low tide
We watched logs fall into the ocean at Nova Scotia
Along with a granite hotel in Quebec,
A gray facade of weather, and the sound of spoken French.
For months the Canadian Government sent us lithographs
Showing all the pines in Ontario forest green,
The red sweaters on the girls, and the blue
Water. Though one could certainly predict
The trees would not be blue, we were cheered
Each morning by more scenes of Canada to have
Beside our breakfast bowls, or beneath our lunches.
The mailman brought well trimmed lawns to Sliding Alley
Every day, and left them in the Seaworthy Arms
Of our mailbox, like a bright bird.
Canada come to visit Boston. "Come from Boston
To Canada," said Canada, and though we never reached our
        destination
We waved to our northern neighbor,
And it smiled back, inviting the thirsty, happy couple
To drink the Great Lakes

Disaster

Something is wrong. The telephone rings.
You don't say what. Only meet you
At home. Is there still a home?
Or a hole? My coat is halfway on.
The day is cold and windy, clear as a Sunday.
I can smell the coffee factory, and pleasure
Comes to me with breathing, impossible to reject.
On the train, I force myself to think of disaster.
We come out of a tunnel, and height calls to me
Across the river from houses where you could be drawing curtains,
Merely watching motes in the sunlight.
Yet, when you said my name just now, you apologized
And something in me perceives what I can't understand,
Knows it is something.

What do I know of disaster?
After the meeting, the women take their cars.
We go out of the house. The cat is dead.
He is shoveled up, and we get another.
Or at lunch, we are eating, and a friend
Suddenly calls on us, her face
Bloody from falling off a bicycle.
More? I even know you slept with someone in a truck.
But you said it was a large truck.
And were you pinched in the subway?
We will learn to think of it as having happened.
Bad things can be replaced in the memory, outlived—I think.
I hit a tunnel, searching for the root
Of a mountain, and have thoughts of Rh negative,
But vow that problem too is solvable.

I have ended, after all, more difficult works
Than a small baby. It will breathe—
New blood! Illogic! Bad construction! My mind wrestling
With the problem will solve it in an evening.
When in love, one knows how the beloved will look
When speaking certain things. News of
Her own death, even. Love is new pain.
The mind allows disasters, beyond what fate
Cooks up: Cancer. "Cancer?" I say,
Knowing even I could not cure cancer
Even for you. But if you leave me
And die, can't we still see Europe?
And swim together at least another summer?
I know the disease is relatively slow.
There will be time to think it will not happen.

Blue Nun

It was in the world's smallest pine grove that I raped you,
(Oh not really nightly, but a lot)
And stones the size of potatoes lay beneath the needles
We arranged. You could not move
Without pain. And there, in the plain air,
Quiet as a jungle, your tiny shorts as warm
And black as night, got taken off.

Where are you now? getting screwed
The way I taught you, or having discovered
That love was a rope trick I used
To climb beneath your skirts, have you refrained
And started drawing class in summer school again?

You have! You are now the blue nun, whose robes are midnight,
Sitting on a stone bench and painting the buildings with diluted
    wine,
And whistling so softly, even the silver medal on your breasts
Doesn't hear. Here I rested my hand

While the dogs searched, and the priest followed in his T-shirt . . .
Where have you been, mingling dust with the essence
Of your black hair (which has departed)
Blue nun—Pride of the drawing class, and maker
Of leather post cards that last two life times . . .

You are approaching me, on your way to the convent;
And in going there—after painting—
You must faint a little, holding out your parakeet
On which you wipe your orange brush,
And call gently to someone for a little help.

As you come, you notice me dressed as a robber
Lying on the stone bench (where you used to set your roses!)
Whispering "Kiss me, Nun! Kiss! Kiss!"
Hissing like a gangster snake,
And you reply, the starched robes flying
From your pure skull, "I'd rather be dead!"

Rian's Story

It took Rian all that long time to realize that the tiny poles beside the wood ocean liner were people. The townspeople had gathered by the pool of asphalt, as tall and dignified as poles, but to Rian, no bigger than whiskers. The foreign dignitaries were packing their belongings into valises, and leaving the premises to board the wood liner in the fake port. Everyone was afraid of him; he was very high. Was he a missile? Was he the sun? The townspeople stood about the pool of asphalt in miniature horror, under the brilliant sky.

Then Rose Klotz said: "Occasionally one is paralyzed by one's thought." Then Henry Caparelli said "Rian nearly put his elbows through the observation glass." Frank Hennings said that Rian was a moron. Dr. Fleigel said that Rian was a moron, undoubtedly, and Dr. Garber, a pediatrician, added that Rian was indeed a moron, with which opinion Isidore Fruct Ph.D., M.D. agreed, saying "Rian is a moron." Drs. Asphault Interstate, Country Inwood, Public Ideas, Manual Mantel, Majestic Pest, Lumber Steinbrook, Killer Leo, Steck Stecker, Arthur Elizabeth Taylor, agreed that Rian was a moron, along with Rian's parents, Rian's earliest teachers, and the following dentists: Samuel Keats, D.D.S., and Samuel Keats (27 Brookfield Drive) D.D.S.

Then Rose Klotz said, "We are going to miss the train." Henry Caparelli said that Rian was a real prick, for he nearly destroyed the model by putting his elbows through the observation glass of the station, and now we are going to miss the train. Kenneth thought the train was a foolish critical notion, and that though Rian was a moron, he had also written "It Is From the Side That I Love You." Philip Bernstein added that Rian was a moron but he was also very absent-minded, having walked in the wrong direction. Rian infuriated all his earliest teachers and his partner Miss Phillipa "Pimples" Bernstein by walking in the wrong direction. Miss Sarah "Virgin" Crown said, "Rian you are afraid to fulfill your potentiality as class treasurer." Miss Ellen "Smelly Girdle-Eagle Head" Thunderbelt said, "Rian you are so popular that you are class treasurer, yet you are afraid to live up to these potentialities and pretend to be a moron." But the school psychologists Alice, Bernard, Henry, Robert, Monroe, Danial, and Xavior Segman said that Rian was a moron, quite insane, and the author of "The Rain Came Down Like Snakes." Sarah "Virgin" Crown said that when Rian stole the class treasury he was a rich man. Mr. Alexander Abrams called him "A Wealthy Man," Rabbi Irving Irving said, "Rian is a truly wealthy man." Smelly Girdle Thunderbelt said, "Rian is a thief." Kenneth said "Rian is the author of This Fine Blue Cat." Albert Stern Ph.D., the academical mathematician, said, "Rian is no thief but the solver of many equations which I did not think of." Pimples said, "Rian you're a moron and a thief." And Braids countered, saying: "Rian you're so tall, I love you, I love you, I love you."

All boarded the train. Rian had to be carried on board the train when the conductor said "All Aboard," for despite the numerous reproaches he wished to continue his thought. Rian's mother explained to the conductor, "Rian is both an incurable moron and a genius." Rian's father said, "The train shall not leave this day until my dear son Rian boards—as he is now doing with the help of eight men." The conductor said, "Rian had better board the train quickly, for have I not said unto you 'All Aboard' which pertaineth to men and women of mean and great capacities alike."

"Precisely!" argued Rian's eight-man crew as they carried him down the station stairs. "Precisely! for Rian is that same figure of both 'mean and great capacities alike.' And must we explain in what way he is man and woman both?"

"All aboard," said the conductor, as the train left the station carrying Rian to the West.

As the train ran through the tunnel Rian's thought ran behind through the blackness, following. He was not yet capable of knowing in what way he was the sun, but he was convinced that he was indeed at the center of the universe. The center of the universe followed the train through the tunnel. From this center lines of equal and infinite length stretched to the walls of the universe, proving itself to be the center indeed. And it was here that Rian was and he could not ever not be. Mother said:

"Rian, you're a little baby; you think you're the center of the universe."

Rian could feel the pleasure in every sector of his body and at almost all times. He loved or hated all smells, was fascinated by everything he saw, could sing back any sound he heard, loved to touch objects both cold and warm—in short, he could feel everything so he was in this way too the center.

From Alamangonoshikucko the sweet candy train climbs up the green hills of Okcukihsonognamala, Ryke, Feltmenshire, and Bomb Bay. From Bomb Bay the big strong daddy train runs to the great valley of Federal. Here the tribes live and the soil is sick and petulant beyond hope of getting well again. Out of the valley it climbs past Federal to Hah Hah. Down the long valley to Bad Manners, past Doo Doo and the black houses of the Turd Peoples to Fabric, the lovely city. Change here for the greatest train of them all, the train for the greatest city of them all, the city where Rian lived, the city within whose boundaries the center of the universe is located most often, and the city named after Rian himself by Rian himself: Rian City.

Rian liked to wake up in the half-light before dawn. The engine was sparking again, throwing blue to all sides of the track. The names are new in this part of the country: Federal, Hah Hah, Doo Doo, Fabric, hard names for a Zulu schooled in English. Though Rian could repeat any sound at all there were some names he did not want to repeat. He loved to say Fabric and

Hah Hah. He hated to say Federal and Doo Doo. He did not care to say them often. He liked to say Rian and Rian City, which was the greatest city and which was named after himself.

"Why am I called Rian?" Rian asked his father. Rian's father was younger than Rian because he still lit matches. Rian was fascinated with his own name, and that he could, if he wished, call himself Fabric or any other name. Rian's daddy lit a match.

"Sweetheart. My son. You are called this name Rian after the brightest constellation which I believe to be in the western sky. It is for bravery and for brightness—for you are the most cheerful person in the house." Then the humble man reached into his pocket for his sacred book and began to read:

> Life is complicated, but can be solved! A money system
> of value will enable men to express a scale of relative
> preference for commodities of different natures.

The humble man closed the sacred book. He was certain once more of the certainty of this world and no other, and that he preferred rubies to human hair.

Rian saw thrusting irises in the stone steps of his father's beard. He and Braids liked to make love with their feet. "Braids and I," said Rian to his father's austerely constructed, melancholic, somewhat peppery beard, "would like to get married."

He was called Rian after the constellation which was the largest his father believed to be in the western sky. "For brightness and for bravery . . . Rian was the most cheerful person in the house." Rian wanted to marry Braids. Rian's father's beard knew that if it made a sign with its hands and ears Rian would be destroyed forever. Rian flinched at the possibility. Braids had feet like swallow's tails and Rian had feet like tree roots. They lived in the woods very happily and Braids called him not Rian but Rain, after the rain which fell like quartz tears into the stream. Rian and Braids wanted to get married. Braids was going to have a child, and had already begun to collect her soft materials—and as everyone knew there must be, ever so much sand.

"Braids and I, Father, wish to communicate into your excellent heedless ears the following unignorable weather bulletin. We are getting married."

Father gave Rian a good swift kick in the pants. Though Rian was eternally old, those possibilities, those slender possibilities of human comfort were denied to him because he was still a child in the eyes of the prime mover. And his father agreed in some manner which is difficult to relate.

"You are a moron my son, yet you possess a wit quicker than an eternal being of your years."

Rian solved many unheard-of equations before his father's fern-like inalienable, ambitious, lonely beard. Rian wrote poems, quick poems, into his father's mosslike, taped-down, porcelain, antique ears. Rian danced and sang the whole Maturation Cycle which he improvised on the spot. Rian brought Braids before his father's beard and Braids braided it. Would he consent to the injustices to be reaped on the world Rian made himself by consenting to this wedding? Father decided to make a continent of serpent shells between Braids' house and Rian's. It was at this moment of despair that Rian knew everything there was to know, and one of those many things concerned that way in which he was both man and woman.

Braids was the woman part of him. He could not live forever without her.

"And so my friends," intoned Rabbi Irving, "we have spoken today about the H bomb, that bomb which is the power God has given into the hands of all of us to destroy that world He made for us out of Chaos," the rabbi searched for his Bible, "As we are told in Genesis: 'In the beginning God created the heavens and the earth. And the earth was void! Can we blame the great gov-

ernments of the world for this bomb, or can we blame ourselves?
The answer is my friends, that we can blame only ourselves and
not the governments. What are governments? if not the manifestation of men's will? with which opinion the great philosopher
Hobbs agreed so beautifully saying that the sovereignty is a great
Leviathan, a great whale, representing the manifestation of men's
wills."

"Remember, if a missile fly through the air from the East
toward the West, if New York our home and a great World Center of Commerce be destroyed, *You* are that weapon!"

Rian's home was Rian City. Why was Rabbi Irving pointing at
him? Was Rian really a weapon? Rian counted the pages. Rian
played shooting the people on the other side. Was that what Rabbi
Irving meant? "That great H bomb God has given into our hands
to destroy the earth." Rian asked his sleeping father why the H
bomb was called H. The father of Rian alerted himself. "H is for
hydrogen, like what keeps the sun burning." B is for Braids, R is
for Rian, F is for Fabric, D is for Doo, H is for Hydrogen, like
what keeps the sun burning. Rian played braiding the strings near
his arm. Rian counted the colors on his grandfather's head. Rian
sang in thirds with the congregation. Rian read all the words
backwards, which he could do faster than anyone else in the
world.

Rian knelt on the edge of the seat. Kicked the wall. Grandpa
hit Rian. Rian played conic sections with the prayer book. Rian
wrote a poem. If Braids were here could he braid her hair?

A boy there was who lived in a
Bank. A bank there was that slept in a
Country. A country there was that got blown to
Damnation. All the poor people lived in
Europe. Europe can be seen from the beach in
Fabric. In Fabric lived the banks'

Grandpa. Grandpa slept. Rian was the
H bomb. Rabbi Irving's first name was
Irving. The H bomb was the responsibility of every
Jew. Rian had two dentists named Samuel
Keats. Samuel Keats said that Rian was too
Little to fill his own tooth and Samuel Keats called Rian a
Moron. Mommy said Moron meant Child
Or still a child. Rian liked to write
Poems. Rian was OK but asked too many
Questions. Unheard of equations were solved by
Rian. Being a child was
Staying alive. Being smart, Mommy said, meant
Timeless. Some people spelt "you"
U. V was for
Victory Vagina Vaporub
W was for World Center of Commerce
X was for wrong and for Christ whose birthday is celebrated
            by all the peoples of the earth at
Yuletide. If you say
Zap you turn into a malted.

Rian was so hungry he plundered the Atlantic Coast for supplies. The rum and slave trade was the most lucrative trade. Was
rum the same color as slaves? Slaves should be freed. Rum was
made from molasses. Four score meant eighty.

Almost all the people in the world were born since Grandpa
was born. Grandpa was mostly dead and 2% alive. Rian was almost all alive. Daddy was half and half. Daddy had a scar on his
left side. Braids was almost all alive too. Daddy smoked Half and
Half. The scar didn't hurt. Almost all the buildings in Europe,
the Louvre, the Pitty Palace, Versailles, the Place de Concord, the
Arc d'Triumph, the Villa d'Est, the American Library, were

built when Grandpa was born. Daddy walked fast, Grandpa walked slow, Rian could run, and got home first.

Rian was not sure there was any bread inside his French toast. Daddy was telling Mommy that if someone made her milk green she couldn't drink it, and Mommy said she wouldn't drink milk now anyway because of the bomb. Then Daddy explained that French toast was omelet when it had no bread.

Rian felt guilty about being a bomb. Grandpa, though he had punished Rian for kicking the wall, lied to Mommy saying Rian was good. If Grandpa was Mommy's father, why did he call her mother? The wall nearly broke anyway when Rian's father leaned his battle ship of gray linen neck-wear against the kind recesses of the salad counter. Rian had found no bread in his French toast. The toast was then all omelet because it had no bread. When Rian's milk came to the table it was green. Of all the things in Aristotle that Rian worshipped the prime mover reminded him most of his own home. Rian felt so bad about the bomb. Was Rian someone's weapon? Was Rian someone's weapon? Was Rian Responsible? Had Daddy and Grandpa seen Rabbi Irving point at Rian? "Can I be called Rian Rian like Rabbi Irving, Dad?"

"See he hates his name," said Mommy. Was she mad about the bomb? Had Grandpa signaled her under the table about Rabbi Irving? "I'm only joking Rian, sweetheart, go out and play sweetheart."

Outside the cat's fur was green, and Braids came. When Braids came

She was wearing America's most perfectly proportioned wedding gown. From the tips of that famous convertible collar, Braids was resilient, pleasant to touch, ruggedly handsome, with a natural warmth. She was wearing an invisible chemical shield that wards off most oily greasy and watery stains. Braids had an uncanny gift for keeping Rian comfortable.

"Braids did you swim here? You look so moist and fresh." Rian kissed Braids, lit a cigarette and fell akimbo into the plush green grass.

"Yes, by underground river," laughed Braids. Braids lit a cigarette and fell into the plush grass with the cat. Rian put his head on her mossy thigh and watched her white hair drift across the sky like Cirrus clouds. Braids was wearing her wedding gown. Rian was so comfortable.

"It didn't go well with Father, Braids." Rian uttered these words and exhaled a cloud sigh. Rian exhaled a tree with birds singing. Rian exhaled a golden meadow, and then tenderly Rian exhaled a crystalline love stream.

What a lovely love stream Rian
So wonderful and clean

sang Braids with a voice like a tiny door bell.

"It didn't go well with Father, Braids."

"I know Rian, but can't you disobey him?"

"He took me to see the Bank, Braids." Braids turned into a raven and flew to the moon in fright.

"Is the bank a terrible place, Rian?"

Rian's liver burst when he said the word Bank. How could Braids misunderstand reality so completely.

"We can live here forever, Rian. We don't need to live in the bank."

"The bank is a terrible place Braids, you don't know."

"We can live here forever Rian. We don't need to eat our meals at the bank. You can build a house of leaves. We will eat your poems for breakfast."

"And in winter?"

"In the winter Rian, my bright Rian, I will weave you a blanket of hugs and kisses," sang Braids, white as pine, white as a new egg.

"You misunderstand reality completely."

"Kiss me my Rian, my sweet Rian . . ."

So Rian kissed Braids on her blackberries. Rian kissed Braids on her fresh roll. Rian kissed braids on her cool honey. Rian kissed Braids on her warbled odes. Rian kissed Braids on her ripe white dress.

Rian kissed Braids in a sunny postcard, in a tall cathedral, at a Brazilian carnival. Rian kissed Braids underwater with his hands and feet. Rian kissed Braids on the George Washington Bridge, at an Italian Restaurant, at a poetry reading, in a baby carriage, on a sailboat. Rian kissed Braids in Canada, at the temple of Solomon, on the New York Thruway, in a small English town, in the garage at Versailles, under a pile of leaves, in a fireplace, in the outfield during the World Series, and in the World Center, and from Fabric along the shore to Hah Hah.

"Are you happy Rian?" said Braids very softly. And Rian danced seven times around the globe and across the midnight sky to show that he was happy. Rian was happy. "Oh Rian I'm so much in love with you," sang Braids. Then she sang an entire Mahler Symphony.

> Rian you are so tall and fine
> I love you Rian, happy Rian.

And Rian loved Braids so much he took her hand and told her twenty thousand times I love you too Braids in a secret language. But now the time comes

The lovers slept under their soft kiss warmed by swans and soft pillows. Sounds of the sabbath meal skipped happily across the lawn. The grownups were drinking turtle-dove soup. And the soft sounds of Rian's family's soup skipped happily and softly to where the lovers slept. Soft soft happy happy soft soft soft.

But all was not peaceful in Rian's heart, for things had not gone well with father. The prime mover disapproved. The Bank disapproved. The doctors, dentists, lawyers, psychologists, fence builders, and railroad guilds disapproved. Rian dreamt for the hundredth horrible time the horrible dream of the purple bank.

The bank was in a destroyed section of town where once minority groups had lived in chaotic profusion. "Apples, Oranges, Blood, Heads." The bank had once been a house where no person knew any other person, a house with a fine hat on its head. In fact Rian and Braids had passed it often on the way to the bakery. The bank had three sides facing the street and one side conjoined to a row of barges. The three street sides were painted tan and trimmed with purple. The shady side had an entrance for the people who lived on the second floor, and if you entered the entrance you were on the staircase.

The cloudy side, which was the broadest street side of the bank, was composed all of brass mail boxes with little numbered glass windows. (Why is the bank in the story?) Rian liked to call this side of the bank the eclipse side because in an eclipse the light is bright but shadowless.

When Rian told a story, the story became a person. The story of the bank sat down in the garden with Rian and Braids, bringing a Boston summer on its cape. There were no trees.

"And the third side of the bank was the bank itself!" said the story of the bank. "It was here that Rian went to put his money."

"What money?" asked Rian. "Why don't I understand my own story?"

"You had 30 thousand dollars that you had to deposit in the bank," said the story.

"Why? I had no money ever."

"You did!" said the story, and the clouds on his cape spun

muddy flocks across the path of white tombstones in the garden. "You had 30 thousand dollars in your pocket and you needed a bank to put it in, because, Rian, a man was chasing you. He wanted your money.

"You argued with the cleaning man in the bank about which mail boxes were his. Then you went into the bank to open a savings account. The teller told you that the bank was only a small branch bank and hadn't enough money for such a large deposit."

"But he wanted to put money into the bank!" objected Braids. "Why did the bank need money to accept Rian's money?"

The story of the bank was angered greatly and rose out of the sea like high tide, covering the garden. "Because because because the bank had to have money to return to Rian in case he wanted it back!" shouted the bank story.

"But," persisted Braids, "the bank could return the same money to Rian that Rian deposited."

"Oh silly Braids," said the bank story, "Banks use their money to buy real estate, convertible debentures, and amortized fiduciaries. So if Rian were to ask for his money back the bank would have to sell property quickly and" said the bank story shaking its gray worried locks, "that would undoubtedly be at a loss."

"But the bank could call the main bank in Fabric to send the money," said Braids very sensibly, "there must be a reserve fund."

"Ah but there you see the problem Braids: It takes money for everything, even to return money," explained the bank story.

"Yes Braids," agreed Rian, "You don't understand economy. It takes money to receive money. It takes money for everything. What happened next?" asked Rian of the bank story.

"Well, then you got into a telephone booth to call the main bank in Fabric and they told you they would allow you to deposit your money after three months time."

"I understand!" cried Rian, for he was amazed at the complications he could absorb by making up a story. "Then what happened?"

"The man outside the bank stole your money."

"What man?" asked Braids.

"The man who wanted to steal my money," explained Rian.

"Yes," concluded the story.

"That's a stupid story and it doesn't belong in the story," concluded Braids.

"You'll see," said Rian.

"48081639, 40121093, 68043179, 28, 513.78, 910543891024, 003001.6, and 15!" concluded "Virgin" Crown. The two candidates for treasurer were seated in glass booths at opposite sides of the lunch room. Pfeffer finished his calculations immediately, but Rian had shouted out "360914703148.789036!" instantaneously. Rian added by instinct, and because he could read minds he was the fastest adder-counter in the school.

"That answer is incorrect!" corrected Pfeffer. "I find the total to be 564738475643948574638!"

Sarah "Virgin" Crown is remembered to have said the following at this most politic moment: "Mrs. Gynzberg, members of the faculty, and dear students, Rian has added the figures instantaneously but incorrectly. Pfeffer has added the correct total immediately but slower than Rian who reads minds. I beg that you remember that Rian once walked in the wrong direction, and therefore elect Pfeffer and Rian jointly to the post of treasurer."

Rian and Pfeffer clasped hands and ran with the money bags to the gymnasium. Mrs. Gynsberg, members of the faculty and students applauded riotously at their prompt exit. Pfeffer took his money bags to the gymnasium floor and spread out the coins according to their value, pennies nickels dimes quarters halfs. Next he rolled them in colored paper and took them to the bank.

Pfeffer skipped and hopped along the sunny sidewalk to the bank.

Rian, however, did not take his money bags to the gymnasium floor. He did not divide count and roll them to the bank, but pocketed the change into the cool dirt of the tulip bed behind his house.

We beg you to remember at this moment that Rian once walked in the wrong direction.

We beg you to remember at this moment that Rian erased his father's name to collect an orphan scholarship, that Rian stole Sanford Herzog's color T.V. screen, that further he did hand in all his sister's beautiful gaudy maps to Mrs. Seman, that he willingly took train tickets from the brown envelope, that he did deliberately cheat on his small plastic checkbook, that he murdered bugs and blackbirds, that he stole the weeder, and that further he handed in the same paper, and that further he read love letters, that he smoked all winter at the golf course, and that he lied with every breath and sentence of his being from birth to death, and that he unzipped the woolens one summer, threw away the plant and never told.

When Rian stole the school treasury he was told to stand forever outside the classroom in the snow and be insulted by the traffic.

Miss Crown came by and she said "Rian you have walked in the wrong direction, Rian you have stolen the class treasury. Rian you are pretending to be a moron in order not to live up to your potentiality." Then Rabbi Irving Irving came by and said "Rian

YOU!"

right into Rian's face.

Through the air the missile came, its gold sides flashing in the naked atmosphere. Below the world was gold and blue like puddles and reeds. The missile struck with fire brighter than the sun.

When Rian got home the house was empty with his disgrace and silent with his crime. Only Braids remained to cook the eggs.

She had redecorated. There was no white dress and no love stream. The wall of serpent shells was wrecked.

Braids and Rian, Rian and Braids.
Married, married, married, married,
sang Braids,
Married, married, married, married.

The garden was newly outfitted. In the first room was a kitchen with a black sink, a free table, a broken refrigerator, and a cold shower. The second room was a living room with a purple board floor, parchment wall paper, a hollow table, and an eaten door. And in the bedroom was a string of beads and a basket.

"Rian, I've remade the garden according to our limited new budget."

Why were the trees yellow?

Yellow paint is good and cheap
I made our dinner from carrots and beets,
sang Braids stoically.

Why were the trees yellow? Why did Braids smell of jelly and rubber?

Rian I made the garden over cheap
So sex won't cost you any money dear,
sang Braids, crying, crying, crying.

Rian heard terrible sad hymns. Why was Braids dressed in beef stew? Why did he want to go right to sleep?

You are just tired from stealing and lying
You'll feel better tomorrow, my Rian.
You are just filthy from stealing and lying,
wailed Braids.

"Shit on you," said Rian.

Through the air the moron missile came, its silly flesh sides naked in the atmosphere. Below Rian's head was gold and blue like reeds and puddles. Rian was a bomb, destructive as the sun. "Come out of there," said Mother. "Come out of there my dear son," said Father. "You!" said Rabbi Irving Irving. "You! You!"

"Now I want you to answer these questions as quickly and as carefully as you can, Rian" said Mrs. Gynzberg of the blue hair. "There are three foxes and six chickens and two huge dogs on the muddy bank of a lonely river. The farmer must get the chickens across, but the dogs and foxes must do the rowing. How does the farmer get them all across in fewer than four trips." Rian saw that there was no solution whatever and that the chickens would have to be eaten by the foxes and dogs. He began to cry. Mrs. Gynsberg went on to the next question . . .

"I want you to tell me why you left me Rian?" When we played in the garden we were so happy," said Braids her face red from crying. "I want you to tell me why you disgraced your family by walking impetuously in the wrong direction, stealing the class treasury and disobeying your parents?" said Rian's father who had died from being disobeyed. "I want you to tell me why you stole the treasury," said Miss Crown. "Why are you afraid to live up to your potentiality?" "You you you you!" said Rabbi Irving Irving. A flock of lacy figures came on stage telling Rian jokes. Then a noisy student group burned Rian's tears in a great bonfire. Then an angry editor ate Rian's children at an anti-Rian banquet. Then Rian fell from a great height, burning as he went, much to the satisfaction of everyone.

It was about to rain as Rian sat on Braids' valise to close it. Rian looked out the window and found himself in the middle of a lifeless sea. He steered with the handles of the window, but his speed was so steady that he could feel no motion. "C'mon Rian," said Braids, "We'll miss the bus."

Rian carried the valises belonging to Braids and all her belongings down the dark wooden staircase. The subway was crowded with delegates from the World Center on their way back to the World Center. The delegates were very tired, having failed to make peace. The delegates were dressed in foreign clothing. The men wore black woolen overcoats and black woolen hats. The women wore nose rings and purple embroidered silk. Each delegate carried a camera.

When Rian heard someone say "Rian" he turned to Braids but she had not spoken. Who called him? Soon everyone was whispering "Rian." Then a blind man stood up and shouted "Rian! It's Rian!" All the delegates regarded him solemnly and took his picture. Rian and Braids got out at the Federal Terminal.

The bus that was to take Braids back to her mountain village was a black bus.

Dear Mr. Rian:

We regret to inform you that your wife Braids was killed early this morning when the black bus she was riding collided with the Peruvian oil tanker "Collide," rolled over the dam, was captured by Federal agents at the Mexican border, was shot at by angry mobs of doves, was glithorized by hydrobenzine bombs, and broken on the back of the Pacific Ocean.

If only Braids had taken a plane, thought Rian as he slashed his wrists in the bathroom sink.

"Rian," the bald doctor said kindly, "we are here to take you back to the time when you were an embryo—we see however that you are still an embryo and we all feel very confident that you will recover from your nasty death in the soonest possible time."

"Rian," the doctor with the green tie said warmly, "We are here to make you understand those terrible things which you have done to help you feel the proper kind of guilt."

"Yes Rian," said the doctor in the plastic blouse, "we want to relieve you of guilt for those things which you could not possibly be responsible."

"And," added the doctor in the quiet chair, importantly, "make you feel a healthy guilt."

"Finally," said the doctor with the crystal bow, "we hope to relieve you of all guilt and all feelings."

"Yes Rian," said the doctor in the scarlet hat. "But since you are still an embryo this should take practically no time at all." He smiled with satisfaction at his brothers and sisters.

In the period following the death of Braids and his own death, Rian was wont to walk the cold Fabric streets each dawn conversing with spirits and phantoms. It was at this time that he befriended the lonely Alpine chamois hunter, Rudolf. Each morning Rudolf and Rian would tell stories of their own deaths. Rian was wont to go on for a long time, for though he was a profound thinker he could not entertain more than one thought in ten minutes. Rudolf, unlike Rian, would tell his story very concisely, at times using no words at all, but only his melancholy Alpine horn.

"Once, I lived with a girl named Geister on the bottom floor of a very old building," Rudolf began. "She hung yellow curtains in the kitchen so that the kitchen was yellow." (Yellow she said was a good cheap color—)

"I know," said Rian.

"And in the living room she hung red curtains so that the living room was red. And in the bedroom she hung white curtains so that the bedroom was pure and white."

"Did she burn spices?" inquired Rian, aiding his melancholy friend.

"Yes. She burned spices. Rose, sandalwood, lemon, kiwi, salander, rare jasmine, golden silner, fragrant apple, all kinds of spices.

Oh, Rian my miserable friend, if only you could have been our houseguest in that heaven."

"And you Rudolf and your Geister would have been cordially invited to our garden," wept Rian.

"But the most fragrant, the brightest, the most scarlet, purest thing in the apartment was Geister herself. She filled my desk with damp old books. She found blue rugs to carpet the floor beneath my feet. She bought plain white chinawear and hung a candle in the bathroom."

"Then what went wrong, Rudolf?" asked Rian though he already knew.

"Geister went to Rome to visit her father."

"Ah!"

"She wrote me 'Dear Rudolf, I am going to stay here in Rome with my father forever.' I wept. But then, Rian, I got an anonymous telephone call from Idlewild and two hours later I heard Geister letting herself in with her dear key."

> Geister, I sang in my joy, you cannot stay here
> You left for another whom you held more dear.
> I'll let you rest a week or so,
> But afterwards, I insist that you go

"Oh I was so happy I sang! But I was firm Rian, and after a week I kicked her out . . ."

Here Rudolf would pause and search the street for broken glass to eat, for at the height of emotion he frequently forgot he was dead.

"You are already dead," said Rian.

"Yes. So as I was saying, I kicked her out. First she went to the naval base and slept with the sailors on the U.S.S. Collide—"

"The Collide! I knew it well," said Rian to himself.

"I was heartbroken but luckily the Collide, you must remember it, collided with a black bus."

"I know," screamed Rian.

"I forgot old man, forgive."

Rudolf made his voice softer. "Well, after the colli—after that incident, she became the mistress of Benjamin Franklin. She wrote me a letter taunting me: 'Dear Rudolf, Benjy-Wenjy, Mr. Franklin, that is, has invented a stove to keep me warm in the winter time, which is more than you ever gave me, Love Geister.' Can you imagine how I felt, how I still feel, when I think of that letter?"

"The way I feel when I think about Braids," said Rian understandingly.

"To think that I gave her the heat of my body, nay, the heat of my passionate love to her, a whore of whores."

"Yes," sighed Rian.

"And she preferred Franklin's silly stove."

"Yes," sighed Rian, "Oh yes!"

"But that isn't the worst of it, my unfortunate friend. Franklin was an old man, couldn't have lived long even without Geister's young body to keep warm, and when he died—she came back to me!"

"Lucky Rudolf!" cheered Rian.

"Nay! not so lucky as you would suspect. Lucky Rudolf! Hah! Better luckless. For, no sooner had I told her to leave me for good and never speak to me again, we heard the sound of my upstairs neighbors getting a divorce."

"My fault," cried Rian, "Oh, I sometimes think I am the bomb!"

"There, there," comforted Rudolf, "Let me finish. Anyway, an instant later Geister and I heard the sounds of Mrs. starting up the motor scooter, never to be heard from again. And what did Geister up and do?"

"She upped her skirt, ran up the stairs, got upped by Mr., bought a pup because you loved dogs, and moved in," wailed Rian in an ecstasy of sympathy.

"So could I help it, my unfortunate friend!"

"No. You heard them laughing above you day and night, bouncing the bedsprings, walking the dog which you could never own, smelt Geister's wholesome cooking. Oh! poor Rudolf, how could you help it?"

"I couldn't. I killed them."

"Yes, you killed them, you could not help it."

"I could not."

"No you couldn't," said Rian, who cried each time he heard the story.

"But you could have saved Braids, Rian!" continued Rudolf insanely. "You could have said: 'Braids sweetheart, I love the home you made for me with no money; I love the yellow trees. My, Braids, that beef stew colored dress is so becoming.' You could have lied, you could have said 'Don't leave me sweet Braids, don't get on that black bus, I fear it, I fear it!' "

"I could not have lied Rudolf."

"Yes, you could have lied, Rian. Only children tell the truth; married people must lie."

"Then, if it would have saved Braids, I should have lied. But what of the treasury? and suppose I had lied, and suppose I hadn't stolen the money, what then? Why did the Rabbi point at me like that? Rudolf, I am an infant, an embryo, a moron, a murderer, a crazy man, why me?"

"I don't know. I just know that you could have helped yourself and I could not."

"What kind of friendship is this? Why don't you lie to me?" In his anger Rian exploded like a bomb and the embarrassing fact of his identity was revealed both to his friend Rudolf and to himself.

Through the echoey tile halls they wheeled him. The pains! Oh the pains! had any man ever felt them before? Beads of sweat sprouted from Rian's brow as he labored. Rivers of sweat twisted down his temples, collected in pools in the shiny hallways, and roared in torrents back to the sea.

"Thy stomach is a stormy sea," said the bald-headed doctor kindly. He clasped Rian's hand in reassurance. "Before we start the operation, there is something I must know. Why did you once write 'the rain came down like snakes?' "

"Did I once say that beautiful thing!" sobbed Rian and he died several times from old age and nostalgia.

"Yes, you did say it," said the doctor cheerfully. "But tell me, Why did you say it?"

"I am, I mean I was, a poet. I used to say many beautiful things like that."

"But why that? Why that particular simile?"

"I don't know, doctor, the mind thinks of many things."

"Well, what are you thinking now Rian?"

"That my stomach hurts from the life in it, and that I wish I had left all my poems, even all the equations I solved, in the places where they were accomplished. If you came to a beautiful bridge in the middle of the woods and you saw an old piece of paper with a poem or an equation, you'd appreciate it."

"Yes I would. That's a beautiful thought," said the doctor. "But tell me now about the snakes—I have to know before I can bring you back to life."

"Well, I think the snakes are my father. A profusion of fathers. They rain on me."

"Why do you have so many fathers?" asked the doctor interestedly, because he thought that he was about to find out the truth.

"Because I fear him. So I make him many. And because I hate him for giving me his life and his responsibility."

"You mean his guilt, don't you!" chortled the bald doctor in glee.

"Yes," Rian admitted, "His guilt. Now I, not he, am responsible for the world and for all the people in it."

"Yes!" said the bald doctor clapping his hands in happiness and smiling at his brothers and sisters. "And do you understand why Rabbi Irving pointed at you?"

"Yes!" said Rian, very peacefully, "Because it was *me*."

"Ah hah," cried the doctor, "Now you are ready to return to life —for now you know the truth." And he sang the following song in triumph:

> Now let us have mirth
> For Rian will give birth
> A son he'll bear today
> To take his guilt away.

And we blush to say it, but Rian did indeed give birth and not to one creature but two and one of his sons he called Rian and the other of his sons he called Rian and that Rian that was a living child grew up to look very much like his father, for he had short chunky legs, wide shoulders, two hands, hair on his head, and he too was a moron given to the deepest thought, yet the other son had not wide shoulders nor hands, nor hair on his head, nor head, yet he too was a moron of the same deep nature.

After the delivery Rian rested and dreamt the most beautiful dream of his life. Braids and he were in a garden of exceeding beauty save that hand soaked bills fell from the sky occasionally like snow, and coins came down with the grease of many fingers, like filthy rain. This garden was a paradise that exceeded all others, for its two inhabitants were not left idle. It was their job to shovel the money into huge sewers whenever it rained.

And it was in this way that Rian and Braids passed

He was suddenly staring at the model in the glass case, towering above the tiny city like the sun above the earth.

"C'mon," shouted Rose Klotz. "The train's leaving in forty seconds."

"C'mon, you moron, you'll put your elbows through the case!" shouted Henry Caparelli.

But Rian, as he was called, felt responsible for reading the sign: "In this new World Center, foreign dignitaries and their families can live together with their families, and the best atmosphere will be thereby be provided . . ." Someone was tugging Rian's sleeve.

"C'mon you moron, it'll take eight of us to carry you to the train. You want that? What are we, your servants?"

"Hey Rose, did you pack everything, all his belongings and everything into his valise?"

"What are you crazy, Hennings, you think he'll need all that where we're sending him!"

"I don't know Rose," said Henry Caparelli, "I don't know . . . They say it gets warm out West. Maybe you should a packed his summer stuff?"

"Are you crazy?" said Rose hotly, "He'd have enough stuff to sink a fleet of ships. Man," said Rose, "you think you're the center of the world, the funky crux of the cosmos, don't you Rian?"

And it was then that Rian realized the poles sinking through the table aboard the wood liner were foreign dignitaries, that all the shadows of the townspeople by the fear struck asphalt pool ran in the same direction, away from his eye! and that because the scene caused in him such intense, blinding horror, he was indeed the sun and had to leave for the West immediately.

AARON FOGEL

Vietnam

1.

After a haircut, feeling the cold wind closer to my scalp.

From the barber chair a series of repeated diminishing reflections
In the opposite mirrors that should technically be infinite
But end at seventy or so.
In the chair next mine, an officer of the college NROTC
Is talking about stocks with the Jewish Barber who owns the shop.
The barber cuts hairs from the officer's nostrils
And the officer turns his words toward Vietnam.
The barber says that the Russians will help the Viet Cong.
"From where?"
"From Vladivostok," the barber says with his accent.

"But we throw up a blockade. What'll they do then?" the officer
    laughs.
The barber walks away from the chair to get lather, and says,
"They came by sea."
His fingers full of white lather.
"But we put up a blockade, right around it.
What can they do about it?"
"The Russians are going to help them with their navy."
The barber is behind the officer, studying his hair sculpture in the
    mirror.
"But we throw down a blockade. They can't get through it," the
    officer insists.
The barber continues to say that, "The Russians will help
The Chinese, no? They'll send in troops."

The officer finally gets his point across while the barber is vacuum-
 ing his head
"Yes, but we throw a blockade and what can they do about it?"
"So . . . then they'll come through China."
The officer laughs. "Through China? Ha!
China and Russia aren't friendly enough. We'll live to see
The day when Russia asks us for help. We'll live to see the day."
The barber sweeps him with a hand broom. The officer says,
"You and I will live to see the day."

2.

All over America today poets are looking up from their
Newspapers, holding their fingers near their ears,
Listening, smiling, saying, "Vietnam . . . the name has a nice
 sound."

A photographer friend of mine said, showing me a photograph
Of Negroes beaten in Selma, "Isn't that a great photograph?
What a strong shot. Look at that white cross. Look at this grey
 up here.
Look how sadly this woman is kneeling."
The old paintress writes
"There is no ecstasy like an ecstasy of compassion"
As she composes her book on school integration in New York.
She later writes, "And then, of course, I thought, if
Death were to be triumphant, what colors should be used
To be the most triumphant?" She chose blue and red.
I would use elephant grey. The elephant is big and has a hard
 hide,
The elephant forgets, the elephant is a gentle creature,
Who loves water. World Book says,
"Like most other animals the elephant dies

Wherever he happens to be at the time."

"The only thing is," he said, "the terrible thing is, I want to help
These people and I can't."
"Yes, that's the terrible thing."

"Art," she continued, "is a state of being.
For instance, one time Picasso was, we were drawing together in
    the park.
Which we sometimes did, and I drew some trees and foliage.
And he said, O Sarah, that looks like a tomato. 'Permit me.'
And he sat down and drew a tomato in my leaves.
Art should properly be the tear-gas of the heart.
It should make the feelings run out of their houses
To do battle in the streets. One time I saw two people
By the sea. It suddenly struck me how beautiful they were,
And, you see, I had this state of being, so that I wanted to cry out,
'You are as beautiful as
Two Egyptian statues!"

In John Jay Cafeteria, reopened now for those
Among us who had been boycotting it
To get union elections—
Now that the boycott is over, I ate there two nights ago,
Sat near a young fellow in NROTC who spoke of the walks in
    space,
Assuring a pale, high-voiced man of thirty,
"The Russians are terrible photographers. We've got much better
Photos of the moon. We'll win."
He laughed happily. Then he described the techniques and his-
    tory of the war
In Vietnam, and said of gas,
"Actually, it's more humane than bullets."

3.

I too love my baby food.
The click of swallowing. I eat sweet celeries
That crackle, I laugh, and when my belly
Is touched by Judaism or by Carol's
It grows warm and I am inclined to smile
I know that there is goodness and peace
In my world in our time but I do not
Even think anything like that sentence
But simply listen with a kind of concentration
On being to the hysteric chirps of birds
In a college morning nesting in the stone library
Above the columns as I walk over the red bricks.

Anna read to her small son the story "Vietnam."

"The red sky at twilight is covered with a blue cover,
Becomes violet, burns itself out
Against the finiteness of its own time.
A smell of burning gasoline comes from the sky
And with it a healthy looking man whose eyes betray
To us that he is in nirvana. He comes in a red
Car and wears white robes that overcome the fine night.

"Among the Viet Cong there are 431,543 kotis of lotus Buddhas.

"He sings, 'The Buddha-field is filled with rice-paddies.'
All over New York this fine spring
A host of white rice and brown rice-paddies
Of yellow rice and cardinal red rice-paddies
Came down.
          "When the citizens of Vietnam woke up
That morning they could find no rice and no rice paddies

Anywhere in their lovely land and they wondered,
'What has . . .?' "

Anna noticed that her son had fallen asleep.
He was drooling on her dress.
She carried him to cot and went to an afternoon movie.

4.
"The U. S. Government will not tolerate
This attempt to destroy our destroyers."

STATE DEPT CITES DISTINCTION BETWEEN
OVERT AGGRESSION AND RETALIATORY RAIDS

"Hot Green Leaves! Burning Bush! Brushed Cheeks!
What Heat! What Light!"

5.
Ray and his friend were discussing Vietnam at a party.
Ray said that we had not given the Buddhists free elections.
His friend said, "Frankly, I'm not interested in freedom.
We're defending our own interests." "What interests have we
Got there? It's strategically unimportant," Joan argued.
The friend thought.
"Well, economically, for one thing. There are a lot of rice-paddies."

Exiting from that trionfi party
Where the team of play and silence triumphed
Over the team of dance and concentration
I heard two "Bastard!"s.
Across the street, two wives stood in the half open doors of their
    opposite houses.
Their husbands screamed at each other on the lawn of one.

In the other house the old wife wept, "Stop it. Stop it."
But her husband pushed the other over the porch
Railing head first into the snow.
A few seconds later they began punching each other and fell onto
    the snowy ground, jaws shaking.
I ran across the street and broke it up.
They lay on the ground for a few seconds. Then one got up.
An old man came out with a rake. He was dressed in tweed
And said to the man lying still on the snow
Who had not punched first
Who had been the one to fall head first into the snow,

"George, get back in your house."
His rake made him appear a vulture
Reminded me of a political cartoon I had seen
Portraying Boss Tweed and cronies as vultures,
With the inscription, "Let us Prey."

George said, "This is my land and I'll stay here
If I want to." He lay on his back in the snow,
Snow as cold as statuary,
Which had lengths of green and purple vegetation running
    through it
It was a lovely suburb, frame houses
Surrounded by a belt of cemeteries
Clean doorsteps and the young wife said
"Sylvia, for ten years this has been going on,
The same story. If you wanted something,
Why didn't you ask for it?"

March, 1965

The Turtle Hunt

Irving insisted that Dan come into the city for only a few hours to mediate an argument between two of the foreladies, both of whom, he said, liked Dan. The foreladies said they were fighting over which one of them was in charge of a worktable that had to be cleaned up. With the voice of a shocked, frustrated and tired person, Irving told Dan how the women wept, gave and received insults, and were "almost hitting each other." Irving owned the factory where Dan was production supervisor, but he was usually away negotiating with other business men. He worked on an irregular schedule, doing a lot of his business over supper, in his car, and late at night. He dressed his dark and stocky body like a dandy, in silken suits, lace-cuffed shirts, and pointed shining shoes; so that it was a joke and made every one uncomfortable the rare time he had a few free minutes to wander out of his office for a tour on the floor among the machines and workers. They didn't look at each other simultaneously, though they exchanged friendly comments. "But he's a straight, honest person," Dan told Abigail, "he just tells you what he wants, and that's all." Irving made rigid demands but never insulted people and never showed anger. He insisted he couldn't resolve the fighting women, though it should be easy for Dan.

Dan told Irving to just order them to do what had to be done, and so with authority put an end to the fighting. On the first Monday of his summer vacation, Dan said, he wasn't willing to make a two-hour journey from his summer home only to have a fifteen minute conference with two stupid and stubborn women who could be easily handled. But Irving continued to refuse and said Dan had to come in and help. Dan asked him once more just to be strict with them. "Look, I can't," Irving said. "I don't know how to do it with them. I don't know these people." This vacation time was supposed to be his own, Dan said; he needed it to work on the summer house he'd finished building, and wanted to be with his wife Abigail when a van came in the afternoon bringing most of their summer furniture; but Dan conceded to Irving and agreed to come in, angry at himself for giving in, then telling himself not to be angry.

When they argued on the phone in the morning it was raining lightly, falling in thin strings, in the city and the country. Because of a drought, no one in the city was allowed to water trees, so that some of the leaves dropped dead, others stayed dry and red on their branches, making it look like autumn or a city of red maples. On the drive to the factory from his home, Dan was enjoying listening to the radio, and was moving his head in time with some of the songs. He responded especially to the music of the "Rolling Stones" and sang with them. It was early afternoon; it had stopped raining, was warm in the country, a pretty day to stay there. Dan was annoyed at having to go into the city now, and angry at Irving's weakness. But the "Rolling Stones" were a pleasure, the landscape was interesting, changing from cliffs and forest to buildings.

About an hour after Dan left his house, a boy of seventeen, who got himself employed in the shop by showing false identification papers, forced his hand through the guards of the small press he operated, amputating four fingers, leaving only a thumb. The boy fainted, parts of his cut crushed fingers still on his hand, parts on the press, and one piece on the floor. Work stopped in his area for a half hour while the ambulance was coming, and the people used the time off for talk. It was clear to a lot of people that the boy had thrust his hand intentionally into the die. The people who thought it was intentional reasoned that the boy did it so he could get money from disability insurance and then move to Puerto Rico, where he would live in wealth and security for the rest of his life.

Carmen, one of the two foreladies Dan had to talk to, was convinced it could only be an accident. "A boy wouldn't do that to himself," she said. She was fat and overheated, wearing a cotton dress of red flowers on blue, sitting tired on her work stool, arguing with sweet exasperation with Bernard, who stood. "A wealthy man don't need a hand," Bernard said, "and I tell you, that's what this boy knows. He is a smart boy," Bernard said without letting Carmen know if he was being ironic.

His angry cold blue eyes made Carmen nervous; but she wouldn't be forced to believe a moment existed when a boy put his hand into a machine to get chopped up. She said that a number of guards put on the machine to prevent accidents would have made it necessary for the boy to push his fingers willfully into the machine, not just let them fall there. "It is like a guillotine," she said.

"What are you talking about?" Bernard laughed. "Jesus Christ" —he was stroking a greasy hinge he held—"you know what you just said? I work at these machines all the time. I tell you something, they only help you if you don't want to get yourself hurt, that's what. You got to be careful. And then maybe they don't work for you." Carmen was quiet for a few seconds without giving any signal she was going to answer. Bernard was filing the side of the hinge, stopping after every ten or twelve strokes to bring it close to his eyes and see how much he'd taken off.

"I show you something," Bernard said, and walked over to his machine about ten feet from her stool. She turned her body slowly to watch him. He was shoving his soiled hand through a guard, into the stamping area. "You see how easy it is. Look at that."

Dan's car was coming over a bridge only a mile away from the factory. When he was halfway over the bridge, glancing at the bay, the angel he had seen in the morning hailed him from the pedestrian walk. Dan stopped his car and pushed open the door for the angel to come inside. The angel gave Dan another talk for three or four minutes, repeating the prophecy it had tried to make a few hours before in the woods in the country. But now it succeeded; in one image the angel made clear what it hadn't made clear before in a long stream of images. It conjured for Dan a vision of people maimed like insects or rodents, revolving on the ground, blistered and screaming. There was grass mixed with blood; there were charred standing houses. Dan's stomach was aching while he listened to this; he sobbed and shook so hard for a minute he couldn't talk. But the angel didn't take pity and relent, because at last it had the agonized conscience it wanted to evoke, and told Dan gently, "You have to do something. You're going to become another Adolf Hitler and destroy the world." Dan stopped sobbing at this incessant attack. "Whose fault is it if I am? What are you asking me to do? You're asking me to kill myself, but I can't. You're able to prevent it. Why don't you do something?" The angel didn't say if it recommended suicide, but a little abstractly, resentful that Dan had gotten so angry and stopped responding, it recited, "You have to take the step from ritual purity to self-control. This is the last time I'm able to tell you, you're going to destroy the world."

"You keep being cruel," Dan observed. The angel got out of the car.

All in white, it strolled on the pedestrian walk at the edge of the bridge. Though the sun was still out it was raining again. The angel was walking stiffly, and because it was surrounded by strings of rain, it looked to Dan like a marionette.

Dan recovered his calm easily by talking to himself for a time, reasoning that there was no emergency, and that he'd have to think a lot till he could interpret the angel's intention.

He drove to the factory. A white ambulance was leaving when he got there.

Carmen and Bernard had stopped arguing and were working. When Dan approached her, she asked him a few sympathetic

questions about his vacation. He always felt she was sexually excited by his presence. She appeared to laugh with delight at his
descriptions of his baby and their lake in the country. When he
was through she described what had happened to the boy. She
gave Dan motherly advice, "You shouldn't come to the place
today. You are always working too hard, you know what I mean?
You come in and look what happened, look what you find here."

Bernard saw them talking and let his machine run for another
half minute, then stopped it.

He walked over and initiated Dan into the argument he was
having with Carmen. "I think you are wrong" he had a staccato
foreign accent. "That's a very sad thing, let me tell you Dan, that
a boy should hurt himself like that." In this argument Dan inclined to Carmen's thinking.

"No, Bernie, I don't think he could have done it that way. He's
only what—eighteen?—he can't be that—" Dan lost his line of
thinking, his mind went back onto the prophecy for a second, he
was only weakly searching for his words, "he can't be that—"

"So he's an old man who is twenty-four," Bernard was pointing
with a greased brown finger at Dan and grinning at Carmen.
He'd underestimated Dan's age by two years; he himself was
about fifty but was subordinate to Dan. Now he was pulling his
age as rank. "I tell you, all right, that is a smart boy," Bernard
laughed bitterly, "he sure is." Dan wasn't going to argue any
more after he felt Bernard pulled his age as rank like that. What
was the point of it? Bernard was a crazed old man ranting about
things he couldn't understand, insisting when he couldn't know
for sure that the boy mutilated himself. There was no point in
arguing with him when he was being so offensive. Bernard's red
face was talking, opening its mouth, expressing its insistent view
of the accident in his peculiar Scandinavian staccato. Dan withdrew himself with a calm surface from the argument by conced-

ing, "I can't know what happened since I wasn't here." He turned
to talk to Carmen. "No," Bernard said, "I worked ten years ago
where a boy did that."

"Mhm," Dan said without smiling and looking just to the right
of Bernard's head.

Dan was hoping the fight between Carmen and Milegraz
would be easier to solve because they might be ashamed to be
petty right after the boy's drama. Every once in a while he recalled the angel's prophecy, became physically so tense and upset
he forgot where he was in his talks with the two women. But
they were both very excited and didn't seem to notice when he
wasn't concentrating on them. He hoped they would be like those
people who feel noble and refreshed by a tragedy, cleansed as if
their insides had been scrubbed with a brush and soap and then
showered with boiling water. The image quieted him. Any one
might be embarrassed to be petty compared to a tragic one. But
Carmen and Milegraz didn't make it easier. He had to talk with
and mollify each of them separately for a half hour, he told Abigail, until they accepted a compromise. "They sound like real
bitches," Abigail said, her large eyes and sweet voice giving the
wrong impression of incredulous innocence; they made the word
"bitches" sound like an artificial, self-conscious slang. Each one
of the women repeated a few insults she'd received from the other
and made a few scandalous innuendos about the other, though
Milegraz seemed to Dan the more spiteful, because she claimed
that Carmen was stealing from the shop. He was convinced there
was some root to the fight neither of the women was readily willing to reveal, so he kept asking gently probing questions, but got
nowhere. Each one only repeated her innuendos and told again
how she'd suffered clawing insults. It was boring, and Dan
thought he'd want to laugh at them if it weren't annoying and if
he weren't himself upset about the angel. Finally he insisted on a
compromise that they both accepted.

While he drove back home he tried to review the day. He told himself it was a good kind of work, though the country was relaxing and much different. The scenery was changing to freshness, greenness, the peace and beauty of cliffs, living green trees and blue water. This work involved physical labor sometimes. But Dan loved working at physical tasks. He especially loved lifting, going at it with the ferocity and concentration of an athlete or an ascetic. This was one reason besides cheapness, he thought, why he'd built his own house. The work also involved dealing with people and coming into conflict with them. "Poor boy," Dan said aloud, looking at his hand on the steering wheel. The angel said he wasn't coming again. "I'm going to have to decide." The plague of the angel's prophecy stayed in his mind, making him think more than was usual for him. So did a lot of petty annoyances. The night before he'd found frays in some new country furniture, which made him furious, as though he'd been unjustly punished. He remembered how happy his parents expected to be when they'd become rich for a time. He'd viciously attacked all wealth as a fraud, because he felt they had remained just as unhappy as before. Abigail said, "No one expects that it's going to make everything happy, but without it, I don't think any one is happy. You shouldn't start being so upset, or condemn everything, just because we found a few frays in a cushion." But he still hated imperfections in new goods. That morning when he woke up he'd studied the red rose design he'd stenciled onto the inside of the back door, and concluded it was uneven, in some way. There were little imperfections. He felt dejected then. He breathed in for refreshment and sat down on a box, complaining aloud that the stencil was imperfect. He moved back and got a splinter through his jeans. He'd had to pull it out with his fingers. Now he began to debate with himself whether he should tell Abigail about the angel.

But the country was still very different. It had a different architecture, a different nature, a different style of life, fresh and green, clearly colored, loving, light and calm. People there took on the placidity of sleeping babies, constantly basking in the beautiful sunlight cast on their flesh, which they had no shame in exposing as much as they were allowed. The factory was hot; the country was warm. In another few years every one would go naked in the country. The people against this were the frightened, overly quiet ones. But society is progressing to an open warmth. Most summer people want to expose themselves, even if they're misshapen, to be accepted, have fun, and have a loving quiet with one another. Every one is on his guard in the city.

On the morning Irving called, Dan woke up into the cold, naked and without a blanket, when a hornet stung his arm. Abigail had seized their blue floral quilt to herself in her sleep in the dark, where it now surrounded her while she held to it with tugging tight fists. She tugged just that way on Dan't shirt or jacket when they walked arms around each other, as if she were trying to strip him in the street. Outside now it was light blue and birds were chirping wildly. Abigail's back was facing him, and though his hornet sting was still receding to an itch, he wasn't concerned with it, and couldn't resist taking some of her soft light brown hair in his hand and kissing it, though, also, he was afraid she would wake up. But it seemed to him that her sleep was voluntary, a consciously unconscious seduction, a game; at any moment she really wanted to she could switch herself awake, become a dry, orderly, too stable person who had to be careful, using the excuse that Dan was puerile and irresponsible for her lack of spirit. In bed she volunteered to lose her power in sleep and, he thought, because she was also naked, she appropriated the quilt coyly to herself without his knowing it, till it was her own sleeping bag, and her husband lay exposed feeling like a monkey with all his black hair, chilling in the air. Feeling he was like a baboon, he lay back and happily spread his legs, putting his left over his wife's covered thigh. She continued in her ape sleep. He gave in to an impulse to grunt and Abigail, though truly asleep, moaned in response. She put her free hand on his hairy thigh, squeezing it a drop. He began to have an erection from this play. Since she was always functioning so consciously in front of Dan, always moving and considering, apparently in control of herself, he was sure this sleeping was a game, planned and understood by the sleeper; which was why she could make love to him even in her sleep.

Dan woke her a few minutes later by putting his arm around her waist. She looked at him and smiled; he smiled at her. "Oh, I didn't take the blanket again," Abigail scolded herself. She struggled to put part of it over him, but he said, "No, I felt very warm, so I threw it off during the night."

Out of bed, Abigail stood in the kitchen, squeezing orange juice and frying eggs on a stove that wasn't pushed into place yet. Dan did exercises in the back yard. His exercises were a symptom of his craving for strenuous and painful work, his love of moments of pain when there is some goal to be reached which causes and sustains the pain. Dan's exercises weren't bouts of "willpower," because it was the painful crisis itself, the last push-up, the last curl, which he enjoyed and needed every day. It was the experiencing and overcoming of pain which satisfied him, especially if he could be rewarded with the knowledge of having done more push-ups, or whatever, today than he did yesterday. Action before the painful crisis began was boring and tense, simply a mechanical repetition meant to work his arms and chest into the ache which made more movement so difficult and so engrossing.

Now, while Dan was doing the first twenty-five push-ups, keeping his back and neck straight, he smelled some fertilizer nearby, and thought it was being used on fancy lawns. He smelled nothing during the last painful eight push-ups, which involved him so completely he felt only the pain and the effort he was making. But when he'd finished the thirty-third push-up and collapsed onto the ground, the smell became worse.

He stood up, and saw that on his bare chest, mingling with the hairs, and on his right pants' leg, were wads of dog shit. It didn't disgust him; there was even a pleasant coolness to the paste on his flesh. At the same time he felt compelled to wash it off quickly, mostly because of how it would look if someone saw him. He went in through the side door of the house, and was making toward the bathroom, but met Abigail.

"Is that . . . ?" she asked and looked down, curious, grinning, but wincing a little. "Yeah," Dan laughed.

"You got it all over you," she smiled. "I think you'd better go wash off." Dan was grinning. She thought what she'd said had sounded too dominating, so she played along with his amusement, making a mock-face to show disgust. "Am I supposed to say breakfast's ready?" she giggled.

"You look sexy today," Dan said. She had just taken a shower, her black hair was a little wild, and on her pretty, slight body she was wearing tight shorts and an amber sweater, obviously without a bra. Dan moved a half step toward her. Now she pulled back, puzzled.

"I'm coming for you, shit and all!" Dan growled.

"Come on, get washed," she told him with annoyance. Dan laughed at her outburst of annoyance, assuring her, "I wasn't really coming for you, you know." "I know," she said.

Dan went into the bathroom and cleaned himself, wetting a lot of pink tissues, smearing off the shit with these and flushing them down the toilet; then he soaped himself, and put the pants in the hamper without removing the shit. He walked to the bedroom, put on a pair of chenos, and made for the kitchen.

During breakfast it rained a little. Abigail experimented, mixing cream in with the egg batter instead of milk; the scrambled eggs came out too rich. Abigail often experimented, never was content to make the same good food repeatedly. Always with the excuse of cooking standard food a new, exciting, interesting way, so as to avoid boredom, she changed and sometimes ruined it for both of them. But Dan said the eggs were "delicious," wanting to make her happy. He thought the orange juice, which had thick pieces in it that burst inside his mouth, was too sweet, and became annoyed at the strands of orange string it left in his teeth. He was trying to extract them with his fingers, while Abigail laughed and finally suggested he use an eyebrow tweezer. Whether it was made seriously or not, he didn't take the suggestion.

They were both watching and listening to the rain for the few minutes it lasted. This activity relaxed them both, so that they forgot the tension they were feeling since their encounter before breakfast.

They talked about their baby's health, and about a politician who Dan said was trying to control the district where they lived in an apartment most of the year. Dan was fascinated with the machinations in local politics, the way certain figures manage to get into powerful, profitable and silent posts; he linked this particular politician with the dope racket. "—He's a bastard of course, but he's a clever guy," Dan said.

Abigail was hardly listening. She absorbed herself in holding and feeding the baby, who during a lapse in the feeding pointed toward his father and said the only word he knew, "That."

"He's smart, isn't he," Dan said. "By next year he'll know how to say 'this'." He shook the baby's foot and the baby laughed. Abigail said, "I think he's pretty smart. He's only half a year old, and you can't expect them to talk usually before much later." "Of course he's smart," Dan answered; then he shrieked in an old lady's voice, "Smart! Smart!" and tickled the baby's belly with his pointer finger.

The three of them were elated, the parents laughing in the same

happy way the baby did. Dan took the baby from Abigail and
held him under the arms, moving him up and down in the air.

Dan sang, "Oh you're so smart you'll get plenty of screw, give
'em one for the papa too," while the baby giggled. "Oh, you little
fucker," Dan sang, swaying the baby from side to side.

"I'm glad that wasn't the first word he learned," Abigail said,
with an affectionate propriety.

"But 'that' was," Dan said. Abigail's head became very still, her
neck stiff and tense, as she concentrated, looking at Dan. "I don't
understand," she said. "I mean, what do you mean that was."

"No, it's nothing," Dan said, paying attention to the baby.

Abigail's head and neck gradually lost their tension. She didn't
like the way he was acting. All Dan thought was that he had a
great deal of energy, and wanted to play in a happy or comic way;
but Abigail felt he wasn't being with her, rather that she was
being made some kind of audience for his games, or was his
straight man in a routine watched by an outside audience. Dan
knew his exuberance was resented, because while he was making
the baby laugh now he was really concentrating on how Abigail
had stiffened. He was a little angry that she couldn't stand his
energy and play, that she thought it was childish and was afraid
of it. Actually she liked his playfulness, but told herself he was
pushing her outside when he made her his audience or his team-
mate in a vaudeville show.

"You really think it's good for him to be learning those words,
huh?" Abigail said with light irony; he felt he was supported,
not questioned.

"It's the best thing for him," Dan answered in the same tone.
He sat the baby on the kitchen table.

"I'm not so sure," Abigail was serious and lowering her head.

But Dan was already moving toward her, and pulled her out of
her chair. She was a frail person; he was eight inches taller than
her, and at least sixty pounds heavier. He lifted her up and lay

her on the floor. She was laughing and pretending to struggle. He sat on her without applying any pressure, supporting himself on his knees, and he held her two hands together with one hand. She was struggling, laughing and making what seemed to Dan a pretense of trying to get out, blushing, saying, "let me out, Dan" with a silly smile.

"You can't get out, you can't get out," he sang, pointing at her face with his free hand.

She sounded wounded and petulant. "Let me up!"

"Ha ha," he said.

"Let me up, the baby may fall off the table," she laughed, wrenching and twisting her body futilely once more. He still knelt over her and still held her hands clasped, thinking how she was even tinier in this position.

Then suddenly she was authoritative and said, "Get off, Dan." They stood up. Abigail didn't go to pick up the baby.

"I have to go now," Dan said. "Okay?" Abigail looked puzzled.

"I should be back by three or four," he said, and kissed her for a second as a signal he was leaving.

"Dan," Abigail said slowly, "I don't think," she wasn't looking at him but at his tie, "it's such a good idea that we should act like this."

"Like what?" Dan asked in a weak voice after there was silence for too long.

"Well it seems like a game, you start jumping on me . . . and then I see myself, I get angry at you because . . . I know I shouldn't get angry like that," she looked at Dan with a smile and a little timidly, "but then . . ." she sighed as though it were a tremendous effort for her to tell him, "then . . . as soon as things seem to be difficult you say 'I'm going'—"

"But you know I don't want to go today, but Irving insisted. I have to go now, it's not a matter that I decided now to leave when I wasn't planning to before."

"But why was it just that second, after I told you to get off?"
Dan had to work very hard to get up enough energy for this
discussion. "Sometimes I don't know what's happening, but"—
now he was talking slowly with a tone of being afraid of hurting
her, "I think you take this too seriously sometimes, because the
slightest little thing that I do which could show that something
was going wrong, or that I wasn't happy with what's happening,
and you bring it up and you get very hurt." Now his tone was
very insistent, commanding and hard, "You see nothing's going
wrong. You have to realize that not each thing should make you
that upset that you're going to . . ." he stopped.

"That I'm going to what," she said, much more relaxed than
before, her voice very gentle.

"No I don't know," he realized.

"I know all that," she said, sounding much more calm to Dan,
"and it's not a matter of me getting upset like I used to before,
only—you know, I think I said this before to you one time, but I
still think it's very true—that we never get things out in the open,
that I feel you never tell me when you're angry, that we never
fight at all really," she sounded puzzled and hurt by this.

"So we do things our own way," Dan said: "There's no should
that we're supposed to fight," he said with a raised voice. Then
they both laughed. "I think we heard this before," Dan said while
they were laughing.

"I know you're right these discussions don't get us anywhere."
Abigail conceded. "You're right."

"Well," Dan said tentatively, not sure he agreed. After some
quiet he said, "The van should be coming about two o'clock . . .
I don't think you'll have to do anything except be here for it."

"Mhm," she said, hugging up close to him.

Now she seemed very soft and pretty to him. They were holding each other around the waist. His hands were on her shoulders,

then on her cheeks. Her hands were on his chest. "I love you my gorgeous baby," Dan said, and they kissed for about a minute, "I love you very much," Abigail said.

Dan walked through a little woods to reach his car in the community parking lot. Most of the trees in the woods were weeping willows, but there were some pines also; bugs were falling from them like blossoms in a wind or a dandruff. It wasn't raining any more, but the tall grasses soaked Dan's grey cotton shoes. This was a favorite place for walking dogs. When he noticed once in a while he was about to squash his shoe into some shit, Dan leaped, vaguely and with amusement thinking he was like a goat. The sun came on and off through the trees, covered and uncovered by grey masses of moving clouds. More and more while Dan walked he saw that the barks of the trees were wrapped at the base in some kind of green slime he couldn't identify. He'd never seen this before; maybe it was some new tree disease, or a new kind of moss entirely, or a mixture of rain or someone's urine and moss. He tested the feeling of the slime with his fingers. Its velvety texture gave him chills. He shook it off; there was still some green stain left on the pads of his fingers that he rubbed off onto his pants. Now he felt there was some bug walking on his left arm, and he looked at the arm. A red creature the size of a penny, thick-legged and confused, was buoying itself and tangling itself in the black hairs it had fallen into, like an octopus in water, not knowing where he was or how to get out. Dan felt a little love for it, and guided it from his forearm onto his finger; then he put his finger in the grass and turned it till the bug was edged onto a piece of grass.

He felt warm and relaxed. He looked around and told himself that this woods was beautiful; he was in love with every thing in it. He looked carefully at the green of the trees, the brown of the

barks, the blue and white sky. He moved his eyes over them as
though he were stroking them with his looks.

The angel made efforts to prepare itself. Its hands were white as
snow, delicate and sickly. But they changed to bloody red—then
they changed to the muted red of terra cotta when the angel held
them up near its bloodless blue lips, and tasted them.

Each terra cotta hand caressed an eyelid tenderly, as if the angel
were exciting itself. It tried on an assortment of bodies, most of
them freakish or diseased in some way. Each successive body the
angel adopted, in an experiment to discover which body would
be least intolerable, stood and explored itself with its own palms
and fingers, naked in the shade of a pine where it had the most
comfort, though it was shivering and chilly; it had been ill and
dizzy when it was exposed to the sunlight.

The eyes were always closed; the hands roamed over the whole
body. It was a perfectly featureless man, poking his own anus
expressionlessly. The albino's white fingers ran over his own
white nipples. A young woman, the angel was seducing herself;
she moved her hands along her hairy thighs and then was squeezing cautiously tenderly and blindly her own vulva, gradually in-
serting a finger more deeply as the lips became more lubricated
and full. She hurt herself and pulled out the finger; she put her
palms over her breasts and stroked them.

But whatever type it tried and parodied, the angel depended
completely for its knowledge of its environment on two yard-long
feelers that emerged from its head and fingered the branches of
the pine it stood and trembled under, or probed in the thin grass,
as if the pathetic selfless creature were blind or unable to open its
lids it liked so much to caress tenderly, no matter what body it
assumed.

When it had finished testing out bodies, it gradually made itself
into a conventional angel: it had no feelers and opened its lids;

the hands felt all around its sexless body, and discovering its wings, which gave off an intense smell of burnt bread, it smiled feeling proud and reassured; it was an angel; its long white wild hair was uncombed and fiery.

Its clothes didn't shine, and weren't the source of any of the warm brightness that penetrated suddenly through Dan's lids, which he'd closed for a few minutes, feeling in love with everything in the woods, getting tactile pleasure in the sunlight on his skin; but there was a splendid, purified whiteness around its robes. Its wings were soft as a swan's, translucent as thin plastic or white petals.

Convinced that it was an angel, the angel felt itself ready to perform its prophecy. "Don't be afraid," it opened.

"I'm not," Dan answered, intent on being honest. "The odd thing about this is you don't excite or frighten me at all, I think; I'm confused, and I don't accept you, I mean I don't get upset about it; but it doesn't surprise me."

"Well, perhaps you should be a little more frightened than you are," the angel said with a certain coldness.

The angel tried to explain to Dan that in about ten years he would be a destructive tyrant modeled after Adolf Hitler, and would end by destroying every thing alive in the world. It couldn't make clear why Dan would be transformed overnight from an innocuous person into a world-destroyer; and because all this went unexplained, Dan didn't completely believe the prophecy yet. He asked why all this would happen; since the angel didn't give any answer Dan couldn't accept that it would happen.

"There is a progression from the will to the emotions and at last to the Spirit." The angel quoted the Talmud, "Zeal leads to cleanliness, cleanliness to ritual purity, ritual purity to self-control, self-control to holiness, holiness to humility, humility to fear of sin, fear of sin to saintliness, and saintliness to the Holy Spirit." It then looked at Dan as though it had communicated something revelatory. But Dan understood nothing concrete from all the words.

"What's the difference between saintliness and holiness?" Dan asked.

The angel was like a psychiatrist trying to tell a narcissist about love; with one difference, that the psychiatrist would be prepared for his patient's obtuseness.

The angel was just silent; he understood that Dan was anxious to learn but he was angry at himself for not knowing how to teach.

"I hope we're not . . . losing communication," Dan said. "I'd like to talk with you. . . ." He was fascinated to find out what this exotic creature was like.

But the angel in a half hour found no way of concretizing his message; he got no emotional reaction from Dan. "I still don't understand all these words," Dan said timidly.

"A picture is worth a thousand words," the angel answered suddenly, smiling happily in a way it hadn't smiled before, as though it had discovered a password to admit it into Dan's company and friendship.

The angel wanted to conjure for Dan a moving picture of Dan's destruction of the world, but it failed. The events Dan saw himself in the middle of, tyrannizing and murdering, weren't as awful or believable as the angel intended them. Little prettinesses shot up here and there in the picture that Dan watched as if it were a news broadcast; he was too passive and entertained, not hysterical or frightened absolutely enough to please the angel. It hoped to see Dan converted, but he was only attentive.

There were red and yellow flowers, crocuses, zinnias, and roses, scattered on the blue waves. There was no explanation for the flowers. The future sadistic Dan commanded a camouflaged battleship, screaming from his moustached mouth orders to shoot missiles to the left and right, contented watching cities and ships explode, three miles away on the shore, and on the horizon.

"What are the flowers doing there?" Dan asked the angel.

"What flowers?" it asked back.

"There were flowers near the ship. The whole scene was violent, but for some reason there were flowers in the water."

"That is not good," it said, "but at last you are telling me what you see. I have conjured up corpses on the waves, people you will execute on the ship, and then throw overboard. You have to make an effort to understand."

The waves were ordered and symmetrical, standardized; the ship was an old craft of wood, and the sea, not rolling but swelling up and down, was the sea of a medieval painting. "Send off the clean bombs!" Dan ordered. There was a fireworks of white detergent flakes from the guns, flying like snow toward the shore. In minutes the water on the coast had churned itself into a foam of soap bubbles.

Dan laughed. The angel said arrogantly, "What is funny?"

Now Dan had a perspective from the shore. His battleship looked tiny on the horizon; then he was back on the ship, saying "shell the coast" to an immediate inferior.

He was back on the coast waiting for the shells. A crowd of maimed people struggled, lamented, and were dying on the shore, panicked after the first shelling. Some of the wounded people were caressing each other and crying. The death vision made Dan more nervous and upset than any of the others; his brows knit together because he was pained, and the corners of his mouth pulled downward because he was suppressing crying. The angel observed all this and was satisfied that Dan was responding deeply, as he should. "You have healed slightly the hurt of the daughter of my people, saying Peace, Peace, when there is no peace," the angel took the opportunity to quote Isaiah.

Every one on the shore could already see the shells coming

toward them, and Dan didn't listen carefully to the quotation. For a moment in his vision the bomb shells changed to sea shells; there were egg shells painted for Easter also; large hot pink spiral sea shells; nut shells, opening up with some grey fruit inside— which, when they hit the sand, metamorphosed into bombs and blew up, killing all the people, making the whole picture smoke and explosion; but Dan was still there and conscious on the coast, though every one else was killed.

"That's terrible," Dan told the angel, putting a certain drama and pain in his voice; what he thought was terrible specifically was the way the decorative shells were so weirdly replaced. The angel said nothing for once and Dan thought it had sensed some insincerity. To destroy the silence Dan deliberately antagonized it.

"The sea shells . . . I thought the sea shells were pretty."

"There is nothing pretty in any of this," the angel began moving its wings. "This is not a television show. You certainly haven't shown yourself a person of great conscience." It had expected from Dan a passionate response stronger than anything Dan ever felt. When all the techniques it knew—direct conversation, scriptural quotation, and visions—failed, it gave up and said a temporary good-bye.

Dan's mother lay in bed tortured by a migraine headache, her brow and left eye bathed by a blue cloth that had been immersed in a solution of boiled water and vinegar. The solution was in a white pot which was standing on a little mahogany bedtable. On this table were four boxes with pink, yellow, green and white pills in them, none of which seemed to be successful in relieving her pain. It was the second day of this migraine, and she cried silently for about a half hour in the morning, terrorized by the thought that the headache could continue, as it had before, for as long as a week. This fear made her so frightened she vomited. Because she hadn't eaten much, most of the time she was just retching, bent over the white toilet, weakly comforted by the whiteness and smallness of the bathroom. The retching made the blood flow forcefully into her head so that the pain increased. While a migraine was going on she usually found light unbearable, kept all the blinds closed in her room, lay on her back with her head on a pillow or sometimes propped up on several pillows, and covered her brow and eyes with the cloth in order to exclude as much light as possible. About every forty-five minutes, her husband, who was near deaf, came into the room and took the pot. The water was getting cool, and his job was to pour it out, refill the pot, and boil it. He asked her how she was feeling, and she always said something indicating both that it hurt terribly and that she was used to it. The rest of the time her husband sat in front of his television, which he could hardly hear; but he watched sports: baseball or golf or bowling, and didn't lose much from his lack of hearing. He didn't spend any time with his wife while she was suffering her headaches: this was traditional with him. Though sometimes he would kiss her on the brow or on the eye with his lips, tasting the vinegar and touch of the hot skin. She said, "That feels so good, when you kiss me there." Her husband, Yanusch, who was in his seventies, refused to get an efficient modern hearing aid, and stuck to his old one, which ran on a large battery suspended from a string necklace over his chest, contoured beneath his shirt like a single rectangular breast. At least ten times this battery had set his shirt smouldering, starting a grotesque scene in which the old man whimpered and shrieked for help, trying to unbutton the shirt, a scene which ended when someone threw a glass of water on him. Only three weeks before the visit Dan was making now, his father's plaid flannel shirt had begun smouldering during a conversation among the three of them, in which the old man took the tiniest part. Dan went into the kitchen and filled up a glass with water. By the time he was back in the livingroom the material had already begun to flame in one place, which had never happened before. Dan poured the water on his father's shirt, wetting also the pants; then he took off the shirt and examined his father's chest, which was a little burnt in one area under the nipple, where the white hairs had become shrivels of black ash. He went for some vaseline and spread it on. "Why should that happen Danny?" his father asked. "How could it happen, I don't understand it." Every one had decided that Dan's father was senile. He sat in front of the television as often as he could, smoking a pipe, which made his lips black. His skin was as close to grey as human skin can be. When anything important happened, such as a visit from Dan with the baby, he seemed conscious, lucid, alert, watched the baby struggle and act. They'd tell him things and he'd nod or smile. But every one who saw him called him senile because the rest of the time he just watched television or sat making no responses. His only expression was a laughter, a sudden convulsion when his lips went into a smile and his chest shook. Dan didn't think his father was senile: he was only retreating. This retreat gave him the advantages of not having to talk to any one, and of being pampered; he could spend his old age in his own good company and every once in a while have a good laugh.

After he left the factory Dan paid a short visit to his parents.

Yanusch laughed inanely. He sat in a soft cushion chair strewn with a flower design of blue and gold. There were horses dancing on television; then there were young girls lifting their dresses and coying their knees, showing parts of thigh and then with a burst of music showing their panties for a second.

Dan embraced his father, and they patted each other's backs.

"Momma is inside," Yanusch said, toward the end of the hug.

Dan switched on the light in his mother's room. Light blossomed from three directions, showing her frail in her bed, a chain of red beads around her wrist; she was in pale yellow pajamas, uncovered, with the blue cloth on her brow. She quickly covered herself and said, "Don't turn on the light! It hurts me."

Abigail left the baby asleep watched by a friend and took a walk over a pebbled road to the lakeside, where she watched the rowboats moving quietly and silently. She was sitting on the shore of the lake for about an hour, watching the people and starting short conversations. The boatboy, at the end of the hour, walked to the edge of the dock with his loudspeaker and called, "All boats in." Abigail decided she'd been there long enough and walked back to the house.

The mystery novel open and turned over on Dan's lap had a bright red cover. Abigail looked at it and read the title upside down, then went and stood over Dan by the side of his lounge chair. She'd observed that he read mystery novels whenever he was brooding. He had stopped reading now and was just sitting in his chair without talking to her. "I think there's something wrong. Isn't there?" Abigail suggested.

"No; I was thinking about the boy in the shop today. That's a strange thing," Dan said in a voice between talking and direction-less muttering.

"Mm," Abigail said. "Joey's asleep" she said about their baby. "Here," she said, taking the book off his lap, "let me sit down on your lap."

"A boy like that maybe isn't so stupid."

"I think he's pretty stupid," she was wry. "I can't believe you're seriously thinking he's done something shrewd." On the wall opposite them they'd hung a painting of an apartment building with linen hung out to dry; Dan was looking at it for a while and not saying anything.

"The swellings are already going down," Abigail said. The baby also had been stung during the night, on a cheek, and they'd taken him to the doctor in the afternoon; Dan didn't have to pay.

"That's good," Dan felt satisfied for an instant.

"His desk is amazing," he said, "that must cost a thousand dollars." The doctor sat behind a wood desk that had many elabo-brown surface that glowed the reflection of a heavy lamp stand-rate curlicue carvings, ridges and round bulbs, and a polished ing on it.

"Yes I know," Abigail said. "He seems so proud of the desk. That red carpet is so horrible! My God, I didn't think any one had such bad taste."

"Hmph," Dan reacted, smiling a little, but feeling he had nothing to answer.

Abigail decided to be blithe and passive to get him happier, and was studying him while sitting on his lap. Dan had the idea she was attacking the red carpet to comfort him, because he'd been complaining all the time they were driving home from the doctor that he wasn't making as much money as he could, and even joking bitterly about the boy getting a lot of insurance money.

Half a minute passed without talk till Dan said, "Do you really think the carpet's bad? I sort of like it." They laughed at themselves arguing.

"Really?" Abigail said. "I don't understand you men. None of you have any taste."

Dan pulled her head toward him so that it was resting on his shoulder, and they sat hugging each other.

At last Dan said, "It's useless to try to work inside somebody else's system, who's in control and which you can't get out of and you can't get ahead in. I know this is all just talking but," he stopped.

"It's not just talking. I know what you mean," Abigail said. "I think that you're saying the same thing you said before."

"No it's not the same thing."

"But if you're not a slave, I mean if you don't have some kind of real responsibility, what are you going to be? I think you just have to accept something."

"No, I know. I don't care about the working the responsibility and so on, but it just makes it hard having to put out all this money for a bunch of doctors—" he was talking about paying for operations for his parents "—and I have to work with these completely stupid people—no that's not true, some of them are good people, but."

"I don't really know exactly what's bothering you." Abigail kissed his fingers three or four short times in between the words.

"I'm not even humiliated any more when I don't pay the doctor."

"But I don't see why you should get so upset," Abigail said, "It's not something where you're not making enough money. You had to pay for them."

"Mhm ... yeah." Dan nodded.

Did this boy . . . did you even talk to him much? Abigail asked.

"No, I just said hello. He was a strange character—You know what I want to do tomorrow?"

"What."

"I want to go on a turtle hunt. Have you ever done that?"

"No what's that?" She snuggled a little into him.

"It's a good thing. They're very hard to catch," he said.

"Well, don't they snap?"

"No, these turtles don't snap—It's not going to be hard, we just take a rowboat and try to follow them and pull them out of the water. I used to do this all the time with my father."

"Oh." She seemed pleased and her buttocks settled into him more, as if she were unstiffening. "I was thinking it was some kind of a hike into the jungle with snakes—well not that, but I was expecting we'd be using knives."

"No, I wouldn't do that," he laughed, pulling his head back, affecting shock that she'd think him so brutal. "We throw them right back afterwards."

"You know Dan," she said, out of nowhere, "I'm very happy you're not depressed any more." There was a silence. "I have the feeling I shouldn't've said that." She put her head down against his chest. He thought she was on the verge of crying.

"No no," he said, shaking his head as if to shake out an ache. "You didn't say anything wrong" in a mothering tone.

"I know," she assured him. "It's just that you seem so upset and silent and you won't tell me why."

"But it has nothing to do with you!"

"I know," Abigail said, "but why can't you tell me? I don't want to feel you can't tell me when something's wrong."

"But there's nothing really. I'm just depressed because of going to work today and then to Mom's. I don't always get depressed because of something that happens."

Abigail put her head down and said, "Okay."

She went to sleep and he read his novel till two in the morning. At six he was up and went out to the backyard to work on the dog-house he was building for their collie.

He had in the basement twenty pine boards to begin the dog-house. He went to the basement through the door that opened from the ground, and pulled on the light. He sectioned a stack of twelve boards and lifted it onto his shoulder, walking up the stairs from the basement bent to one side. The bottom board was digging painfully into his neck and he panted. He walked stiffly to the corner of the yard for which he planned the doghouse and let the boards fall freely because his neck hurt so much. His arm was throbbing. The air had a wet tree scent. Dan put his hand to his stinging neck and felt the sore dent.

He still had to remove a large stone embedded in the site which would annoy the collie. He dug with a shovel around the stone

till its belly was revealed and he could seize it to lift it up and
away. He grabbed on. The stone was a little slippery, but he got a
firm hold. Abigail was up and watched him from the kitchen
window. She came outside and said, "You'll strain yourself."

But Dan knew the correct way to lift. He avoided back-strain
by making his arms and legs do the work. He crouched, knees
bent, then slowly stood up back straight, thighs doing most of the
lifting. Arms aching, he walked badly to another corner of the
yard and set down the stone, again by bending his knees, letting
it drop only a few inches before it reached the ground. He stood
up, his brow sweating, breathing very hard. "Well hhh I got it
cleared anyway," he said.

"I just squeezed us some fresh oranges," she said.

It was so hot in the afternoon that people horded by the water-
front, and there was a long line of residents waiting to take out
rowboats for an hour. The boatboy—it was his first year as a boatboy—to keep out the sun put on a Mexican hat whose brim was
so wide it was as good as an umbrella over his tall frail body, but
still, he twice felt faint.

Abigail had met him the afternoon before. "His name is
Lenny," she told Dan. "He tried to pick me up yesterday. It makes
me feel like a baby." She spun her arms in circles. Lenny was
only twenty, she estimated. He had been wearing his crazy hat,
she said, and was carrying a single longstemmed rose; "so I
thought it was for his girl-friend—and I felt so happy watching
the water and it was all so nice that I smiled at him, you know
like at a little boy. But he walked up to me very properly, and he
swooped off his hat—" she imitated his stiffness and gesturing—
"with a bow and said, 'Would you like this rose, madame?' Then
I took the rose. He asked me where I lived, and it was all over.
I told him where and I said I was married; so he laughed and
said" (she made her voice bass) "I guess I want that rose back."

But there was very little spirit in her parody. Dan made himself laugh. "So what'd you do?"

"Well, I offered him the rose but he said I should keep it; and we were talking for about fifteen minutes. And he's a very sweet boy; he used to go to the same camp I did and we talked about that." "Mhm." "—Anyway maybe I can ask him to let us have a boat first. Otherwise we won't get one before four o'clock."

Abigail took Dan's hand and dragged him to the front of the line. The people were all studying her; Abigail was lovely. She was wearing a white bikini with small red and yellow flowers on, she had a slight body with full breasts which Dan talked proudly of. He said in her ear, "Every one's looking at my wife's tits." The woman on line, especially the old, were staring at her with still faces. "They're feeble people" Dan whispered to her, and she laughed. She wore a red band in her hair which she tore off while she was walking, and she shook out her light brown hair.

Abigail touched Lenny's naked back. "Hi, Lenny."

"Hi, Obby." He had turned around.

"Dan, this is Lenny." The two men shook hands. "Lenny, do you think you could let us go out sooner? we'd like to. We're all the way at the back," Abigail asked.

"Sure, I guess so," Lenny said, half seeing the people on line who could hear him, who didn't object.

At the end of the boating hour about twenty boats were pulling into the bouncing dock; almost all the rowers had difficulty steering their boats, so that the process took at least ten minutes.

Lenny told Dan and Abigail he thought this system should be changed, because it concentrated all his work in a few minutes each hour, and made the boaters wait. As a boat coasted toward the dock Lenny knelt and grabbed the rope at the prow; he pulled the boat toward the dock and strung the rope through a metal loop affixed on the dock. Then he ran to another boat on its way in. Occasionally he offered a woman his hand to help her out, though usually the men came out of the boats first to do this.

Abigail and Dan stepped into a wooden boat. They could have had a new aluminum one, but the seats were so hot from the sun that Abigail couldn't have sat on one in her bikini, without burning her thighs. As it was she was uncomfortable at first.

Lenny said, "Hey, have you people got yourself some hats? No fooling, you could get a sunstroke today." Dan had already rowed out a few feet; he rowed in reverse back to the dock, while Abigail said, "No, we haven't."

"Well, I have some towels here you put over your heads."

"O wonderful!" Abigail said, sticking her arm out, hand open, over the dock.

Lenny opened the lid of a green wooden oar-box on the dock, and pulled from it two white towels which he threw to Abigail. She was seated in the back of the boat, facing Dan, who looked at the lake, his back to Lenny. Dan turned around and said "Thanks a lot."

"That's okay," Lenny said.

Dan oared, moving the boat backwards, away from the dock. Out on the open water and rowing easily he said, "This is a terrific way to relax." "O! it's so wonderful to be with you for a whole day!" Abigail closed her eyes and leaned back, her face getting sun. Dan had a feeling of love and tranquility inside his whole trunk; he watched Abigail. She opened her eyes. "Have you been watching me this whole time?"

"Mhm," he said. She lifted her leg and caressed his knee with her foot.

Dan told himself to stop thinking. He was knitting his brows, and shook his head quickly to get a painful thought out of his brains.

Abigail said " 'No' what?"

"What?" Dan returned.

"No, I mean, why'd you shake your head? Is something wrong?"

"No no."

"Have you got a headache again?"

"No, there was a fly on my neck—" he laughed at her.

"Oh," Abigail said. "Because you could always use a towel."

There were large dark green turtles sitting sunning themselves on rocks that came up over the surface of the lake. The rest swam in those parts of the lake that were quilted with white water lilies and green lily pads; they came up once every few minutes for air, sticking out only their snakes' heads, keeping the rest of their bodies hidden under the water, flailing their fins to keep buoyed. Unopened lily buds looked almost the same as their heads. Dan told Abigail to survey the water very carefully for movements of "buds" or ripples in the surface that might betray the camouflage. He had rowed the boat into the lilies. In clear water the boat's movement made no noises except the splashes against the sides and quiet rush of the oars in the water. But the lily pads and other vegetation where the turtles hid scratched on the boat's bottom loud enough to be a warning. The oldest ones were the most daring. They were black-green and about as big as a hand. Their oval shells got soft and black when they were dying, sometimes covered with a white ooze. The young ones lived by the shore, basking on little stones there, never swimming out as far as the middle of the lake. Their shells were light green, the size and shape of big coins.

It was hot midafternoon and for a half hour Dan and Abigail hadn't detected one turtle, in an area full of lily pads.

"Let's try to catch one off a stone. You see them over there?" He pointed to a rock about fifty feet away.

"No, I can't; where?"

"We'll get closer." Dan rowed from the lilies into clear water and, very slowly and quietly, putting his finger on his lip to stop Abigail from speaking, he tried to move up on the turtles without their hearing him.

When they were about a boat's length from the stone Abigail finally saw the three turtles basking. Dan stopped using the oars and let the boat coast toward the stone, extending his arm as fast as he could. The turtles walked into the water, their shells knocking against the stone. Dan and Abigail started laughing. "This is so ridiculous," she said, laughing without control for at least a minute. Dan thought the turtles were contemptuous and they aroused in him a guilty feeling that he was a stupid, a vicious one, chasing them.

This feeling that the turtles were his betters didn't stop him, because he had it rarely. More often he felt an affection toward them and laughed at them; the affection drove him to want to catch them and play with them despite their fear. "I really enjoy this," Abigail said, recuperating from her laughter.

"I see one," Dan said, pointing at the water to one of the turtles he had scared swimming below the surface. "Do you see it?" he said.

"No," she said, looking into the lake. "Wait, yeh, I see him!"

Dan used one oar to get her close enough to the turtle to grab him. The turtle began swimming away from the shadow of the boat. But Abigail was close enough to catch him. She put her hand into the water quickly, held his shell for an instant; but her hand was shocked and frightened by the touch and she withdrew it. "I almost had him," she said, very conscious of her forearm and the cold water on it.

Dan was watching the turtle, who was now aware he was hunted. "That's an old monster," Dan said. The turtle was swimming wide circles, always just enough ahead of the boat, giving Dan a hard time rowing in the right arc. "Are you sure it won't snap?" Abigail asked.

"No, he won't," Dan said, leaning over the side of the boat. The turtle hadn't come up for air for at least five minutes, was tiring and getting out of breath.

"You take the oars and I'll catch him," Dan said. It took them a few seconds to change places, in which time the turtle had swum far enough from the boat to come up for air. Dan saw him, and instructed Abigail whispering, "Left oar!" She gave one full pull on the left oar, brought Dan close enough to lean extravagantly over the boat and grab hold of the turtle who was just beginning to submerge.

He pulled the dripping, openmouthed turtle, who was flailing his legs furiously in the air, out of the water. Dan shrieked, mocking at the turtle, "We got you, hey? turtle!" trying to look right into the turtle's eyes; but the turtle kept averting its snake head this way and that, as though it were impossible to stomach looking at a repulsive human head.

Dan held the turtle toward Abigail to show her. It opened its pointed mouth and showed a small black tongue, then closed the mouth. It spat turning its head from left to right. Abigail said she didn't want to hold it. Dan set the turtle on the bottom of the boat, and it began trying to climb the vertical sides, its feet still on the bottom, pulling itself up along the side till it made a forty-five degree angle with the bottom, then dropping back making a clacking noise, the outer skeleton crashing against the bottom.

They watched him and listened to the scratching of his naily fins not able to hold up its own weight against the side of the boat. Dan picked it up and put it back in the cool water, holding onto it for a few seconds while it was submerged. Then he released it. This time was a joy for the turtle, but it made Dan a little lonely.

Abigail kept her hand in the cool water and had been making comments to Dan about the turtle's struggles on the floor of the boat. All this time during the turtle hunt Dan had been feeling once in a while that he remembered the prophecy, as though he were zooming his camera to a close-up of himself; and what was he doing enjoying himself? He had asked Abigail to go rowing with him because he wanted to talk with her in a beautiful environment, but he hadn't decided that he would tell her about the prophecy. Now he felt the prophecy impinging on what he was going to be saying to her, and only halfheartedly suppressed it.

Dan rowed around over the clear parts of the lake. Abigail put one of the towels on her head and leaned back against the v of the prow. They passed by a cliff of trees which cast a dark green reflection on the lake. Dan rowed closer and closer to the shore to see if he could get them inside the reflection. Then he rowed out toward the lilies, enjoying using an alternative stroking of the oars, so that the forward movement of the boat consisted of movements forward to left, then forward to the right. Abigail was watching Dan and the scenery behind him, which was the lake and short trees and a red and white farmhouse among the trees, shifting a little to the left, then to the right. When they came into the waterlilies, Abigail pulled one from the water. It had an elastic stem. She held the stem in her two hands and pulled her hands apart till it snapped; there was water in the hollow stem. The petals were white at the top; the tender inside of the lily was pale yellow, with three water ants crawling in it. She sniffed but it had no odor.

Abigail had been comfortable in the scenery and silence that prevailed for the last minutes, but Dan was agitated. Despite the fact that it sounded artificial to him he opened by talking about race riots in the city. He had put his hand in the water and flicked water in her face while he talked. Her face tightened up for a second when the water hit her and smiled and she didn't splash him back. She said she thought maybe it was a good thing that people were getting frightened by the violence and that it was necessary to have riots. "Anyway," she joked at herself, "we're safe up here." She plucked a petal and tried throwing it at him, but it fell a few inches after leaving her hand. Dan said it was pretty obvious that nothing could be done if people were full of hate and anger; he splashed her violently while he said this and she laughed. "Don't you . . . think hate sometimes accomplishes something" she asked, shoveling both hands full of water and drenching him. They sat wet and laughing, Abigail breathless.

After a silence Dan was serious again. "It doesn't work that way, it can't, because then the hate's only going to become more hate," he said excitedly, but then he was calm and tender, looking at her, "you hate everybody and then you stop what they're doing wrong, and even though sometimes what they're doing is wrong, but then you just go on with the same amount of evil there was before. And the only way you're going to get anything real done is if that hate is taken away and you can make some small improvements by some kind of good feelings."

"But that doesn't . . . you know that's very saintly and everything, but that really doesn't . . . that's too wishwashy. Because it's human to hate, and I don't think you'll be able to just throw it away like that because it's not pretty."

"Mhm," Dan said, not continuing the discussion, listening to Lenny calling the boats in through his loudspeaker.

"We can stay," Abigail said; Dan had taken hold of the oars. "It's beautiful here. . . . I don't want to talk about this," she pleaded.

Dan hadn't told her about the angel yet.

"I saw an angel yesterday."

"What?" she said.

"When I was going for the car," he was looking at ivies on the shore a few feet away, "I met an angel who said I was going to become an Adolf Hitler, and that I'd destroy the world." Abigail felt embarrassed by the slow seriousness of his confession.

"I don't understand," she said. It wasn't clear to Dan whether she meant she misunderstood him, or what he'd told her.

"I had a vision," he said.

"Well . . . what did you see?" He laughed at this but she didn't.

"Well—you can't really believe that this is true?" After Dan had sketched the vision for her, Abigail felt she was making an obvious and frigid point. He had stressed the incongruous flowers and the murdered people, telling the story clearly and convincingly enough to make Abigail see pictures of some of the things. Now she was giving him her inept skeptical answer, the only one she could accept. "I feel I'm being sympathetic" she said with irony intended. She had been considering saying the last sentence several times, and meant it to be, "I feel I'm being unsympathetic." But when she said it she withdrew the *un* and ended the sentence by drawing out the last word. His silence made her hear her own words and brood over them and their sound; if he'd answered she would have forgotten them. When she finally spoke her sentence she put into it a terrific amount of energy and work; but it was a spastic on his way across an avenue; she was forcing herself to move from word to word, not making a strong even stride but thrashing about. "I think you were working very hard for the past week." Dan felt pleased and relaxed by this care and looked at her, stroking her cheek by extending his arm out, between their seats, and she felt the talking was easier, "you were up so early and went to bed so late . . . I asked you not to do that." They laughed. She deliberately took this offensive although she was convinced his hours had nothing to do with his hallucinating, because she expected her scolding would show him she knew the event was trivial, and would relax and comfort him. "I want you to go to a doctor," she said. She stood up in the boat, and tilting the boat left and right went and sat next him on the rower's seat. He was looking at the seeping floor. "I think you think this is real, but it's ridiculous. And then you even tell me this—I think you're chasing me away," she said, hoping he would look at her, "I feel as if you want me to laugh at you or go away. Why do you tell me this?"

"I don't know why I'd want to chase you away," he said not looking at her.

"I don't think you do, but I feel that way."

"I didn't tell you this because of you. This really happened to me," he laughed.

Abigail was entirely serious, "I really think you should go to a psychiatrist once."

"You think so?"

"Yeah, just to see what he'd say; because I'm sure he'll tell you just what I am."

"Well then why do I have to go?" he laughed.

"No, because he understands it and I don't."

"I don't think I told you this to chase you away. I was thinking for a long time whether or not I should tell you. You realize I couldn't keep it from you."

"I want to hear about it more, because I didn't get a clear picture from what you told me."

"This angel was a kind of ordinary looking thing; I mean he had wings . . ." he laughed. "You know, it's a joke!—So he started talking to me, he was talking to me for about a half hour; and he was telling me I was going to destroy the world . . . and . . . I didn't understand. Actually it didn't do anything to me. I just listened to this just took it without feeling any excitement or any pain or you know . . . without it upsetting me. Then I told him I didn't understand and he saw that I didn't, or that I was getting it, and so he got very upset about that, he got really, he started acting very you know haughty about it and everything and he said that uhm . . . he would have to, he would have to show me pictures, he said that with contempt, almost like, 'I'm gonna show you pictures.' " Here Dan laughed, mimicking the way a sweet old lady would talk to a child. "But it wasn't pictures, we were in, we were part of it, you see? We were part of this, of what was actually happening. And what happened was that we were on this big battleship," he laughed. "It sounds like a joke now, but at the time, it was very real, and I think it did happen. It's not that it's a dream or anything like that. I mean it's not a hallucination either, it actually happened." He thought Abigail sighed. "I can tell the difference between when it really happens and when I'm imagining it. And . . . um . . . so we were on this battleship, and he said in ten years I'd be, I would be an Adolf Hitler." "That's the part I don't understand," she said. "It's so stupid!" "No, it isn't that stupid, I just can't tell it.—And uh and uh . . . at any rate, we were on the battleship, and I was looking at this, at this picture of myself, there, or I was looking at myself. I was ten years older, and I had a moustache, and grey hair, and I was very angry; I looked very angry. I . . . and I was hopping up and down the way Hitler used to," here Dan wasn't laughing any more, though it was a funny part to Abigail who made a little exhaled laugh. Dan felt himself very pained remembering this part about himself looking like Hitler, "and I was making an idiot out of myself, and I was screaming and yelling and everything," he sounded as if he might cry, "and there were all these other . . . and I was wearing a uniform, and there were all these other people running around I was commanding. And then . . . yeh . . . the angel said the battleship was called The Clean Bomb and then we were standing on the shore. The thing was it was very pretty, it was a lovely shore. See that's the whole thing—the whole thing was so pretty. And . . . uh . . . we were standing on the sand, on the beach there, there were large waves, ah . . . there were shells all over the beach. And the ship . . . I could see the ship far out, I could see it on the horizon somewhere, you know, slightly misted over. All of a sudden it exploded. And the thing is you see I can

tell you all of this and it seems to me now almost like it's a joke!"
"Yes, I know what you mean," she encouraged. "—And it doesn't
even bother me, that's what's so horrible. It doesn't mean anything
to me, Abbi. . . . The whole thing exploded, and . . . um. . . ." Dan
puzzled for about ten seconds, not talking. When he began to
speak again he spoke so oppressively slow that Abigail felt sick
and angry about his pitying himself so much, and she shut up
and let him talk. "Of course later on he told me, he told me some
things. I just remembered that now, I mean he told me some
things that were very sad and that I didn't think were funny. But
this first part I remembered more clear, and . . . maybe because
we're out on the lake now; the uh . . . the water. And um . . . so
the ship exploded. And the thing is that it exploded and it was
like snowflakes of, of soap. And the soap was raining and the
whole ocean was filled with some kind of detergent, and it was
bubbling, and it was bubbling onto the shore." Abigail laughed a
little laugh again, but wasn't smiling. "He showed me a tree on
the shore, he said it was a sassafras tree. And he said that these
leaves all lived together on the same tree, that there were four
kinds of different leaves. I can't figure it out at all. What do you
think that was." "I don't know" she said bitterly. He laughed.
"And then um . . . then . . . yeah. There was this headline in a
newspaper saying Navy Shells the Coast. I saw all these sea shells.
I was looking at the sea shells, they were actually flying into us
on the shore there; he was showing me newspapers from the time
I was going to be destroying the world. And . . ." Dan was getting tired from talking and didn't want to relate this part. "This is
what hurts me the most, this is it, this is the part where I stopped
seeing it as sad, so I said that was very pretty, because I thought
that he wanted the, that he wanted to entertain me or amuse me,
and I said the shells were very pretty, I wanted to make him feel
good, and so well he got very angry about this. He looked almost
vicious. And he said that everything—um, something like that—

that everything that he tries to show me comes out wrong, or that
I saw it wrong." Abigail sighed now wanting him to hear her.
"And that I see everything as being physical, I see everything
taking place only physically. And then he told me that he'd
wanted me to see, the picture he wanted me to see, was pictures
of bombs; bomb shells; you see, and I saw sea shells. But at any
rate he got very angry, and now he started showing me pictures
of people who were dying. And this part, this was very strange,
because, also here it was like watching it on a film or on a movie
—not like in a dream, because in a dream I'm always moved—
because I didn't believe it. And there they were, you know,
women like insects, and they were bleeding, and I was sort of,
just watching them. And this was what I was causing, you see, or
what I would do. And I asked him how it was, how I'm going
to be the person, it seemed to me completely ridiculous." "Mhm,"
she said, "that's what I don't see." "He didn't explain that. At
least he didn't make it clear to me. The ocean was really pretty;
and there were torches." He struggled for something else to remember to relate, looking up. "And, it was very pretty. But I
really saw. It wasn't a matter that I didn't see it and . . . But it's
not more important to me than some dream. It wasn't a dream,
but it's no more—"

Abigail felt he was pounding on her chest with adolescent fists.
It hurt and frightened her that he could be so completely blind,
picking on himself with so much mockery. "But it was! Don't
you see that?" Abigail was crying. "I mean if you heard someone
else saying this wouldn't you know it was?"

Seeing her cry, Dan decided that he had been torturing her.
"Yeah," he said. They talked for a few minutes more; he assured
her he would consult a doctor about what had happened. They
embraced a little, and when it was over he patted her behind,
signaling her to go back to her seat. "Okay, you little slut," he
joked, "we have to take the boat back." She suggested that each

of them take an oar and remain together on the same seat. Having trouble coordinating their rowing, they zigzagged back to the dock, where Lenny scolded them for keeping the boat out for two hours. "Is it that long," Abigail said, climbing from the boat. She sounded a little stern, "We had something to talk about."

Dan came home after his first session with the psychiatrist, and talked about it for a long time with Abigail. The psychiatrist's eyes were small, wrinkled and wet, behind the frail lenses of bronze-rimmed glasses; he'd been stylishly dressed; Dan thought he might be wearing perfume. Dan felt the smiles were dishonest and studied the decor of the office. The waiting room, used by a group of doctors, had been a colder room. He'd sat next to a priest reading a magazine, and put an old copy on his own lap but couldn't concentrate on it, and gazed around the waiting room. He'd sat on a cushioned sofa, but everything else in the room, chairs, magazine racks, a coffee table and side tables, was made out of pink wrought iron. But the office was a more placid room, its white walls decorated with seascapes, some abstract originals, probably by patients, Dan said, and diplomas. All the furniture was upholstered, soft. Dan sat facing the doctor across a desk; something in the psychiatrist's tone had incensed him at first. The indifference was pretending to be gentleness and control. He had the spirit of a river eroding a wound. The gentleness was appealing even if it was phony.

The doctor hadn't said if the vision had been a hallucination; that didn't matter, he said, and there would be no point trying to persuade Dan it was. But he thought it was "interesting" that Dan assumed the angel meant for him to kill himself, when the angel didn't say so. Dan hadn't understood the doctor's drift, and felt the doctor was forcing it. But the doctor had clarified himself by saying that prophecy was usually a warning, not a prediction. Dan got that point and was deeply pleased. "I'd never thought of that!" he said smiling; he told Abigail he felt relieved. He thought the doctor was implying that psychoanalysis, not suicide, was what the angel had been pushing him toward.

Dan didn't know how long it might take, or how expensive it might be, but he went a second time, because he believed he didn't have an alternative, and because Abigail wanted him to.

ARNOLD EGGERS

The Wax City

GRETA: The booming of the guns is not so far off as it was yesterday.

ALBERICH: You notice it, I don't. When you're at the front, you hear too much noise. I only listen for silence: the fir tree outside the window, the comb you move through your hair.

GRETA: Let me take your hand and place it—here—feel? Our child is growing irresistibly.

ALBERICH: Let's go outside, the guns boom less at night. Can you walk? You are not too heavy with the child. It's not very cold. The city will be taken soon—the people are already fleeing—and in a few nights we won't be able to go out at all. Do you want something to cover you?

GRETA: You are so always trying to think or not think, to feel or not to feel, that you don't understand how to be peaceful. When I don't say anything because I don't have anything to say, you think there's something wrong.

ALBERICH: Look!

GRETA: The city is turned to wax!

ALBERICH: The room too. Only we are not turned to wax. What about the war? It is still there; the booming is louder than ever. And what is this? a wick! everything has a wick!

GRETA: The clock, the radiator, the window shade, the fir tree, the blades of grass in the lawn. Help me through the window.

ALBERICH: Ah, there we go. Now, wait a moment—let me take some matches, they're here somewhere, in the drawer. The matches are wax, maybe they'll work anyway.

ALBERICH: I'm going to try to light this phlox. Look how real the wax petals are: dark pink with an edging of white. The flowers are so fragile I can knock them off with a touch of my finger. The light has taken, the floor is burning.

GRETA: The floor doesn't smell like wax, it smells like phlox. The petals are dripping down the stem. Light the other flowers.

GRETA: Look how beautiful our garden is in the twilight! Small clusters of flickering yellow lights, the assembly of shadows, the mixture of the fragrances, the pale glow hovering and beating its wings in the air, the leaves dripping in green drops to the ground.

ALBERICH: Let's go down the street, lighting trees, streetlights, everything we pass.

GRETA: Let's light the wax lanterns hanging in this cafe—the people are still here with their drinks. This man's laughing: he's leaning back with one foot off the ground, one arm in the air, and the other arm slapped on the table.

ALBERICH: The young couple embracing: they're clasped together chest to breast, they have only one wick. The man's brooding: he's slouched over with his elbows on the table and his nose in the top of his glass.

GRETA: The chain of gaslights we lit stretches down the boulevard. The band we passed and lit is melting. The cymbals have fused into a silver contortion, the trombone player's spectacles have melted in a stripe down his pants, the tuba player's tuba is filled with globules of glowing wax.

ALBERICH: There is no sound from the band: the only sound is the splash of wax falling from the trees and the boom of the artillery.

GRETA: The trees have burst into ten thousand flames—each stem a wick, each leaf a drop of wax. The flames swirl with the wind, a shower of wax drops to the ground.

ALBERICH: The artillery is loud—there is something coming—a tank! Do you see the tank coming down the boulevard? Can you run.

GRETA: We don't need to run, we can hide in the cafe.

ALBERICH: Down! (*In a whisper.*) That was machine-gun fire. It swept by overhead in an arc. The tank is still drawing closer. Put your head beneath my arm.—Again.—It is passing now. No! Down again.—It is gone at last. The soldiers must be entering the city. We have not held out as long as expected— what is that on your foot?

GRETA: The lantern was hit by the machine-gun fire; it fell to the ground, splattering its wax on my feet.

ALBERICH: Can you get them apart?

GRETA: With difficulty.

ALBERICH: The band is destroyed—the tank mowed it down. The players stand in architectural ruins or lay smeared out in stripes down the street. This looks like the trombonist's head, how did it get over here? It's still burning, but there's only the bottom part of it left, the liquid of the top part splattered. Damn soldiers! I tremble to see what they've done: the street is disfigured by the grooves of the tank wheels, the buildings are peppered with artillery fire, the band is destroyed. And the tank is still rolling on, one tank of many rolling into the city.

GRETA: The tank shot down leaves from the trees; they are lying about, quietly burning themselves out.

ALBERICH: Let's go to the old part of the city. The tanks cannot penetrate there; the streets are too narrow.

ALBERICH: The river is a stream of molten white wax solidified. The fish are yellow flames burning within the white wax.

GRETA: Here is a general on his horse, forever watching the river and the plaza and the bridges over the river. The trees are not lit yet, the plaza is dark and open. The gaslights are passive observers and the cobblestones are untrampled.

ALBERICH: The old city rises beyond the plaza.

ALBERICH: The buildings are cool here, the walls crooked, they smell like wax. Nothing is lit, the streets rise up the hill.

GRETA: Why are we walking so far? We have zigzagged so much I no longer have a hold over what I am doing. I am tired.

ALBERICH: Come in here—first, a canary is hanging in a cage in the open window. Before we go up, I will light its wick. Both plumage and flame are yellow. . . . The stairs? I will carry you. There seems to be only one room on a floor, let's go up to the top.

GRETA: Lie beside me. My body is already asleep. Be careful of the sheets, draw them gently. They crack.

ALBERICH: I don't want to lie in darkness.

GRETA: Why not?

ALBERICH: We passed an old man in a rocking chair on the last floor. I will bring him up and light him to serve as a rocking chair. I'll be right back.

GRETA: You smile and turn to look out the window. Now you will turn back and jump on me.

ALBERICH: No, I am watching the lower part of the city burn: the flames are fusing together and swirling into the sky. A grey cloudbank hanging low over the city and singed by the flames, prevents them from rising higher. Candle fumes are trapped between the clouds and the city and a glow of candlelight hangs in the impure air. If the clouds rain, the city will sputter and go out, the wicks will drip water instead of wax, water will flow in a film over the streets, collecting in the low parts of the city in deep puddles. In the morning there will be a circle of tanks about the city, tanks on the plaza. The city will be one color: light blue, pale grey, dirty white, ruined buildings, wax-filled streets. The cloud-bank, thin and pale grey will move away anxiously and swiftly in the morning light.

KEITH COHEN

Mission at Cam Ranh Bay

Major Atherton sent an order to the clear-minded captains.
There were seven captains of the battalions, and with each
A hundred infantrymen moved out, armed with rifles and
  grenades.
And Major Atherton brought the officers together into his shelter.
They laid their hand to the refreshments lying ready before them.
(Later, the guards had poured water over their heads
Before they started away from the Major's shelter, Tempo
  3977-BB.)

But these two, O'Donnell and Jacksby, walked beside the lighted
  sea.
When they stood before him, Ky, dazed, sprang up
With his binoculars, leaving the cushion where he had been
  sitting.
And so Nang Ho, when he saw the men, likewise stood up.
Magnificent Ky, having spoken then first, led them forward,
And they sat down on chairs spread in purple
(He had thrown the maps into the fire),
And they laid their hands to the refreshments lying ready before
  them.
Then staunch Captain O'Donnell saw his chance,
And filling his cup with wine he toasted Major Ky.
"Once I load the ships and command them out
To the oil-pocked sea, while inside my men, who did great
  damage,
As usual, to the Da Nang coast, reverse their meters;

Once we have blown vast forests to the shores, roots and all,
Early one morning as the ships pull out of Cam Ranh Bay,
You will see, if you should wish to and if it matters to you,
Soaked raw roots and the peach blossoms themselves."
After he had spoken, Ky nodded quietly to Nang Ho
That he should lay out the warrant before Franks,
So that the others might soon take leave of the ministry.

They went hurrying back to the enclave; and O'Donnell led the
    way.
And when they were inside Major Atherton's shelter,
The officers, rising, favored them one after the other
With gold stripes and started to question them.
"As for himself, he only nodded at our threat of dragging
The full-gunned shellers back out to sea at dawn.
He said that Franks should sleep there,
So that he might go back with them to his adopted homeland."

Charred mute before maps, whole roots, peach blossoms,
Staring silently through water, or binoculars,
One after the other with gold stripes.

Caribbean Sabotage

Geraldo walked silently beside the gate of the sugar mill.
Fernando Anuncios had come from the peaks near Bánica
When Angela took Pelegrino's son by his yellow hair.
She has gone back to Bánica.
Pelegrino's son has gone back to the canals and the *posadas*.
As they sprayed the sugar and threw the washings out of the mill,
Don Ajobe led Briscada from his *posada*.
Celina rose like steam from the gray water,
While Osmundo was coming into San Pedro.
He guided Briscada to the gates.
They threw down the bruised barley
And crept out next to the dock-cables,
Underneath her arranging the long props.

After Celina had sat beside him and with her left hand embraced
his knees,
She leaped from bright Bánica into the sea;
But Geraldo was then on his way to the chambers,
Where, beginning from the left Hechizero poured drinks for the
others;
And they laughed as they saw Hechizero bustling through the
ministry,
But Geraldo went to his own bed.

Strands Growing Downward

The bow ran easily across the thick strings that rose irregularly with the body of the cello. The movements of the bow were still long and even, while the body of the instrument now moved erratically, sometimes with short jerks. The cello would rise higher and higher as the bow swept back and forth across the E string, and then it would fall haltingly when the bow alternated to the A string. The body of the cello not only moved up and down against the cutting of the bow, but it also wavered slightly to the E side with each upstroke. In all this, the extent to which the patterned bust panel of the nightgown was visible was constantly changing. The embroidered flowers of this panel, though large, were in thread of nearly the same flesh color as the nightgown and could be discerned only at close range. The flowers were all the same, consisting of five petals in the shape of ovals drawn and pointed at the ends, around a circular center. Each flower was connected to other flowers at one side or another by a common petal, so that the eye could never distinguish one whole flower without seeing at least one petal as the constituent of another apparently complete flower. The flowers appeared in an effusion. The only continuous movements in the design were four vertical lines of flowers that curved slightly to meet one another at the upper and lower borders. Sometimes the curved neck of the cello would cover exactly one of the curved lines in the design, but generally it landed elsewhere, covering a random group of flowers, a few in totality, the rest only partially. And the short jerks of the instrument alternated constantly the position of the neck against the panel.

In another part of the hospital a young nurse left the orderly's office and started down the green linoleum hallway. Her white shoes were soled with dark red rubber formed in a series of seven rounded and parallel ridges. The heels were of the same material but had a flat surface. Her left leg went forward; the heel and the back three sole-ridges on her right shoe came up. Her right leg went forward; the heel and the back three sole-ridges on her left shoe came up. With each step, the firm red ridges angled up and then came down perfectly flat upon the green linoleum of the dim and spotless hallway.

The cello and the bow stopped moving altogether the moment that the nurse appeared. This black stare. Say something. Move. Nodding to the nurse and keeping the bow in one hand, Maria carefully lay the cello against the chair and went to the window. The nurse went ahead to straighten up and clear off the medicine table at the side of the bed. The firm red ridges of her shoes squeaked as she moved from side to side and finally turned to leave. "The hot water is back to normal, you know. There will be some this afternoon."

The fields stretched out on three different levels, coming up at the highest level to the edge of the hospital property. They were yellow and almost too bright, Maria thought, against the steep green background of the Pyrenees. Fine sand-like dirt had been spread over certain areas, and yellowed grass grew in other areas; this coloration itself suggested the goal posts which she finally noticed at either end of two of the fields. The largest of the hills behind the old brick asylum below her was part of a succession of hills that led to the heights of the Pyrenees. It blocked nearly the entire view of the town of Mont-Louis, which was indicated merely by the gap in the hills. Further back in the mountains Maria could locate what she suspected to be Prades, again by noticing the relative gaps between the peaks. She traced with her bow against the window the general pattern of the trip she had taken back from her family's summer cottage on the Costa Brava. She pressed the bow firmly against the window at certain patches of road she could identify for sure. She noticed immediately, however, the group of boys that swarmed from the asylum onto the lowermost field, just as one notices an insect cross the far side of a room. Some of these boys were chasing one another. Others simply ran straight ahead toward one of the higher fields. They ran well. Other boys followed these out of the building more slowly. They walked onto the field as one might walk into a cluttered room never before entered. A few of these last boys ran a little; they made jerking motions with their arms. Some didn't really run at all, but just lifted their knees high up into the air as they walked. They all seemed weighed down by their hands. The majority of the boys wore long-sleeved sport shirts buttoned at the wrists and the neck, dark trousers, and smooth leather shoes. Many, especially the older ones, also wore dark jackets that looked old-fashioned and too long. Another young nurse walking the halls of a large hospital. Visiting a class; riding an elevator; asking directions. Celia, her sister, another Dutch girl living for the time being in a foreign country. Of course, Celia was in America to study. Maria had already studied abroad, sometimes for a year, sometimes for a summer. Two of the boys barely went out onto the field; they stood and talked, one of them making a frequent slapping gesture with his hands and rocking his head back. Maria had copied Richard's address into the small address book she gave to Celia as a going-away present and even felt happy she could do it. That was a month ago. The summer ahead of her at the Mont-Louis Hospital. The summer to prepare for September classes at the nursing school, to get used to New York. Why not talk about Amsterdam the same way as New York? the same way as Grenoble? Because she hadn't even met him until far into the second semester at Grenoble. Yet the spring outings on Mont Rabat. . . . Some of the first boys to come out were now running up to the farthest field as one of the instructors or doctors caught up with them and threw out the ball. The nearest boy kicked the ball toward a group of several boys, one of whom redirected it straight out into the emptiness of the field. The boys in Amsterdam were coming through the college gates. It was the first year for these students, so they didn't have any hair on their heads. Some, riding bicycles, faintly jerked their cycles up as they went over the curb of the driveway and looped, some to the left and others to the right, down the suddenly sunny street. The head of one of the bicyclists who had turned left was curved smoothly from the top of the forehead back to a point approximately level with his ears. Here both sides of the skull curved sharply downward to meet at the center of the neck and left a small rounded protrusion. It was off this point of the skull's downward moulding that the new sun reflected, as the bicyclist overtook on one side a decelerating trolley. From one of the side windows, Maria smiled down and pointed out the bald bicyclist to Richard, who sat next to her on the shiny green seat. The same boy who had kicked the ball far out into the field reached it and tried to dribble it back. His kicks were not light enough, though, and the others who had been chasing after him took possession of the ball immediately, one of them soon kicking it again down the field toward the far goal. They hadn't started a game. Out of the wide cement steps a small group of boys could still be distinguished in the darkness as Maria pushed open one of the swinging doors that led to the masses of people dancing and to the clouds of smoke that might have seemed themselves to be exuding the electric vibrations audible even beyond these doors. One of this group, with his back to the street, was standing on the stone siding that projected from the building. He was able to lean pretty far back simply by holding his hands flat against the sides of the stone protrusion, which were used as bulletin boards. He was held there by the friction created between his hands and the rough, almost sandy surface of the stone. He let himself way back and then pulled himself upright to call a few remarks to his companions, who were talking among themselves on the steps. He liked repeating the word

"enfin"; almost every sentence began with it. He leaned back
again, putting his rigid body at a forty-five degree angle with the
building, and then apparently saw what he had been watching
for. "Enfin! Enfin!" he yelled.

The body of the instrument now moved even more erratically.
The cello would rise higher and higher as the bow swept back
and forth across the E string, and then it would fall back haltingly
when the bow alternated to the A string. The body of the cello not
only moved up and down against the cutting of the bow, but it
also wavered slightly to the E side with each upstroke.

The silky, flesh-colored nightgown settled down across the
chair, the lower half falling down around the forward right corner of the wooden seat. It hung straight from here and rippled
only once at the actual point of the corner. It also lay straight
across much of the surface of the chair. At the point, however,
where the natural gatherings began, the nightgown had been laid
down less carefully, so there were certain additional folds and
overlaps here. The number of gatherings that normally would fall
from the lower border of the embroidered bust panel seemed to
be reduced. This was because, at the right, the entire upper edge
of the nightgown had been turned over on itself. The bust panel
itself, which extended between the two arm openings and all the
way up to the shoulders, was partially covered at the right by this
same overlap. From this point the embroidered flower pattern remained unfurled as far as another fold that stretched from near
the lower left corner of the bust panel to the narrow neck slit. In
the remainder of this panel the flower pattern was obscured by
innumerable wrinkles that lay generally parallel to the large fold
near the corner.

It was shiny black hair that the doctor had. His deeply tanned
face, somewhat less brilliant than his hair, stood out above his
spotlessly white, neck-buttoned uniform; yet his face was more

pronounced because of its naturally greater proportion as compared to the hair and because of its greater proximity to the white,
stiffly starched material. The nurse, from whom he took the ster-
ilized hypodermic syringe, was entirely invisible. Once the elastic
bands were in place, he spread alcohol over the hairless area at the
crook of the arm. There was a slight twinge of pain that shot up
both arms. Then nothing. The doctor removed the needle. There
was the squeaking of firm, rubber-soled shoes. When the squeaking stopped, there was another twinge of pain, followed by a
slightly greater pain concentrated at the point of penetration—
the pain to the ears of a certain high sustained note on the flute.
But after a moment it became a great flushing pain, and the doctor, squeaking, withdrew the needle again. Maria at last looked
down at her arm, from which thick streams of blood spewed in
smooth, even intervals.

"A long, even motion across the strings. Your arm must be relaxed, your fingers poised. Keep your arm widely curved around
the instrument, your fingers poised. Even, now, back and forth.
Back and forth. Back—forth—back . . ."

As the doctor thrust the needle, only slightly filled with blood,
onto the tray, the nurse rushed up and unfastened the lower
elastic band. It was Celia. She held tightly to Maria's wrist, and
the doctor quickly raised and tightened the upper band. These
were Richard's hands, as deeply tanned as his face. The hair that
covered only three-quarters of the back of the left hand was continued as far as the second knuckle on each of the four fingers
that were clamped around the elastic band. The smaller bone
beyond the second knuckle was visible only on the index finger
and had no hair. The hair line proceeded from the fourth finger
joint to the ball of the wrist in a gentle curve that hooked most
sharply just before the wrist. It then disappeared under the silver
watch band and the white sleeve. The watch band itself, as well
as the watch, was half covered by the sleeve. Only the hours from

twelve to six were visible. Neither of the hands was on this side.
The sleeve was perfectly pressed and unwrinkled from the wrist
up to the elbow, where there were three creases presently held in
place by the position of the arm. The upper sleeve was similarly
unwrinkled as far as the shoulder seam, where there was an irregularly spaced series of parallel, scallop-shaped creases, probably made by an electric hand iron. At the end of this series was
a slight indentation created by the right thumb of a female hand.
The other four fingers lay across the top of the shoulder. The nails
of all five fingers, cut short and carefully filed, were clear-glazed.
The heel of the hand rested on the backward curve of the
shoulder.

The high flat region extended from the Spanish border, running
northeast between the Mount Carlit range and the Prades range.
Mont-Louis itself was located amidst the high, rolling hills that
led up to this second range. There were three principal hills that
surrounded Mont-Louis. The two higher ones, to the east and to
the south, led to the peaks of the Pyrenees. The smallest of the
three was to the west and constituted part of a long succession of
hills leading up from the flatter region. The rolling terrain on the
west side of this hill, along with the dry air common to the entire
region, invited large country estates, small rest-hotels, and health
centers. A large area at the western foot of this hill was occupied
by two institutions, an asylum for mentally retarded boys and a
private hospital that specialized in respiratory illnesses. The
asylum was more directly at the foot of the steep slope, but, because of secondary hills that existed immediately adjacent to the
drop, the hospital was situated higher. The border between these
two was a high wire fence that ran approximately north and
south, parallel to the foot of the mountain. Although all the natural foliage had been preserved on the hospital grounds, much of
the land on the opposite side of the fence had been razed and

leveled. On each of the three terraces that led down to the asylum was a playing field, the yellow dust of the lowermost one only now settling back to the ground. The recreation period was over, and the instructors were leading the boys back into the old brick building.

The young nurse lifted up Maria's arm and pressed the uppermost towel back against her side. She moved the wet cloth gently along Maria's arm, and a vague film of minute soap bubbles appeared up and down. She then wrung out the cloth and rinsed the arm. She placed the arm back under the towels and then pulled the uppermost towel to one side.

"How long will you go on with the cello?" she asked.

"Do you mean today or in general?" said Maria.

"Both."

"As long as necessary, I suppose."

The bow lay on top of the nightgown. It extended from the smallest wrinkles at the upper left of the flowered panel up to and past the corner of the chair, at which point the bottom part of the nightgown hung down. It cut the lower border of the panel a bit to the left of the third natural line in the flower design. Nearly one-third of its length extended beyond the corner of the chair and stuck out over the green linoleum floor.

You Froze the Light and Flew

"... behind the high sustained note, he said he heard now and then the suggestions of a melody."

The next night they were there again. It was difficult to believe that they would stay so close to the building, though a few more yards and they would have been lying against the rusted fenders in the used car dealer's back lot. He did practically nothing at first. Once he was down on the ground with her, it was little different from previous nights. Even after he had unbuttoned her blouse and fumbled with her skirt until it was down to her knees, it seemed ages that nothing happened and that they were more or less still. Thin clouds began rushing across the sky near the horizon, about level with the top of the steam stack rising from the huge burner in the adjacent lot. And at the same time, a particular species of black bird began congregating, as they always did when it rained, around the top of the steam stack. They were briefly alighting on the lip of the stack and then relooping several times in the air and swooping down into the stack itself, when it was suddenly apparent that she had unloosened her garter belt by herself and pulled it down. At once he began to work frenetically on her panties, then on his own pants and underclothes at the same time. Within a few seconds, he had eased himself on top of her. They both had their clothing simply pushed down from the waist to the knees, so that she could barely spread her legs. Nothing happened then; again there was no movement. After about five minutes, he moved back over to one side of her. She pulled her clothes back on by herself. They got up rather hurriedly, and he pulled his raincoat up over his head before they reached the sidewalk.

As Katherine walks away and goes through the double glass

doors into the apartment building, her hair swings across her shoulders and flashes reflected light in the manner of the three fountains on the front banks of the property. The crests of these fountains are now visible above the low wall that encloses the parking lot. They appear in irregular spurts, sometimes, though infrequently, disappearing altogether below the wall. Their color is constantly changing, probably depending on the light thrown up at them from some cyclical source below. All three fountains seem to be colored by an identical source, since the blue, for example, of the fountain at the left will appear several seconds later on the middle fountain and then in a few more seconds on the fountain at the right. This pattern of horizontal motion, though not at once detectable, can be seen repeated with every color.

"Ten, nine, eight, seven, six, five, four, 3, 2, 1, DONE."

Katherine turned over again, this time getting up on her knees, and pulled the covers from under the pillow down toward her ankles. Before she could sit back down, Alan tucked his fingers into her thin skirt at the waist and pulled down with one swoop all that remained. She slowly flattened out as he dragged the clothes entirely off her legs and then all at once turned herself over to face him. She pulled him toward her at first, but he remained propped up above her by his arms, so she raised her legs and with her feet tugged at his underpants. She got one side partially down. Then with one hand that she unloosened from along her side, she relieved the tension in the front so that the other side would slide down. They both kicked at the underpants until they flew from his ankles.

While Katherine sleeps, an airplane is passing. It crosses the suggested shapes of three radio towers visible from the bed through the window. These towers, formed solely by red lights along their sides, appear to be in the backyard across the street and on the edge of the horizon at the same time. The red lights seem to go out now and then as nearby trees obliterate them. The

airplane cruises past their peaks, flashing first a white light on the
tail, then two sets of red and blue lights on either wing. The white
light continues flashing, and after the plane has passed the third
tower a red light near its nose is lit and remains lit.

"He said the crack had started from one point at the bottom of
the pane and exploded into thin vessels all across the top."

They were falling from the fifteenth floor. Katherine kept looking up through the hole in the top of the elevator to see the sky-
light shrink in the distance. They were illuminated by the momentary flash of each passing floor. Alan kept walking over to
the control board and pushing the button marked "1."

The drugstore is just beginning to close up when Katherine
goes in. Most of the front lights are turned off; then the outside
lights. In this way, that which is reflected from the outside disappears almost altogether from the glass, immediately inside of
which only the dim lights remain that will stay on all night. They
are bluish fluorescent lights, which tint the elastic supporters and
half-girdles nearby, at the far left of the window. Some of these
foundations simply hang from pieces of cardboard inscribed with
tiny diagrams indicating their correct position on the body and
arrows indicating the support they provide; others are stretched
onto shiny plastic torsos that reflect the lightbulb itself and thus
indicate where it is located. The revolving circle to one side of
these has a smaller white light of its own. The light shines up
from the front of the base, illuminating each side of the revolving
disk as it faces forward. On one side is a woman's face, smiling,
with bright blond hair in a puffed style that comes in just below
the ears; on the other side is another woman's face, smiling, with
bright brown hair pushed up tightly on the top of her head and
braided. The blond's face is narrow, and small jowls are apparent
in spite of the hair that slightly covers them; the brunette's face is
similarly small-jowled, though it is less narrow and more rounded,
particularly at the chin. These light eyebrows extend partially

across the upper bone of the eye socket and are uniform in width; these darker eyebrows stretch from two proximate points of thickness to a narrow width beyond the eye socket. This nose, barely detectable, is formed principally by the two brown oval nostrils; this nose casts a dark shadow to the right that widens above the mouth. These lips are a light pink with streaks of white; these lips are a deep red with circles of reflected light. There are innumerable boxes of facial tissues stretching from this revolving display to the far right end of the window and backing smaller boxes, slightly elevated, of toilet water, cold cream, petroleum jelly, hand lotion, and dusting powder, around each of which is a circle of the same product. The blue cardboard boxes of facial tissues are piled in steps, so that they are eight deep at the bottom, seven deep on the next level up, and so on, the single row being closer to the back of the window than to the front. To either side of the structure, this arrangement becomes irregular, and both the depth and the height are decreased. On the side facing forward of each box that can be seen are printed the name of the tissue in black cursive letters both at the top and at the bottom. The same letters are printed on letters, the first letter, "F," extending out of line with the rest of the top of each box, but on a white rectangular background, the borders of which are perforated. On the end of each box, the name is printed in white letters on a smaller scale. Above the name is a coat of arms, outlined in black and divided into four parts. In the upper left-hand portion is a white bird on a blue background, in the upper right-hand portion a blue sword on a black background, in the lower left-hand portion a blue castle on a white background, and in the lower right-hand portion a black branch on a blue background.

"He told her that the mirror on the opposite wall could be tilted up and down."

From the ruined banks before *Tannhauser* . . . the horses under green lights . . . green-lit trees . . . sprays of hot swimming, the cobblestone way . . . single-file for the following arias, as the numbing at the heels . . . cascade . . . we eat green grass under Pompey . . . further down the flashlights reveal . . . the "Thunder March" at "demitarif" . . . exhaled by the cannon; at the first stepping wave . . . heads, or rather, skulls . . . these green eyes, are they ours . . . we wanted antiquity . . . from the fumes, the salty recapitulations . . . who hobbled over these dark squares . . . the keys, the window, your friends, the German boys, the gate, the highway, the quai, the well, the coupon, the keys, the window . . . onto firmer cement and blacktop . . . weak wires . . . soil that swelled, or so they said . . . going first . . . "scrambling" . . . would endlessly tell on . . . from one soft point to another . . . these pans on the ledge, but has he gotten over them . . . "friends" . . . the warden, the warden . . . posters frozen on Lake . . . rising, the ground out back . . . sprays . . . from the first reflected shoulder . . . would the final aria have . . . we were on the . . . I am in the . . . the keys, check . . . that light . . . is she . . . flew. . . .

(The hairline at the back of the neck consists of two slight curves, almost scallop-shaped, that make a long sharp point in their meeting. A small drop of sweat rolls out from under this point of hair and slides haltingly down the length of the neck. It stops for several seconds at the top of the back, where the spinal column barely begins to make itself seen. It then continues more or less regularly down the back, decelerating with each new ridge of the spinal column and then, once past it, regaining speed. The drop rolls faster down the lowermost portion of the spine, where it suddenly disappears in the thin sheet of light-colored hair.)

EUGENE SCHWARTZ

The Interpretation of Dreams
or Superboy at Sarah Lawrence

(*What has come before*: *The hero, Jonathan Carter, has met the fabulously wealthy "post-deb" Eliza Scattergeld and engaged in a "thrilling" conversation with her, only to discover that she was committed to go to a party in Bronxville that night. He then decided to go to the Mixer with Arnica Barron and David Tuchman.*)

Chapter 5

It's unbelievable! You walk through the winding roads of this infarcted town called Bronxville and climb a hill and suddenly . . . you're just *surrounded* with these girls! It's as if every White-Anglo-Saxon-Protestant hippie, replete with Newboy Blue eyes and maize-yellow hair and just *dripping* with elegance and *l'aesthetique du chic* had come to settle down in this fortuitous clump of New York Neo-Elizabethianism. To insiders (and that means most of Yale, some of Columbia and a splattering of the rest of the East Coast that's *with it*) it's known just as the Place, even though its official name, as the nineteen-thirtyish photo says on top of the fireplace in the main building, is Sarah Lawrence College. There they are—just so . . . tough . . . and so youthfully *lovely* and girding their lily-white progressive loins for the (to them) Onslaught that everyone else labels the "Mixer."

Tall, blonde . . . *elegant* Arnica Barron walks across the lawn, arm-in-arm with Jonathan Carter, the thin and sadly beautiful

Teen Thinker, while David Tuchman follows behind, content to watch girls swing their hair over their tight bottoms as they go up to their rooms. Arnica Barron—the Girl on the Discotheque Floor! Chic America's Hip Goddess!—can look straight ahead and know that when she walks on campus people will *stare* . . . and nobody, but nobody . . . stares . . . at Sarah Lawrence. It's that straight lemon-yellow hair, bifurcating the oval head, covering one ear, leaving the other open like a sculptured labyrinth . . . or it's the cold eyes, a sort of dark aqua, piercing and withholding at once . . . or it's the permanent pout, that almost imperceptible air of . . . sensuality.

But there's a sort of tension, too, like her own fear of her beauty, her need to bury herself in her hair and to look like she's always falling *into* her clothes, losing herself in the rich, rolling folds of her fuchsia-colored Jax shirt with its modest ruby pin, falling over the legs of her Geinrich bell-bottom pants that look like a long skirt when she brings her legs together. It's almost as if she were protecting herself against . . . against the *world,* sort of.

Jonathan just might know her better than anyone, better than the nouveau-riche little girls who see her picture in *Seventeen* and know that they want to look *just like that,* better than her friends at school who see her as sort of . . . cold. They had "made it" two years ago (for chrissake in this crowd everyone, but everyone "makes it" just out of habit, if nothing else) and it was just so . . . depressing . . . Not *bad* exactly, nothing tragic for either of them, but just enough to blow Arnica's cool and get her to admit to Jonathan that, well . . . sex was pretty s———, after all. But exactly! Appearance vs. Reality (*Sein und Schein* to put it the way it's learned in school). She's sterile, but by God, she's got *style!*

"Have you heard anything from Alima?" Jonathan asks.

"I got her letter the other day," says Arnica. "She's in Delhi, and says that she loves it."

"Does she . . . Did she ask for me?"

Arnica doesn't answer at first, as if she were weighing her frankness against her tact and not being . . . certain . . . of which was better.

"Uh . . . no, she doesn't."

Again Alima's image comes to Jonathan, as he looks away from Arnica and his thoughts go back to the intense doldrum fury he lives in. He's so . . . contained . . . in his dark jacket and black jersey, in his hair, his eyes. Somewhere, deep within it all, everything that was Alima, the ash-blond hair, the grass-green eyes, somewhere it's all . . . *preserved* . . . and he can sort of unlock it and see her and it would seem nothing else whenever he wants to . . . it just all clicks, the past, the present and future and . . . the *sadness* of it all!

David walks up to Arnica's side and the three sit down on the lawn, orange-green in the decaying sunlight. On the road, two boys in army uniforms walk by, followed by a big crewcut football type, a transistor radio screwed on his ear, breaking the evening calm as though it were ice in a cocktail glass. Ratty people with ratty hair and dermatitis and corroded thoracic boxes and so forth. What are *they* doing *here?*

David motions towards the athlete.

"Hail the Goyische Golem!" he says, "The Final Product of American Civilization." David is sort of an heir to *l'asthetique du schlock*, that . . . Yiddish way of naming things that hits you over the head, or something.

But Jonathan's eyes stay glued on the boys in uniform. Suddenly all of Asia looms up before him like a clutching Hokusai wave . . . napalm shrieks, pig mantas, the indescribable . . . *thrill* . . . of war. He feels very . . . sick.

"Let's go inside," he says, "I feel warm out here."

David is first to stand. He stretches, opens his mouth wide and releases a comfortable yawn: "A-a-a-a-a-a-o-o-o-o-o-o-o-o-o-o-o-o-o-h-h-h,

Oooh, babee!"

The Insurrections are warming up, tuning in their electric guitars and turning up the amps, while restless couples mill around the floor, hesitantly moving arms and legs in preparation for the Dance.

The "Calf," half snack-bar, half-lounge, has tables set on its upper level so that everyone can see everyone else, so that the dancers bobbing below become a sort of show for everyone on top. David and Arnica and Jonathan have a table that looks over the edge—selected by David, whose main concern is . . . seeing what's happening.

Twee*ang!* Like Edwardian morticians the Insurrections condescend to begin, wailing out their first notes like they're about to pop the vessels in their collective temporal fossa and bleed all over the floor. They survive, though, and wail out their cacophony of Dark Meaninglessness, the thoughts and rhythms of the kind of people that no one at Sarah Lawrence has ever seen. But of course! It's America's first unconscious avant-garde! Marvelous! Coming right smack out of the Vinyl Deeps and surging forth in a sort of Plastic Free Form! What . . . *style*!!

> Ah-h-h-h-h-h know there's people crying!
> Ah-h-h-h-h-h know there's people dying!
> But ah-h-h-h-h-h got your love:
> An' that's all ah can think *of* . . .

A girl walks by the table, shiny hair flipped just slightly, lacy blouse, cone-shaped dress, her little bottom shaking all the way to the ilial crest. She looks at Jonathan, then walks on, confident and . . . hip.

David and Arnica are talking, lightly, commenting on the music, the hip cantilations, the people around them, but Jonathan still seems sunk in his thoughts. There's something very beautiful and . . . bitter . . . about him. He lifts a tabescent hand and runs it through his thick, coarse, sienna-colored hair. He wants to say something, to express a ... thought ... but this just doesn't seem to be the right place, what with all the ululating and assorted statication going on. The friendly chick walks by again, this time looking more pregnantly at him.

"Listen," he finally says, "Listen, I want to say something that I'm thinking, but the very fact that I really won't be able to say it shows that it's true ..." His voice meanders quietly, almost shaking, through his doldrum fury, out to somewhere beyond cynical, beyond cool, beyond ... teen-age world-weary ...

"Don't you get the feeling, watching all the people on the dance floor, looking at yourselves, that we're all searching for some common ground so that we can just talk to each other, someplace where our thoughts and ideas and bodies can meet for an instant before we run away in an infinite number of directions again?"

> Yes, ah-h-h-h-h-h got your love,
> An' that's all ah can think *of*:
> Ah-h-h-h-h-h got your love,
> And that's en-*nuf!*

David and Arnica look at him with expressions of annoyance mixed with a sort of amusement. Jonathan always *thinks* so damn much about things that ... well, sometimes you wonder if he ever really *experiences* them.

"But the trouble is," he continues, and he gropes for words in that tormented world behind the beautiful macerated face, "The trouble is that we never *can* reach one another, even begin to know one another as self-contained individuals. All that we can do is look at each other's lives as an assortment of states of mind being acted out by indifferent performers—if you try to understand people, you end up interpreting dreams. We try to force our own realities on other people and it becomes oppressive, and then they run away into their own dreams ..."

Arnica smiles indulgently.

"Why don't you dance, Jonathan?"

"But it's all so *mindless*," he protests. The Brooding Horse of Western Reason! He sits there, an alienated thin young fellow, uninspired by even the Voice of Eighteen-year-old America crying out in a pre-adult contralto as the Insurrections finish their song:

> Oh, ah-h-h-h-h-h-h-h got your love,
> And that's e-e-e-e-*nough!!!!*

The girl walks by again, this time smiling with Teen Modesty. She practically . . . slithers . . . across the terrace and sits at a table across from Jonathan's.

Arnica turns around, then looks at Jonathan.

"Jonathan, that girl is after your a—," she whispers.

"I don't want to dance."

"Give it a try, goddammit!" says David.

Jonathan looks over at the shiny head a table away. She darts a quick glance at him and turns around.

"She has nice eyes," he mumbles, and he seems to have left the tight fury of the past behind him. He looks at Arnica, who smiles with her perfect teeth that fifty-dollar-an-hour smile. He gets up and walks over to the girl.

David smiles approvingly and drawls, "Go-o-o-o-"

> o-o-o-o-o-o-o-wha, o-o-o-o-wha,
> o-o-o-o-wha, o-o-o-o-wha,
> Got a little girl, across the way,
> Pretty little girl ah'm gonna get some day!

It's that time of the night when the Insurrections reach their orgasmic peak, and their voices pass like a current through the Beautiful Teens dancing all over the room. Her name is Cynthia Forsythe and when she dances with Jonathan her little mary poppins shake at right angles to the curving motion of her arms. And her eyes—they shine like black arc-lights, the long lashes smoothing over the glare . . . that girl's got style!

To hell with "dreams" and "reality" now, in this narcoleptic hour, electricity surging through bodies like synthetic blood . . . Everyone seems to be run by the current, dancing and bobbing in a sort of lopsided order, all young and beautiful and alive. A style of life!! Gone for them are the good grey burghers, the poor old arteriosclerotic lawyers with sagging layers of fat hanging over their ribs, trying to dance with almost . . . pathetic . . . clumsiness.

They're all so young and they've taken over and—holy cow—it's like a *revolution* or something!

> It won't be long before ah get her alone,
> Never a girl ah woulda love at home!

Jonathan is lost in it, his arms and pelvis moving by themselves, suddenly feeling himself so . . . free . . . in the vast impersonality of it all. By God, the current!! Undulating against Cynthia, those almond, long-lashed eyes, those nice breasts, that shiny hair . . . Rapturous agony! The music gets louder and the tempo more fevered, it sounds as if the next note will break the amps—blee*ang*!—but instead it goes on and on . . . Oh Nirvana!! This . . . music.

> Wella Louie, Louie;
> *OH*, baby, well we gotta go!
> Yeh, yeh, yeh, yeh, yeh, yeh!

It gets faster, and Jonathan feels nothing but this . . . release . . . that makes him feel immersed in Cynthia or something. Now *everybody* is out there, bobbing up and down to the plugged-in music. The whole floor begins to bounce up and down, like a lemon-colored trampoline, the whole floor, some people are afraid to edge off to the side, but most keep bobbing and—pow!—glasses and beer cans begin to hit the floor, but everyone keeps bobbing up and down, crushing the glass and metal underfoot. So many heads bobbing, so many bodies jiggling this way and that, so many arms thrown up and around, so many faces one wants so desperately to see . . .

Jonathan shouts something above the clangor of the music, but Cynthia only smiles back and shakes her head.

"I can't *hear* you!"

"I said that you have beautiful eyes!" he cries again.

"Oh . . ." she pauses and throws her whole torso back on this loud tweeang that suddenly breaks out the amp, ". . . Thank you!"

Jonathan throws his head back and laughs, thin and free, a young Teen Savage.

"Thank you," she cries again, "Thank you!"

Chapter 6

I WAS A COED OUT FOR FUN
Could I Have Known It Would End This Way?

I guess that I should have realized what a "Sarah Lawrence Mixer" was like as soon as things began. My heart sank as the girls and a few of their guys began pouring into the "Calf." Some of them were in dungarees. A couple of the girls looked like they were dressed for Hallowe'en—gobs of make-up and sweaters two sizes too small.

These kids didn't even try to be nice. The guys just elbowed their way to the marshmallow roast, grabbing up all the food, then eyeing the girls for a dance partner. They were even worse than I feared. All, that is, except one.

I had spotted Jonathan the second he came into the room. For a long time, while he sat with his friends and talked, I looked up so that his eyes were in line with mine. Finally we had danced, and I thought that I could hear him whisper, "I like you, Cindy. I don't know why yet, but I liked you the first time I saw you tonight. Just chemistry, I guess."

My knees went weak. I stammered out, "Thank you," and realized it was happening! The thing I didn't dare dream about was happening so fast, I was scared to pinch myself!

The dance floor was so crowded and hot that my eyes began to smart.

At last, Jonathan said, "It's stuffy down here. Why don't we find a cooler place?"

I don't know how Jonathan and I got upstairs. On the way, we stopped off on some benches and the lawn. But some of the crowd already took over there, so we moved on.

"What's in here?" Jonathan asked, when we reached the second floor of Titsworth Dorm.

"Like you say in the big city, this is my pad," I laughed, swinging the door open. "Want to take a look?"

TOO FAST ON OUR FIRST DATE!
How Could We Tell Our Parents?

Jonathan let out a low, approving whistle at the big, beautiful room Sarah Lawrence had given me. And Mom's patchwork quilt made a hit because Jonathan had an almost identical one at home. He even noticed the crazy collection of dolls that I outgrew years ago but couldn't bear to throw away.

"I hope that my 'collection' doesn't offend you," I said, keeping my voice real throaty and sexy, "I realize that it's *so* silly!"

The way I said it even surprised me.

Jonathan liked the sound of it too, and he got up and walked over to the bed and pulled me close and slipped his arm around me. So I was right—all I needed was a little 'college graduate' talk to make the boys go for me!

The next thing I knew he was pulling me down on the bed.

"Just a few minutes," he begged, "I want to kiss you, Cindy. I've been wanting to all evening. I thought I'd never have the

—— Advt. —— Advt. —— Advt. ——
DON'T BE FAT!
An Amazing Scientific Discovery
Guaranteed Safe!
KAL-X REDUCING GUM AND PLAN
Introductory Offer—Good for a Very Short Time Only!
—— Advt. —— Advt. —— Advt. ——

chance to meet you."

I knew it was dangerous there on the bed. But somehow, it wasn't wrong. The first boy I ever fell for wanted to kiss me, and I was trembling all over.

"I'll shut the door," I said, in a voice that wasn't my own.

I closed it and fell back into Jonathan's arms, whispering shakily, "Jonny, Jonny, it's crazy the way this happened. I've been watching you, too. But I didn't have the nerve to talk to you."

"It's beautiful, Cindy," he laughed huskily, "And you're beautiful, too. Only let's get some kissing done before somebody walks in."

All the sounds around us seemed to fade, and a hum filled my whole body as only Jonathan's lips and the soft darkness seemed to matter. Jonathan had a way of kissing that turned your insides to butter.

"I'm crazy about you, Cindy," he said, "It doesn't even seem real."

It wasn't real. It was my first visit to that other world I had heard so much about. In a matter of minutes, I whirled into love. Before I realized what was happening, we were going too far.

"Jonny, we mustn't!" I gasped, "I'm not like that!"

Jonathan looked angry, and I got scared.

"Please," I whispered, "Let me tell you about myself before we do anything wrong . . ."

"You girls, you're all the same," he sighed, giving up. "Okay Cindy, I'll listen—*for a while.*"

DOES ANY GIRL DESERVE TO BE TREATED LIKE THIS?

Not Many Boys Would Put A Girl Through Such Horror!

I told Jonathan all about my three years at Central High. Me—Cindy Forsythe—not the greatest looker in the world, but fair game on the personality end. I guess that's why I had no trouble fitting in with what Central High called the "speed crowd"—you know, the kids with cars and fast money—all the big wheels. One of my best friends told me that I could talk my way in or out of anything!

I told him about Mom, how she had worked nights at Joe's Diner after Dad passed away, in order to support me, and send me to a "good school." She's the greatest mother in the world, and, as I was soon to learn, she's always right. She never approved of all my friends and parties and used to tell me:

"Cynthia, if it makes you happy, do it," she would say, and I noticed how tired and old she looked. "I can't tell you what to do. Nobody ever could, except your father. But just remember, you're only fifteen. Don't get in over your head."

"Don't worry, Mom," I said, hugging her, "I know what I'm doing."

But of course, I didn't know. It was only later, when it was too late, that I realized that Mom was right all along.

After I finished this much, I shot a glance at Jonathan.

"You're not annoyed, are you?" I asked.

He said something so vile just then that I couldn't answer. "I'm thinking about someone else," he said. I was frantic! To think that Jonathan would say such a stinking thing to me! I found out right then and there, he wasn't such a dreamboat after all. Only, what was I going to do?

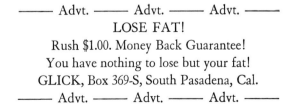

I WAS A TEEN MAKE-OUT QUEEN
Living This Way Was Enough To Drive Normal People Crazy!

My heart throbbing, I kept on talking, even though I could see how impatient he was for me to stop. How could he be that way, I wondered, me, Cynthia Forsythe—who had never really been angry in my life!

I told him all about the first big party I had gone to when I was sixteen, on the swanky side of town—all the rich kids lived there. The party was fabulous. They really had some set-up. Most of the lower floor was just for the kids. And, of course, there was lots of room to dance, and a super hi-fi playing every kind of music. The rumpus room was really big with long windows that opened onto the lawn. They even had a pool for swimming!

The party was really swinging when I got there. Kids were all over the place dancing and even drinking. There must have been three snack bars—and liquor wherever you looked. Jim, a boy I met, was drinking what looked like soda, but I knew better. He tried to make me drink it, but I wouldn't. I was just on top of the world being with all the rich kids.

The next time I went to a party with Jim, he ordered drinks for both of us—and was I scared! Me—Cynthia Forsythe—who never had so much as a sip before—not even a taste of beer! I tasted the drink, and it was terrible. I noticed that lots of guys were there watching me so I pretended to like it and acted as if I knew all about drinking. After awhile, the drink tasted better, and I started to relax. It was getting late, and I knew I should be getting home, but with the liquor warm inside me, I didn't care about the time.

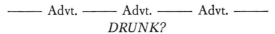

—— Advt. —— Advt. —— Advt. ——

DRUNK?
DOCTOR'S MARVELOUS MEDICAL DISCOVERY!
"World Famous Since 1943"

Guaranteed Pure! May be used secretly in Whiskey, Wine, Beer, etc. Not represented as a permanent "CURE" but as a doctor's recognized method for interrupting the drinking cycle. A happy SOBERIN AIDS user writes:

> Please send me another bottle of SOBERIN AIDS. I had a bottle of Soberin Aids two years ago and my family lived in peace. Now my husband has started to drink again. God Bless You.—
> Mrs. N. K.—Toronto, Ca.

DO NOT WAIT. ORDER SOBERIN AIDS NOW!

WE WILL RUSH ORDER!

—— Advt. —— Advt. —— Advt. ——

I guess I must have made out with every boy at that party, even with the ones whose hands wandered. I soon got the reputation of being "fast," although I would never go any further than any other sixteen-year-old girl. I always managed to hold the guys away. Of course, I never admitted to them that I wouldn't go that far—I'd just tell them I didn't care for them enough. That was usually all it took to stop anyone. But I still made out with almost everyone, and was called the "town make-out queen." I was so embarrassed!

Deep down, I knew I shouldn't have acted this way. But I couldn't help myself. This was the way I always acted with boys. If I didn't make out with them, what could I do? Sit in the corner, with my hands folded? I guess I thought so little of myself, that I was afraid no boy would like me for just being me.

I even hung around the places where the college crowd went, and picked up the lingo, and learned how those kids dressed and acted. I met lots of boys that way, but I knew that the junior college in my town was small potatoes. Along the East Coast were the big fish. And I was going to land one of them, no matter what.

In just a year, I made myself smart so that I could get into a good girls' college—and the swankier the better.

In a way, I guess I had run out of challenges and wanted new ones. Even while all the kids laughed behind my back, I had thoughts of what it would be like to go to Sarah Lawrence. In a year, I changed myself from a shapeless little girl to a grown woman—in every way. And here I was!

—— Advt. —— Advt. —— Advt. ——

WANT TO *KEEP* SKIN WHITE?

Mercolized Cream is specially medicated to help you. Don't hide your complexion beauty! Use *Mercolized Cream* nightly and keep your skin white and feminine looking. Buy some!

Money-Back Guarantee!

—— Advt. —— Advt. —— Advt. ——

ASHAMED TO LET HIM SEE MY FREAKISH BODY!

Does A Girl Like Me Have A Right To Fall In Love?

"Are you angry at me . . . ?" I struggled out, "Angry at the way I really am?"

Jonathan didn't answer, but just grabbed my arm and kissed me. He kissed me so hard and so suddenly—that I was stunned for a moment! But I still hung back. My heart was pounding like crazy. I knew Jonathan wanted to make love to me. I wanted to be set on fire by his kisses, but I was scared.

—— Advt. —— Advt. —— Advt. ——

ARTIFICIAL EYELASHES

The Latest, Greatest Thing In Modern Eye Make-Up!

When you look out of long, silk, flirty, curled lashes, your femininity comes on strong! Luckily, you don't have to be born with them. And they're made of Vulon, a new hypo-

allergenic material that has a permanently built-in curl,
that can be washed and worn in a wink. Don't wait for
evening to wear them. Why not catch the eye of your
favorite guy at lunch? Can you think of a better way to
get the attention all girls want? Money-Back Guarantee!

—— Advt. —— Advt. —— Advt. ——

"Your eyes," he murmured softly, "Your beautiful eyes," and
moved his lips, kissing me tenderly on the forehead. Suddenly he
coughed—my false eyelash had stuck to his mouth!

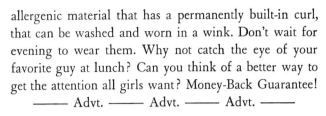

—— Advt. —— Advt. —— Advt. ——
BEAUTIFUL HAIRPIECES
Custom Matched to Your Own Hair
Give Yourself a New Hair-Do Instantly!!
A Variety of Ready-to-Wear Styles that Add Luxurious
Fullness to Limp or Thin Hair, Curl to Straight Hair,
Length to Short Hair—Just $4.99!
Send No Money—Fully Guaranteed!!
—— Advt. —— Advt. —— Advt. ——

Then, before I knew what was happening, Jonathan was running his hands through my hair, even before I could warn him
about my hairpiece which he ripped out of its setting. It fell on the
floor and he looked surprised—but still held me tight in his arms!

I tried to struggle away, to stall for time, hoping that he
wouldn't try to go too far. He held on tight to my hand and
squeezed, and I heard a crack—three of my false nails broke in
his grip! I was terrified. He was really strong, and could do awful
damage!

—— Advt. —— Advt. —— Advt. ——
STOP UGLY NAILS!
Build them up—*In Minutes*—into Long Beautiful Nails!
NOW! We can bring you, for the first time at just $1.98,

the amazing scientific liquid nail builder called MAGIC
NAIL FORMULA No. 77. It actually BUILDS up fin-
ger nails to ANY LENGTH desired—in *MINUTES!*
It is now USED by MILLIONS!
DON'T HIDE YOUR HANDS!
NOW YOU CAN SHOW THEM OFF!
GUARANTEED 100% TO GIVE YOU LONG,
BEAUTIFUL NAILS—NOW!
—— Advt. —— Advt. —— Advt. ——

And now his lips were crushing down on mine the way I had
always dreamed about. Only now it wasn't a dream—it was a
horrible nightmare! All I wanted was to get away, so that he
couldn't see what I was really like. *Please God,* I prayed, *Let me
out of this mess, and I promise I'll be a good girl from now on!*

—— Advt. —— Advt. —— Advt. ——
"WITH GOD
All Things are Possible!"
Are you facing difficult problems? Poor Health? Money
or Job Troubles? Unhappiness? If you are, then here is
NEWS of a remarkable NEW WAY of PRAYER that
is helping thousands to glorious new happiness and joy!
Just clip this message now and mail it with your name
and address and 10 cents to cover postage. We will send
this wonderful NEW MESSAGE OF PRAYER abso-
lutely FREE! We will also send you FREE, this beauti-
ful GOLDEN CROSS for you to keep and treasure. This
MESSAGE IS GUARANTEED!
—— Advt. —— Advt. —— Advt. ——

But even as my prayer screamed in my brain, Jonathan pulled
me closer and his hands ran over my quivering body. Suddenly
my dress was off, and he ripped at my bra—so hard that the foam-
rubber pads came out!

"Please, Jonny!" I cried, "Let me explain!"

Now he brought his hands lower and squeezed the padded seat of my "Two Timer" miracle panty girdle that clinched in my tummy while it added ounces to my hipline and derriere! All at once I knew I was his—I wanted to stop, but Jonathan was too strong! My heart swelled, and I folded into his arms! It was suddenly what life was all about! But then, in a flash, I understood that it could never be ...

—— Advt. —— Advt. —— Advt. ——

HAVE
YOU
OVERLOOKED
SOMETHING?

When you've gone to all that trouble to be Miss "well turned out," doesn't it seem a bit silly to cling to bulky, noticeable sanitary pads? Tampax internal sanitary protection is out of sight, out of mind—never interferes—never makes anyone (including you) conscious of its presence. Try it. You'll be delighted. And it's guaranteed!

—— Advt. —— Advt. —— Advt. ——

He was angry, but he just turned around and left. I don't know how long I just sat in my room and cried. At last I cried myself to sleep—in agony.

When I woke up the next morning, as I looked at all the make-up and lingerie thrown around the room, I suddenly realized that I had tried to grow up too fast. I all at once made up my mind that only when I can handle my emotions in a sure and grown-up way, will I get involved with anyone. Any boy who asks me out now will find that I'm a quiet girl who doesn't push herself, who doesn't go further than a good-night kiss. It's hard to depend on people liking you for yourself when you've had the experiences I've had, but I know now that it's the only way.

—— Advt. —— Advt. —— Advt. ——
YES! WE NOW HAVE THE NEW, GUARANTEED
VIBRA-PEN!
Created by a WOMAN for WOMEN the VIBRA-PEN
is completely safe and satisfying. Only after years of scientific research has modern technology been able to perfect a battery powered vibrator that is guaranteed for *all*
women! Especially made for women with Elderly Husbands, or husbands having undergone Certain Types of
Surgery. Also perfect for Women with Working Husbands, and that certain Kind of Woman whose Husbands
through Necessity have to be Away from Home a great
deal. And, of course, for Single Women and Widows
who are prevented by our needlessly strict Social Code
from finding Outlets. Just 50 cents provides you with all
Information on this new Vibrator, Guaranteed to provide
Years of Pleasure. This could be the best Investment you
will ever make. Thank you for your time.
—— Advt. —— Advt. —— Advt. ——

Chapter 7

When Jonathan left Cynthia's dormitory, he noticed that it had
suddenly become warmer. Dry grass and twigs crackled under
his feet as he walked, and when he stood on a mound in the
meadow, he could see a gently sloping hill slightly shimmering in
a purplish haze. A fire, he thought. The moon seemed larger in
the warmth, and its light made the sky glow green.

The mild evening had become a hot, laconic night which, as
the haze implied fire, only suggested that it was soon to be summer in the city. Summer in New York, Jonathan thought, and
immediately envisioned a window caked with soot and flaking

grime undulating slightly with the vibrations of a blackened air conditioner, the sacred machine whose electric pulsations were the thin and solitary line between "normality" and madness. Polluted air, dusty walks, hot gusts that seemed to carry malignancy as though it were perspiration; from this the only recourse was a "conditioned" antiseptic atmosphere that felt like cold metal against the skin.

Then he thought of Eliza, how she had looked on the train, and later, in her room. It would be impossible to imagine her in the city during the summer; she seemed surrounded by an aura of cool blue, or green, not compatible with the harsher reds and yellows of New York days. It was like a massive thermal exchange: his existence in the decaying heat of the city somehow making possible hers in the Maine backwoods, or at Martha's Vineyard. He began to resent her with the same bitterness with which he resented anything that he envied.

The blond football player, earlier labeled the "Goyische Golem" by David, stood outside the "Calf" with two friends, both in service uniforms. While he attempted to tune his transistor radio, apparently oblivious of his friends, one of the soldiers had borrowed his gun-shaped cigarette lighter and was playfully directing it at whatever girl walked too near to his seat on the steps. Regardless of the girls' reactions to the menacing tongue of flame, both the uniformed boys laughed loudly, moderating the girls' cries with assurances of, "Come on, it won't hurt you!"

The Golem finally tuned in a station relatively free of static and turned up the volume of the set, sending its jangling, metallic sounds echoing against the buildings and walk:

Hah! Hereweare,backagainrightafterthenews,boysandgirls. Hey! itspartytimetonightsojustphoneinfor*your*requests, andwe'llplayem itsthetoptunesthat*you* wanttohear! Andnowfellas, c'monlet'stalk straightyouguysgot ACNE? Don'tbeshyaboutitguysgooutandfight thosepimples. That'srightguys—usenew*Burn-Off*. Speciallyformu-

latedbyadoctorfor*you*guys, sothatyoucanfight*ac*ne and pimpleslike
aman. Andnow,forourfirstpickhit, wegotagirlcallinginfromFlat-
bushAvenue,whowantsustoplay KissofFire, thegoldengoodiethat
*you*wanttohear . . .

Perhaps, thought Jonathan, it's just this unending stream of
word salad, this electrical insanity, that keeps a semblance of
sanity alive in New York. There was never an instant of silence
on that radio station; but then, neither was there an instant of
silence anywhere in the city. The horns, coughs, motors, screams,
brakes, neon buzzes, aluminicron music, senseless dialogues, am-
phetamine giggles, the mutilayered stream of *noise*—it existed
only to hold off a still greater noise, to hold back the pulsating,
cadaverous shriek that would escape from the lungs of every in-
habitant of the city as he collapsed on its fluorescent streets.

"You see them all over New York. In the library, they stand
near long rows of books and debate, openly with themselves,
speaking their own language and staring straight ahead. Or, at
other times, they open book after book, moving their lips, and you
think that they're reading to themselves, but the pages remain
unturned and you see that they repeat the same phrase again and
again. They leave the table glassy-eyed, still repeating all that they
have been saying, as though the phrase were theirs to memorize,
when you see that it has memorized *them*.

"They murmur sullenly in empty subway cars or rage almost
defiantly at the streets. You see them, and ignore them without
being self-conscious, because you learn to ignore everything unpleasant when you live in New York. And you almost never feel
that they are just a part of you writ large, your own oppressive
madness revealed when all the veneer is peeled off."

Alima said this, in a slow, sad voice and then, as if she were
part of a film, turned and waded into the Ganges, looking back
only once to laugh.

". . . you don't believe everything that you read, do you?" "But

I can't *decide* how I should feel, or how one should feel in general . . ." ". . . it was *her* diaphragm, I'm positive!" "Vietnam." "I'm glad I'm not a boy—now, anyway . . ." "Watch out you'll *burn* me you bastard!" *But ah got your love an' that's enough!* "She's still a virgin—as of an hour ago, anyway . . ." "Asia." "Would *you* go in?" ". . . they've got a good beat." "It's a matter of conscience . . ."

"Back so soon?"

Arnica was first at the table to notice Jonathan's return. He shrugged noncommittally and sat down, accepting the cigarette she offered. "She sat and smiled for five minutes," he said, lighting the end and burning his fingertip slightly, "And I smiled back, and then I got bored, and left."

"I've just been telling Arnie about someone I hitched with in France last summer," said David, "I don't think I've ever told you about him—a Marine."

Jonathan shook his head and moved his chair closer to David's, whose voice had been slightly drowned out by the cacophonous emanations of the Insurrections:

> When ma girl knows that ah'm up tight:
> She tries ta please me the whole damn night!
> We get so hot! (We really get burned!)
> We get so hot! (We really get burned!)

David lit a cigarette and began:

"He picked me up about forty miles outside Paris and immediately started to talk about the war in Vietnam, only to listen to him it was like he had just come back from the Crusades. He had 'served his time,' and was 'goddamn proud of it,' and he knew we'd win if we had to kill 'every mama-fucking gook to do it,' and so on. I was going to ask why he wasn't still there instead of driving around in France, but I felt that I had *tzuris* enough without asking for more.

"So we kept driving, he doing all the talking—everything but the Pledge of Allegiance—and me all the listening, hoping that he wouldn't notice my long hair and put two and two together and murder me. Then he said that he was getting hungry and why don't we stop in some 'bistro'—he said it like we were going to eat an illegitimate child—and of course he'd pay for it all. So we stopped, and I decided that I'd order as much as I could, since I pay taxes and so was paying for myself *anyway* . . ."

At a table to their left, two girls sat drinking beer. The girl sitting closer to Jonathan was an attractive blond, dressed with methodical chicness in a short, loosely hanging dress and white boots, while her friend wore dungarees and a lumber jacket. They both looked young, which might have accounted for their being alone this late at the mixer; but as though to emphasize their maturity, they each had four or five cans lying next to them on the table, and were gulping the beer down at a steady rate. The casually dressed brunette seemed to become more sullen and albuic with every taste of the drink; her friend began to talk louder, with an air of forced cheerfulness, attempting to control her disappointment by laughing at it.

"I want to go back," the brunette mumbled.

"Oh come on, Lois, we're having a ball tonight, aren't we, aren't we honey?"

"I hate this fuckin' place!"

"Oh, live it up kiddo—have another beer! They're free with Sarah Lawrence tuition."

The unhappy girl took a sip from the can and stared ahead, expressionless.

"—drunker and drunker on the wine and kirsch and liqueur and whatever else they stuck in the food. First he was just loud drunk, then sad drunk, then he began to cry. The *maitre-d'*, who hadn't seemed altogether too impressed by his uniform to begin with, came over right away and told me that I would have to get him

out of there, so between the two of us we got this sobbing load of
Southern manhood into the car, and it was decided that *I* better
drive. I took it pretty slowly and he began to sober up and talk
and talk, and then I found out why he wasn't defending us any
longer in Vietnam.

"His unit had been assigned to 'liberate' a small section of Com-
munist-held land near the Mekong Delta. For about a week
before, American bombers had given the place all they had, so
the territory was supposed to be pretty safe, if a little charred.

"He was put on night patrol duty in the hulk of some village
they had just about razed to the ground, since they expected that
the Vietcong would try to set up headquarters there. On the first
night, he heard what sounded like a human voice coming from
out of the rubble. He was scared shit and began to run—this was
his first time out on combat—but then remembered that he was
there to 'serve and fight,' etc., so he started back and swore to shoot
whatever moved. He kept on hearing the voice, weaker now, and
searched all around the village—finally he found the girl.

"He said that she was about fourteen, and very pretty. From the
way he described it, she probably was in shock, but other than
that she was almost uninjured. He tried to talk to her, and was
surprised that she didn't speak English—for Christ's sake, they
don't have time to teach these boys *everything* about the people
they're defending!—and she was probably too scared to talk anyway. So he gave her a candy bar, and she stopped crying and ate."

"Oh God, isn't life just so wonderful?" The blond's voice was
louder now, and her enunciation less certain.

"Its marvy, positively *marvy*."

"You know what I have to get? Those great tan boots that
General Hy's wife was wearing when they were inspecting the
battlefields last week. I'm sure Courreges must make her uniform
especially for her!"

"I want to go to sleep!" She wailed this out, and moved her head to the table. "This goddamn music hurts my *ears!*"

> We get so hot! (We really get burned!)
> We get so hot! (We really get burned!)

". . . that he would have to wait until morning to bring her back to camp. She didn't have anything on but a coarse shift, half of which had been torn so that her breasts were exposed. He took off an overshirt he was wearing and moved to cover her, and he accidently touched her nipple so that it became hard. He immediately looked away, and began to walk around the village, fighting the urge to go back and touch her again. He said that he must have run all over the village, hoping to sweat, hoping to tire himself completely . . . When he came back to her, she was lying just the way she was before, and shivering in spite of the oppressive heat. She began to cry as soon as he bent down. He said that all that he could think about while he fucked her was that he was strong, and she was under him.

"He got scared when he was finished, because he didn't know what to do next. Sometimes you wonder whether Americans were ever designed for war. War is nothing but sex and murder, one after the other, until you're through, but the poor dumb cracker couldn't bring himself to kill her when he had used up his sex. It would have been suicide to bring her back to camp, since she would have been questioned and almost certainly would have told them about the rape—so finally he just tied her up, gagged her, and stuck her in the shallow pit of a makeshift bomb shelter . . ."

Gotamessage for little AnnieHurwitzoutthereinFlushing QUEENShappybirthdayhoney!!mmmMMOW! Iloveyakids!and nowforthebigSUperHIToftheWEEK wegottheCoolBlowerssingin

PUTOUTMYFIREBABY!! RightafterIgiveyouthismessagefrom
theModWearShopinRockville—

The Goyische Golem slowly tramped into the room, flanked on
either side by his uniformed friends. He held his radio close to his
cheek, caressing the dials with methodical tenderness. The army
boy had appropriated the Golem's flame-throwing cigarette lighter,
but now seemed content not to direct it at anyone; the boy in the
Air Force uniform, gadgetless, trailed behind and sat down. The
other two stood above the dance floor for a moment, then, ex-
changing glances of mutual approval, descended the stairs and
sauntered towards the band.

> And whenever ah'm in misery:
> Ma baby wants ta get high with me!
> We get so hot! (We really get burned!)
> We get so hot! (We really get burned!)

"—an unbreakable habit. He would go through the motions of
'patroling'—probably as much to allay his guilt as to 'do his duty'
—and then run to the shelter with whatever rations he had been
able to swipe during the day. He would feed her, and then fuck
her, or whatever else he happened to feel like doing: he told me
that some nights all that he wanted to do was talk to her, and not
be concerned as to whether or not she understood. She was, after
all, 'his girl,' in the best American tradition of the word, and I
suppose that, in his own *mishuguna* way, he needed her, maybe
even loved her. Anyway, our boy from Bogolusa had really found
happiness with his Mekong maiden.

"Then one day his unit was instructed to break camp and move
five miles south, as a precautionary measure against expected
Vietcong infiltration. They began hiking back in the early afternoon, and had gotten about three miles south when they heard a
roar above their heads—the sound of a squadron of bombers going

back to the Delta for a saturation raid, just in case there were any VC in the area. The raid lasted less than an hour, but even in the late evening, from four miles off, they could see the bright flames of napalm reddening the sky.

"They didn't go back to their old camp for another day, and even then they were ordered to stay within one mile of camp area. He disobeyed—that was the technical reason they relieved him from service—and he ran back to the big clump of ashes that indicated where the village had been before the raid. He opened the shelter, and found her tied and gagged and burned to death."

> When ma girl knows that ah'm up tight:
> She tries ta please me the—

"Dance with me, Jonathan."

Arnica pressed her hand onto his cheek and he turned around on his seat so that he faced her. She smiled, and walked slowly towards the dance floor: he rose and followed.

The noise of the band and dancers, no longer merely disconcerting, now became oppressive, like the humid, smoke-filled air that wafted sluggishly through the room. Arnica's mouth was curved upward in her beautiful, frightened smile; Jonathan wondered if she were intuitively reacting to his uneasiness or just attempting to communicate her own. He moved his pelvis, his arms, wrists, threw back his head—but the actions were no longer free or spontaneous. His mind seemed to be working separately from his body, separately from the ceaseless maenadic movement that enclosed it. His mind stood still, and looked at the upturned corners of Arnica's lips and sensed that it was not freedom, but an uncontrollable madness, that pulsated through the room like an electric current. Then the song became louder, and, caught up in its undulating rhythm, he threw his head back, and danced.

Chapter 8

THE BOY ON THE GRASS
When You've Never Known What Love Is, Finding It Can Be An Awakening . . .

Now, back in my room, I finally understand what people mean when they talk about just *"having* to write it down." Maybe I ought to write it as a note to Mother—or maybe not, since she would never *really* understand. Here, inside, are the prints on my wall, the Picasso, the DaVinci, the two small, fanciful Degas. And out there, a boy still lies on the grass, and looks at the night sky . . .

If I *did* write, my family would probably wonder what had gotten into me. Since my early teens I have automatically bucked mother on every issue. The core of the chronic argument between us has been that I wanted to be left alone to brood and paint and Mother wanted an everlasting round of parties, boys and dresses. Shopping for me before a party was her idea of heaven.

Actually, I got all the art supplies and lessons I ever asked for, but with them I got the lecture about how I needn't expect to have a normal social life if I remained so aloof and self-centered. And Mother got the parties (arranged by her), but with them she got the absolute guarantee that I would go out of my way to have the most miserable time possible. We arrived at the dreary impasse where I was depriving myself of things I really wanted to do because they would give her pleasure. It was sick.

My repulsive brother was right about going away to college. "Breaking the umbilical cord will be the making of Lois," was the unattractive way he chose to put it. (He, the senior at Yale; he, the All-Wise.) Tonight, after learning so much about life from Jonathan on the lawn, I have to agree.

Breaking the umbilical cord hasn't exactly been easy. Now that

I look back on it, I can see that when I arrived at Sarah Lawrence in the fall my whole way of life depended on having someone to resist. I needed a new candidate and my roommate was closest to hand. I had to find out the hard way that Lana wouldn't fit the bill.

Every Friday night after dinner we have a Mixer in the "Calf." Lana naturally assumed we'd be going together.

Lana is a lot of things I'll never be, and blond is just one of them. She is wonderful looking, thin and tall. Striking, a boy would call her. She's concerned with clothes in a way that I could never understand, and always wears the latest, whether it be white leather boots or canvas skirts or angular Mondrian dresses. She does her work competently and finds it mildly interesting, but she is quick to tell you that she came to an exclusive girls' school for one reason only—to get a man.

Lana's urging was too close to home for my comfort. I found myself automatically explaining in my loftiest tones that I didn't care for that type of affair and preferred to spend Friday nights working on my art contract. "After all, that's why I came to college for," I added unbearably. Lana gave me a big surprise, though. Month after month she kept handing out the same package: "Well, darling, I must admit that you've got my admiration!" she would exclaim in her deep, sophisticated New York tone. And she meant it and she didn't try to push me around and she always accepted whatever I wanted to do as being every bit as right and sensible as what she wanted to do. Seven months of this had thrown me off balance. Lana went to Mixer after Mixer and had a ball. I stuck to my books and papers and as much as I love painting, I had one miserable, lonely Friday night after another.

Tonight, as I sat on the bed watching Lana brush her bangs back with a characteristic little twist and almost smelled the warm spring air that flowed in through the window, I thought: if she really tries to persuade me this time, I'll go. I still dressed as usual, in my paint-splattered dungarees and mouldy old lumber jacket, almost as though I wanted to limit my chances.

"It's an awful shame that you don't want to come, kid," said Lana.

What could I do but start to pile up my books? Music and voices came floating from across the lawn and through the open window. Lana snapped her fingers, syncopating their beat with the music. I fitted a new cartridge into my pen.

"I'm too shy to go," I announced, to reopen the subject of the Mixer in a negative way.

"You're not shy," she said, reaching into the closet for the black Courreges dress that she wore with her white boots. "You know that the mob scene is a bore, but you'd like to meet some beautiful fellow and talk about art."

I knew I would. I balanced my books on the edge of the chair. She had urged me, I had only given in. Then, if I have a horrible evening I can always say, "See, I told you . . ."

My books dropped over the edge and I jumped up and out into the hall with Lana, where we linked arms with another girl.

It *was* a horrible evening. Even Lana, running around from boy to boy, seemed depressed, while I sat alone and brooded. I thought of the warm security of my books and prints, recreating the fine lines and subtle colorings in my mind's eye, and wishing that I were back in my room. I saw a Picasso *Still-Life,* and suddenly the after-image of a Vermeer came to mind. Then I realized, just on these mental impressions, that the two paintings had the same basic structural organization. "Yes!" I said excitedly to myself, feeling sudden goose pimples of surprised pleasure and recognition.

Lana was sitting across from me now, trying to be her usual carefree, witty self, talking endlessly to bring me out of myself. I was wiggling uncomfortably in my chair, as much from my sudden understanding as from the unpleasantness of the Mixer. If only there were someone I could *really* talk to! Painting has been my whole life, but it wasn't until that moment at the Mixer that I realized that, like most people, I've looked only at the surface.

"Oh, God," Lana cried out, trying to act *blasé,* "Isn't life just so wonderful?"

"It's marvy, positively *marvy*!" I almost shouted out, and then saw that the boy was looking at me.

I had forgotten him. He had been to Mixer earlier, left with another freshman, and then come back only minutes before. He sat now and talked to a boy from his school and a senior from ours, and I couldn't help but notice the way he sat, and smiled, or seemed to be lost in thought. His face had character.

I looked over my shoulder. He was staring at me, examining me. I swung my chair so that my back was square to him. I felt my face warm, but resisted the temptation to turn again, and probably meet his glance. I don't know how long I sat, nervously listening to Lana talk, until I turned around. He was gone.

I thought how he'd be walking along the cinder path outside, or perhaps sitting on the lawn, the warm wind blowing his straight brown hair. And how, if I'd had any sense at all, I would be walking along beside him, asking him the superficial beginning questions: "Where do you come from?" and "Where do you want to go?" I wanted to be there so much it hurt.

You miserable mess! I thought to myself, Whatever makes you so obstinate? Why didn't I look back at him? I'd never had a real date in my whole life, the kind where someone asked me out because he liked me and enjoyed my company.

My life was arranged and rearranged by my mother, my brother, my friends, until the only independent thing left for me to do was to say no, even to the things I wanted.

Mother worried, and she tried to talk about it. "When you're at college," she said, "remember that people are going to believe that you are exactly as you appear to them. Anything you don't show might as well not exist."

"Sartre," said my brother, who was sitting sideways on an armchair tuning his transistor radio.

"Looks and manners are very important," said Mother, "Don't ever say, 'I'm shy.' Don't—"

"Project the wrong image," said my brother.

The conversation had ended with me in tears, and as shy as ever.

And now I was like a depressing picture surrounded by pretty ones. If there was something good inside me no one cared to look for it. Why should my friends care? There weren't any courses about what to look for in people. College was teaching me an important lesson: the surface was all that mattered.

What did they want? I wondered, What do they like? *How should I be?*

Just sitting in the midst of the loud Mixer wasn't going to help me at all. The "Calf" seemed to have gotten very crowded, and I felt as though I would be smothered by the heat. I looked at Lana; unperturbed, she was talking vivaciously and smiling at everyone. Maybe *that* was the way I should be, I thought, but knew that I had to get away from the Mixer.

"I'm going out for some fresh air," I mumbled, and ran through the maze of crowded tables and out the door before Lana could even reply.

I needn't have left my table, since it was almost as hot and crowded outside as it had been inside. Couples sat all around the building and the path, talking and laughing, but all seemed listless, like the night. I have to get away, I thought, and quickly walked up the path. Three soldiers, shining in their black uniforms and gold braids, passed by and grinned at me. I turned around and ran onto the lawn, not looking where I was going and almost tripping over a boy who lay on the grass. I stopped just in time—and saw that it was *him*!

I sputtered out some kind of apology, but realized that I sounded like a dizzy little girl.

He looked up at me, and I noticed that the amused, almost bored expression he had worn earlier had been replaced with a more intense, saddened one.

"What's your name?" he asked.

"Lois," I said, having composed myself enough to brush my bangs back with a little twist like Lana.

"I'm Jonathan," he said, almost sighing. He stared at me, and the clarity of his deep brown eyes drew me down, so that I sat next to him on the grass.

"Look at the moon," he said gently, and I looked over to the west, where the waning, two-dimensional disc was giving off a cold light that wasn't its own.

I suddenly wanted so much to say or do something that would impress him, that would make him feel I was as sensitive and sophisticated as the other girls at the Mixer. But I was at a loss as to which image I should project.

"Have you ever known someone to become so inseparable from a place that, to you, they *become* that place, that the grass, and the air, and all the other voices should seem to be aspects of the persons, of the one . . .?"

His voice slowly trailed off, and I tried to think of some way to answer him. I shouldn't be too serious, I thought, so I tossed my hair back and tried to appear smart and flippant—just like my brother. Jonathan just looked more deeply into my eyes, as if unconcerned with my surface and only interested in what lay beneath.

"Did you ever meet Alima Redford?" he suddenly asked.

"No," I replied, "I'm only a freshman." I almost immediately regretted saying that. After all, why would a boy who sat with seniors want to even associate with a miserable little freshman? But Jonathan didn't seem to care. In fact, his voice sounded softer, and he looked more relaxed.

"That was last year," he said abstractly, "We had met in early autumn, and would walk through Bronxville in the late afternoons, avoiding the roads and houses and instead going through the musky woods that shone brown and red in the orange sunlight. We would sit and talk over coffee for hours and then she would dance for me on the meadow, like a nocturnal maenad. The winter meant nights at the Apollo Theatre, or cold Sunday mornings running aimlessly through the streets of the Village. Afternoons were in overheated rooms of old tenements, eating whatever we could buy or what was left over from the weekend. We walked through streets and the City and schoolrooms like two aliens, neither understanding those around us nor understood by them—nor wishing to be understood by them. What we shared was indescribable, exclusive, perhaps not meant for the ears of anyone else.

"There was a night in the spring. We had gone into the "Calf" to watch the Mixer, because, aside from our own acts, we were always observers, never participants. There is something beautiful about stepping into the midst of noise and crowds after just having made love: the tiredness, the serenity are so opposite the disjuncted movement and agitation of the single dancers. We were quickly bored, as we always were by people too self-conscious of their pleasure to be possessed by it, and left the "Calf," walking out over the road into a field of trees and rocks. Alima began to sing, and run, and turned to me and laughed the laugh that was a signal to pursue. As I chased her, I suddenly *saw* her beauty—her smile, her blond hair falling over her face as she dodged me, her long, loose dress shimmering one instant with the moonlight falling on it, darkened the next under the shadow of a tree as she slithered under the branches and re-emerged, still laughing."

Thereareplacesah'llremember: somearegah-ha-han,andsomere-
main; Allthoseplaceshavetheirmeaning—Wellboysandgirls that's
*your*PICKHIT   tuneandnowIwanttoaskyoukids,   doyoueverfeela
littleoutofthings—then   maybeyououghtausenewBURNOFF   for
yourPIMplesandACne—

A tall, heavy blond boy had just walked by, his transistor radio
blaring all over campus. Jonathan frowned, and I wanted to somehow shield him from all that awful noise. Soon the boy had
walked off, and all around us was quiet again.

I now wanted to say so much, to express the sudden rush of
unexplainably similar feelings I experienced when he talked about
the girl he loved. But I remained silent. He had felt so much, had
probably lived so intensely, that anything I would say could only
sound like childish jabbering.

"She left me," he said suddenly, "Suddenly, inexplicably, as
though she somehow had to confirm her feeling that happiness is
not possible in our lives. She taught me how to laugh, she taught
me how to understand so much . . . and now she's in India, having
run away as if from a crime."

I followed his gaze and we stared at the moon, now rounder
and giving off a richer orange light.

"But I can only feel that she's still here. I see her every time a
girl with blond hair walks by, hear her voice, catch a scent of her
skin or perfume in the wind and suddenly she is all here again,
and the campus seems nothing more than a tarnished mirror
throwing Alima back at me wherever I look. I imagine that tonight she would have been walking through marble caverns
under onion domes, the leaves of tamarinds and the tangled roots
of banyans merging with her hair and legs as she slowly grows
into the ground and makes all of Delhi and the Ganges smell and
feel and exude nothing but Alima. Well; it doesn't matter . . ."

He said this last as though it were a moaned lament, a last, futile effort to recall a lost illusion, to recover an image that had crumbled in his hands. He stared blankly ahead, looking beyond comfort—and I wanted so desperately for him to understand how deeply I felt! Without saying a word, I ran my fingers through his long, straight hair and kissed him. My arms thrown tightly around his neck, I thought of all that he had once had and lost, and found myself holding on to a moment in time, not wanting it to slip through my fingers, not wanting it to dissolve into a half-forgotten illusion.

When we drew away, Jonathan looked at me and smiled gently.

"You're very innocent, Lois," he said softly, touching my cheek. I blushed fiery red in what was probably the first genuine moment of shyness in my whole life.

"I was," I said, and then added, "Once."

I don't know how long he held me in his arms, how long we stared at the setting moon and the stars. I remember that I suddenly understood I would have to go back to my room, that I had to leave Jonathan in the loneliness that I, in part, now shared with him. We kissed again, and we spoke, and then I was walking back to the dormitory, slowly, as though in a dream.

That was almost two hours ago. I've just reread all that I've written, and feel that I can grasp at a little of its meaning. Being a pretty picture is all right, I think, as far as it goes. But what matters most is finding out what's below the surface and learning how to show it clearly. Only then is it possible for two people to make the goose-pimple-raising discovery that beneath two dissimilar exteriors lies the same, and sometimes beautiful, basic composition.

DAVID SHAPIRO

Every Night: Another Note

We—we feed them, because they're only slightly mechanical
compared to us, and then they've sealed up the rocket
and the elders say space will not allow them a return.
So how were these star-people ever permitted to travel
The oldest (most narrow?) people in the world.
I look across the gym and think, honey.
Children keep playing with a smelly toy monster whale
But the stench is ridiculous; it cheers me up.
I thought you had forgotten me.
But returned to the clitoris from within.
Ahoy! There's drinking in my ship!
I could stay here forever, teaching philosophy. But then
you've gotten the plate of your share. What tears have you cried
over the arrival of my lines? What papers have you already
        burned??

Poem

Three fresh horses being unable to love
were parked a short distance from the others,
feeling the embarrassed urge to duck bumps
in a high school. You've come for a good time again,

You're white and distorted. Where else could you find
these horses?? Gallop in the hope of reaching shelter
up to the hills, for the hour or the day!
You're being taken to headquarters again! Open the stars.

For Son

1

I kept spinning in all kinds of grass. An unmarried woman
came and pointed out the stems to me. In my light fast
motorcycle, she read each letter in order. My hands are
resting on an arched roof, horse allowed to roam at night.

2

She gave me a damp cheek, to explain why her copy didn't
fly through the night. The telephone operator heard a
coin, "This is very good." A bread accused me of the
hatefully long absence. In this, was I fit to be imitated?

3

A soft unbleached ape in the carburetor due to weak
mixtures, while being launched. You blunt-nosed dolphins—
Decorating hat, shoe, etc. Who supported the vessel
while being launched? The Bishop of Rome of gas and air.

4

The peony is a plant with showy flowers, no it is a race, a com-
        munity
stocked with irritable qualities of red, pink, and white.
So back to the rules of penance, that shed standing with its roof
against the higher wall "Enter a place, somewhat young."

5

She gives body to the words. She will come into the camp of
retired governors, she will insert herself between the mould and
the emotion. Bright green is her hair, and the shadows follow.
A husband carries on, I love you, the tide of the river said.

6

The course of life on earth tends to repay an injury in kind.
Silent man takes a repeated test, a second photograph.

"She made him quiet, she will again, stars finding amends in
    stagnation."
Gravel is the ship's bottom, and the fireplace its frame of bars.

Poem

We have come to be saved. From a pest.
And so we are constructing.

From this altitude, it seems as though
we were swimming, rowing a boat.

Later a girl named Julie grows up
in a blue dress. She walks past our perishable fort.

How new she looks! We hardly recognize
and in this we are ascending in the play.

I'm talking about the New Jersey shore,
her hands evidently excited, while the flag sinks.

"She held out her white hands to us,
but remained in the bitten world."

from *A Poem*

For Joseph Ceravolo

"We muffle whatever is ripe. Then light up their lives in pastry
"the cold nasal cone, the fluffy faces. Yes, you have beaten your
"way to a cup, showing how to lug a vendetta half way up the
       mountain.
"Who was coming? A monster doing presto, through the green
       moss
"thence to her private verandah on the stiffening porch. 'She
       dallies
"in a private parade, her human in a circle of moss.' Her human
       star
"quintuplets launched in a private parade. Her showed her the
       circle.
"The shape of a shell. The vulva of a pig. Gate of composition.
"(as in a mine) returning after the work shift. Pillory 1.
"Bullets are not scattering over the plants. March is carving. This
"forms a thin hard crust. Young idiots cannot recover in the next
       ring
"what would be most agreeable, given for free and nothing,
       delicious.
"So I said, 'My cap of green, my cap is cut. Record this terminable
"light, the tutti I played on the banjo of light and zinc . . .' Ebb.
"Evidently there are days that assemble in the desert, demand
       summits
"say Virgil—but what I saw was a limp crocodile walking in
       eternity.
"A choppy sea, partly blind, wholly blind. Then the ultimate
       principle:
"a feeble light arouses the universe of grey-white. Statements:
" 'Feeling so great, the penumbra has featured its own veto'

" 'She is the articulate companion, she embraces her bowels'
" 'The heartwood lumber of the yellow birch divides in the
    springtime'
" 'You cheat your legs, you make new complaints from the uterus'
" 'The pale blue falcon suppressed a smile after being stuffed'
" 'It comes from Malheur and it makes a new edition of The
    Malebranche'
"So leave your baby in the pond which I will sketch on my skin
"under which the bones. Do you fall persistently, will you rush?
"All roads to Deal have dried up, return to your wings. The state
    of one
"Dead is not locating, exploding is not the underwater near the
    sea."

For Chagy

Tefilot Chagy

1. Moses and Aaron needed a blind animal to shame the chorus.
   They found the animal in the black mud. But none were
   there to help them with the beast. They almost choked before
   God put them to sleep. Was it a lion, an elephant, or a mule?
   Nor do you sleep alone in the hospital.

2. Moses was dying on his blue bed. Near the council of Israel
   the sea was rolling, and heat raised tse-tse flies over the faint-
   ing man. He did little to reach them because of his idea of
   justice in the world. He commanded his men to step over an
   iron road. This man analyzed the shimmering light; another
   sent rats along the iron road. Closed the ransom of all friends.

3. The rowers on Weequahic Lake lift up hands to Moses,
   shadow of the God of pity.

Dagda

4. Back at the rushes the children went forward. The kites were flying above the mat of the lenient deserters. And remember the teacher who showed me my minimum self at the becalmed rim of the magma chamber.

5. Oh what did you give to leave, story of the fish and the land. The odd smoke nails the elect to their donor, as the haves err from the sign they were given. I didn't give the delicious year the summer to kill my pottery on the poor trays. Lazy soldier, walk to school before the derelict wall can be torn off for a minute of being and the not-so.

Johannesburg: 1935

6. Misery wears a shirt and has the bus cry hi-you to every fish. On the street the police shut the oven at home. We are to him what the baker tries to eliminate in his work. The afternoon you bit me I slept around the corner from the imitation noise. The flower-sucker at this period wears diminutive blue scarf threads. A slender doe drinks in ivory and egg and then chats. The kid says giddyap to the shore, and the river obeys the boy.

7. The baby hammers as it pipes human misery.
    A pie is in the oven.
    A pie is cooking; so listen to the disheveled gardener,
    While the potatoes shine in his hand.
    We are the happy kerchiefs of the shamed barn.
    The best of the shot-giving men,
    The beginning of hatred, lime and tar.
    Who plays with us and tantalizes us,
    Rising to rinse its hand in the Thames.

8. Who are you so slim and so slow on the chalk of the voice!
Oh you value me so much sister of Lamarck and kin to his
chosen ideas. Sleep of the bird the boat crews shook out of the
struggle one morning. Touch me with the hand that latches
on to the grave of geology.

Pompeii

9. So the dog went near the dish and died. The morning followed with a nude teacher and a bad noise from the crater.
The lobe and fin of yesterday's fish, how the teacher dives to
satisfy himself. Dim Roman, you were right to stay and clean
out your desk. So the dog kept following the dictator and died.
The rim being fire banishes the hope of a hasty swim. The
diminutives thought better than to think of the sweet. The
suave dog died, and the rain followed. Crowds painted the
room forty-seven times, but a synthesis has disrupted them.

D. 1954

10. Oh have you been in the world Israel?
Anchored to the letters sent and the revitalized kin
With shock God came to the bean garden
(It kept—Make the division so ordered to see
My foot has the same age as this land!)
         *   *   *
Come to me marriage folded together. As a gift that tries
urgently to put my hand in yours. The role in general is
the goal. To God the goal Israel.
         *   *   *
Bad chooser! I kept my hand from the insanity
But I shivered because I was so malformed
And a naked bean and ashamed.
You succeeded with the grain of badness my superior

Lenient when you recovered me from a going dream.
Their friend is the dead usher,
Peaceful laughter and the hand of the maze way.

Song of the Plague

11. I am the famine chased across this land
    How do the masons see me? As some chimney
    They shape the lava from the rim
    Into yellow and blue blocks in competition.
    Massy the storm above the crab
    On mission to the diatomous bottom.
    Momentary the scream of your own mouth
    But you will go on until the conclusion.
    The ash tree goes to sleep,
    The houses are filled with his students.

12. A year of loving deduction came to her because she was
    designed for the stellar ridges with their cambrian peaks
    Because the train says How light you are! hasn't shone
    under the sign of roosters where the major and the decoder sat
    raising up a shot of violet wine, a shot of happy hands
    Bad chooser! You have won the upshot. Being a dog relishing
    his prayers for the dog I didn't marshal a side to rave
    about the choice or the desired effect or stain in limbo yet
    I've grown so much to see the sash around his delicious
    Borders of the mouth of Israel.

13. The arrow wakes up Mozart odious life that sunk the Vedas
    tulips where my pistol goes and reason daily prayers for the
        dead
    brush and dream you to whom the ray of tallow is shining
    milk the day-old Moses and revive the nationalities past yeast

Have you a dog that lived—him—the least of life's musicians
Oh to see their little ones dashed among the rocks
To divide your name from the page of the man who gave it
But she is a male, and the libel lights up this bizarre
Quarrel between the Arab and me

14. The game of mirrors the children played developed at another
    time. Opening her hands, she put tatters on them. The gov-
    ernor ran the island with his sisters. He was too lenient to be
    vetoed. She welcomed him home. Nike rockets massed by the
    dam. OK! Followed by the sorrows, Peter and Ishi, and the
    yoke of the nations. Amo! "I cried by the reservoir in Balti-
    more. I have the communist dove, the brown tse-tse flies, per-
    verse, to me, amo, venal love." Yes to the God of possession
    who has dominated the day of their death and the day of the
    Hague. Pagodas and bags of the nations packed like horses
    pointing to water. Bidden by the heat, as one of their kind,
    you rushed to the "ring of fire."

15. One day Ruth designed to go into the patch
    for the ovaries under the rocks that
    connected to the nuclear court.
          We were neighbors for months,
          breaking the blue eggs.
    He castles in that position. But
    his hand rests on the elephant square
          by the ocean that plays
          with us and tantalizes us.

Elegy to Sports

Orestes pointed out what was despotic
    In youth and stingy hunger.
From his golden injuries he got
    What he wanted from you.

The key used to dial was at last in place,
    The house asbestos.
And he dressed up like a piece of human candy
    With great hustling.

Last stop! Your clothes fill up the trunk
    With a pitiful hand.
The seer in old age follows the raindrops,
    Touring an inhuman scene.

The Swiss have no wars, though they lose combats,
    The English are hemmed in by waves,
Those who drink the rivers Po, Tagus, and Danube
    Are found on the river bottom.

And so the vaulter, who rebounds into gravel
    Dragging his pole behind,
Like gasoline sets the hurdles on fire
    Jumping and jumping again.

The pianist whistles during the accompaniment;
    Mrs. closes her eyes;
She retires from us, seeing you dislike her
    And her rowboat collection.

Now you are happy, and you are more than happy,
    You swan of Lancaster.
Don't complain about the dull apartment life
    A thousand times a day.

The gnome brought suit against the cedarwood,
    And Libya owes money to a tree.
Your father has received the gems amber and garnet
    For a year's work on his bed.

You beat your hand, you jump out of line,
    And you say among yourselves:
"This is what Italy and Greece dumped on us
    In a thousand poems."

So you give away your violin, the other his trumpet;
    The girl gives you away.
And the women, the pedestrians, and the detective
    Desert the champ.

Irresistible Poison

Two families lived in a
    simply furnished house.
But they didn't make
    their own clothes.
These were given for work,
    like necklaces and food.
A healthy young baby boy
    added to their happiness.
But one day his non-sister
    hid a poisoned fork
In her new dress, and
    later the boy collapsed.

MITCHELL SISSKIND

I Worked for the Old Central Electric Company

I worked for the old Central Electric Company.
Later, I went into the manufacture of tables

But Lou was a young executive slated for the top.
I remember coming up to the company and selling Huber,

Who at that time purchased tables for Central,
On the idea of buying one thousand of them: I said

It was a terrific opportunity and everything went fine
Until the order got to Lou. Lou had become vice-president.

When the order came back it had been cut to fifty.
Incidentally, Lou was right. We still laugh over it.

    If you have ever seen him play golf
    You must realize he does this
    Intensely, yet with an easy manner.

    I joined the Villa Moderne Country Club
    And found Lou's name on the roster;
    I got after him and we went regularly.

    I can still see his short, choppy swing,
    With the ball always on the fairway.
    It never traveled far out but it traveled straight.

And I shall never forget the way we used to putt,
And I know Lou has never forgotten it:
There was an incident, when he and I

Were playing in a tournament,
Both of us on the green,
He on one end and I on the other.

I honestly believe there was
A thirty-five foot putt on each side.
Lou was away. He putted first and sank it.

I was next and, putting mine
From the other end, sank mine.
This so demoralized our competition

That they flubbed easy putts
And we won the match. I know Lou
Remembers this incident very sharply.

Lou and my son, Harold,
(Incidentally, now a fine attorney,
Who was at that time only six)
Were listening to the Cubs play St. Louis.

The Cubs were having a mediocre season,
With all the breaks going against them.
But they had three men on base and no outs;
Harold, jumping around, was a Cub enthusiast.

Lou said, "The next one will be a triple play."
If you know baseball, you know triple plays
Are as rare as holes-in-one in golf.
But that is exactly what happened.

A triple play!
And I shall never forget the awe
In my son's eyes, as he looked up
At Lou, a terrific prophet.

We joined up with Joe Wais and Gustav Golding.
This foursome stuck together through bridge,
And then pinochle, from 1928 until last year
When Gus passed away. The threesome is still at it,
A little bit older but just as active and as ornery.

If you would listen to us play pinochle,
You would swear that we hate each other:
Each man is the other's mortal enemy.
Every hand is a matter of life or death.
The desire to win is great

Yet the amount of money is small.
I have never seen friendship such as exists
Among Lou, Joe, and myself. It is needless
To say what I or my family thinks of you, Lou,
Because it is shared by everyone who knows you.

The Plan of the Day

1

A caster and the great, "Fell near me."
But I had thought each was rising by now
Toward a patched-up diagram of the crash

Whose human sides could not exclude us;
Still, out of the brush ran a white snail.
This morning you get cold from watching it.

Then there was the important feeling:
I had now accidentally cut your hand.
Buzzing each crude feeling in a dish.

2

There was a soft gash, too, in the pool.
Light from it dropped carefully; the glow
Of a late autumn sunset appeared at one wall.

I lay face down. There were two big girls.
Finally the room was full of aunts and uncles
And then to have a secret tenderness for it:

True attention, the fun plan, the cell,
The luminous cell we have only visited:
You must try to love it more for this.

A Wrist Lock

1.

A wrist lock
A hammer lock
A chin lock:
A head lock.

A chin lock
A hammer lock
A wrist lock:
A step-over toe hold.

A wrist lock,
A hammer lock,
A wrist lock,
A hammer lock.

A head lock.
A step-over toe hold.

2.

A drop kick
A flying mare,
A flying mare
A drop kick.

A forearm smash
A forearm smash:
An abdominal smash.

An abdominal smash
An abdominal smash:
A drop kick.

A forearm smash
A drop kick.
A flying mare.

An abdominal smash.

3.

The Full Nelson.

A Boston Crab
A Kiwi Hold.
The Full Nelson.

The Boston Crab
The Kiwi Hold.
A Claw.

A Claw,
A Boston Crab:
The Boston Crab.

A Claw
The Kiwi Hold:
A Boston Crab.

The Full Nelson.

The Dawn of a New Day

Three years ago Myrna met a man, Charlie, and she called him a lion. Charlie was crazy about Myrna and her boy. Once he came from the coast just to see them.

Myrna sat on Charlie's lap.

"I hope I'm not too heavy," she said.

"Not at all," said Charlie. "It feels good."

"I'll bet it does," Myrna said. "What are you thinking about?"

"I am thinking about your breasts."

"The lion," said Myrna.

Myrna realized that with Charlie life could be good. She needed a man who could help raise the boy, who would go places, who could show a little consideration. She wondered: Should I grab my son, leave Nate everything—the home, the car, the furniture—and walk out?

Myrna was losing all pleasure in life. Apparently so was the boy: he became hideous.

Because this home is his funeral, thought Myrna.

Nate's sister was going to have a birthday party. Myrna was excited about going someplace. Then at the last minute Nate decided not to go, and made excuses. He said:

"Myrna, meat you cook is good. You like to walk around in your black slip. Instead of going out let's have meat. You won't have to wear no dress. We won't have to leave the boy. Don't cry."

After a while Myrna called the sister and said that Nate was sick. Of course I was not believed, she thought.

That night she decided to phone Charlie.

"I can't just ignore Nate," Myrna told him. "Shall I put the dream of a good life out of my mind? Shall I just go on living this way? On top of everything the boy has become hideous."

"Listen," Charlie said, "I don't believe Nate is interested in you. Probably it is impossible for him to be interested in you."

Myrna remembered sitting on Charlie's lap.

"Nate promised he would live like other people," she said. "But he hasn't kept his promise. He won't go anywhere. Charlie, I remember sitting on your lap."

Charlie said he would take the next plane. He would get Myrna and the boy away from Nate.

"Some story," he said. "Myrna, this is really something."

"You are truly a lion," said Myrna.

"Well, see you tomorrow," Charlie said. "I am thinking about your breasts."

Charlie arrived. Nate was at work. A heavy, wet snow was falling. Charlie stood in the doorway, the snow falling behind him straight down slowly in the still air, some melting on the shoulders of his coat.

"Come in," Myrna said. "Dry off."

"Like to walk around in your black slip?" Charlie asked.

So they lay right down. Charlie got started. He kissed Myrna's neck, and her dark hair, and Myrna moaned and giggled.

In the afternoon Myrna packed her things and the boy's things. When the boy came home from school, she told him: "Let's go on a trip. What do you say!" He was a blond boy and when he came in his distorted face was red from the cold.

"He looks like a good Swiss," Myrna said.

"I'd say that boy is big enough to carry a suitcase," said Charlie.

"Sure," said the boy.

So Myrna put on a dress. They went to Charlie's hotel.

Myrna called Nate.

She told him that Charlie would help in raising a son and would show some consideration. She told him that he, Nate, just

wouldn't go anywhere. The boy had become hideous. That home
was a funeral.

"And would you please wait one minute please," Nate said.

"Just eat shit," said Myrna.

Myrna and Charlie talked to the boy. Myrna said:

"Charlie is our dad as of now."

"Try to understand," said Charlie.

"Sure," said the boy.

He sat in colorful pajamas. They knew he was trying to understand. What to say? wondered Myrna. Everyone sat.

"Like to sleep on it," Charlie asked.

"That's all right," said the boy. "I'm not tired."

Myrna could certainly imagine how confusing things were.

"Do you know," she said, "that your new father is a lion?"

"No."

"Imagine a lion," said Myrna. "Imagine that a lion is going
across the desert."

So in that boy's mind there appeared a jungle and there was
around the jungle a desert; then out of the jungle a lion came
with a short black mane, and at the edge of the desert he stood
staring with his yellow eyes straight ahead brilliantly into the
sunshine. He started to walk, and started to run.

"Crossing the desert," Myrna said, "the lion meets people. He
says: 'Well, so perhaps you've committed a few atrocities . . .' "

The boy's lion was hungry all his life. He had a golden coat
and a short black mane and clear unblinking eyes that stared
straight into sunshine. Well so perhaps you've committed a few
atrocities anyway they are in the past he said and was all exquisite
but his strange claws.

"Sleeping," smiled Myrna, "our boy seems less hideous." She
sat on Charlie's lap.

"And I am thinking about your breasts," he said.

"On the coast he will improve," said Myrna.

"But right now I am just thinking about just your breasts."

Outside it was already getting brighter. The sky seemed oddly lighted.

"All right, oh yes," said Myrna. "Thank you."

A Mean Teacher

There was no chalk in Miss Carter's room. It was gone. She wanted to write on the blackboard. I'll send a child to Miss Baylie's room, thought Miss Carter, to get some chalk.

Still, she remembered: Miss Baylie is like an elephant. Who shall I send there, she wondered.

There were no troublemakers.

The children sat in blue desks, thinking: There is such a thing as ghosts. They read of other lands.

"All right, Paula," said Miss Carter. "Four times eight."

"Four times eight," Paula said. "Thirty-two. You scared me." There was a general flying laugh. At that Miss Carter changed colors.

"Less noise, if I were you," she said. "Maurice, give me five times eight plus three times eight, in your head. You had better know the eights, my friend."

"Three times eight," said the boy. "Twenty-four. Sixty-four, I guess it is," he said, thinking: I have nothing to be ashamed of.

Outside mothers pushed their babies past the school. The pupils heard them crying in their carriages. And safes fell on those carriages in Miss Carter's mind.

"Maurice," she said. "Can a man on foot escape an elephant?"

They look slow thought Maurice, but they are not.

"No," he said. "They look slow, but they're too big. Why, with one step of their giant legs. . . ." He was humiliated quickly.

"The answer is sometimes!" shouted the children. "It says in the book sometimes you can: Bumba was chased by one!" In their minds men were escaping.

Miss Carter roamed the front of the room. There was her hair, the color of a radiator. Then there were her metal lips.

"Maurice," she said, "go down to Miss Baylie's room and ask nicely if you may borrow some chalk."

Maurice was fat yet loved to hum when he ran. This makes it like a movie, he would think. But he walked quietly down the hall to Miss Baylie's room and knocked on the door.

"Come in," said Miss Baylie. Maurice opened the door, thinking: She is more like the dinosaurs. There were the big kids, so awful.

"I'm sorry to bother you, Miss Baylie," Maurice said. "But Miss Carter would like to borrow some chalk."

A mean teacher, Miss Baylie took the boy into her cloak room, a belly. She beat him up there, asking: "How would you like to go down to the office, and see Mr. Wadsworth?" Outside some laughed to hear the thuds. "My glasses, my glasses!" shouted Maurice, in her clutches. "Really, it's hilarious, Charlie," said a big kid girl, and whispered: "From inside there she can't see us, darling." "Let me take you to the land of dreams," responded a young man. That night Maurice told his mother what had happened.

What kind of a woman is Miss Baylie, anyway, she wondered. Where does she come from?

Miss Baylie lived with her father Jake. She had become a big fat one through the years.

When Miss Baylie was small her parents would walk with her

around the block. In those days her mother would hold the right hand, and her father would hold the left hand. Those were the days, too, of her mother's strange infection. Those were the days that Jake was out of a job. Once an old man approached him.

"I'm not going to tell you a long story," said the old man. "I want a quarter for a drink of whiskey."

"I just don't have a quarter to give you," Miss Baylie's father told him. He put one hand on the old man's shoulder. "I just haven't got it. I'm out of a job."

"Then we part friends," said the bum, moving along. They heard his spitting. Just then Miss Baylie's mother made some noise: she claimed her whole body itched. One day her life collapsed like a chair.

"We have to be brave," said Jake, thinking: I've got to find a job. Then he found one.

With time things became easier for Miss Baylie and her father. They moved to a neighborhood where the dogs were not quite lovely collies, but neither were they chows. And on Sundays when Miss Baylie and Jake walked around the block he no longer held her hand, but it was displayed for all the passers-by. And they thought: So light brown! One day an old man approached Miss Baylie's father.

"Give me this moist daughter of yours," he shouted, his arms on her shoulders, her face in his mouth. Miss Baylie covered the man with punches.

"All right, mister," said Jake. "Okay for you." This is no fun, the bum thought. He forgot about the whole idea.

It was a hot day for April. The trees made short shadows on the sidewalk. Because it is almost noon, thought Miss Baylie. But then: I hate that old man, whose lips dripped. They went ahead.

"Well, what do you want to do with your life," Jake asked. "Say, I hope you're not hurt."

"Be a teacher," said Miss Baylie.

"That's a good idea," her father said. Yet one day he would rip her heart out and eat it. One day Miss Baylie would turn around, and she would be shaped differently. Then Jake would ask: "How was work today? Well, I know there's nothing wrong with working for a while when you're eighteen or nineteen years old. All the girls get jobs in banks, or they become secretaries, or they become teachers. But they don't just let themselves go! You just let yourself go! By the time a girl is twenty-five she's married, and has a girl of her own. And believe me by the time she's thirty-five she's mighty glad to have the children around; they bring some cheerfulness into her life. Do you think movie actresses don't have kids? Well, sometimes the studio doesn't want the public to know how many kids an actress has because it might make her look like an old woman to some people. Listen, every one of those actresses has plenty of kids! Do they know how long their careers are going to last? How do they know when some young actress is going to come along and steal the audience? And a lot of them get killed in accidents. But one thing is for sure: no matter what happens, they've left some kids to carry on, and provide them with grandchildren if they're still here. And most of the time, if the mother was a beautiful actress, the daughter will turn out to be beautiful and probably will go into acting herself, or if it's a son he'll be a handsome actor. And neither of them will have very much trouble getting married and providing a few kids, that's all I know. Well, I could stand to hear the laughter of children again. Is it too late? What's your plan?" "I don't feel well," Miss Baylie would say. "Shut up."

Maurice's mother grabbed her son and went to see Mr. Wadsworth, saying: "You're the principal, aren't you?"

"Why yes," said Mr. Wadsworth. He listened to her organ recital. Then he sent for Miss Baylie; she appeared at his door.

"Come in, Miss Baylie," said Mr. Wadsworth. "This is Mrs. Minor. I gather you know Maurice."

"Yes," said Miss Baylie.

"And in fact Maurice has a lot to do with my asking you to come down here this morning," Mr. Wadsworth said. "That is, it concerns your relationship with Maurice. Now correct me if I'm wrong, but this seems to be the situation: last night the boy here told his mother that he'd come into your room on an errand from Miss Carter and that you took him into the cloak room and punched him. Is that right, Maurice?"

"Yes, Mr. Wadsworth," he said.

"Now then. Miss Baylie, what's your side of the story?"

"Sir," Miss Baylie said, "I was trying to conduct a class, and I was interrupted. I don't mind, of course, as long as the child is a gentleman. But I'm afraid . . . "

"Is that the kind of school I'm sending my son to?" asked Mrs. Minor. "Is that the kind of thing that goes on?" Once she had witnessed the beating of a horse.

"Now Maurice, did you provoke Miss Baylie in any way?" Mr. Wadsworth asked. "Did you knock on the door?"

"No . . . yes," said Maurice. Suddenly he burst into tears. "Yes, I did. She knows I knocked, too. She might not say so." His mother flew to him.

"You see, Miss Baylie," Mr. Wadsworth said, "this kind of thing creates a lot of problems. And really, is there any excuse for it?" He studied his folded hands. "Now I want to make myself crystal clear. We cannot . . ."

"Excuse me, Mr. Wadsworth! Excuse me!" said Miss Baylie, standing up.

"Now don't get upset," Mr. Wadsworth said. "I'd imagine there are enough people upset already, wouldn't you say? Well then."

"It's not that," said Miss Baylie. "It's just that my body has begun to itch. It's happened before. But . . ."

"Itch?" sobbed Maurice.

"Now, Miss Baylie . . ." said Mr. Wadsworth.

"It's all right," Miss Baylie said, sitting down. "Pardon me."

"Well, as I was about to say . . ." Mr. Wadsworth continued.

"Just one thing!" Miss Baylie burst out. "I know the children dislike me. I know they tell their parents about me, and make jokes about me. I don't need to be told that. But I want one thing to be clear: whatever I did, it was to help them. I knew they would often misunderstand, and be hurt, but I hoped that someday in the future it would become clear to them, that someday they would think kindly of me, or—if not that—at least remember me. I felt I owed them something which no one else seems prepared to give—the feeling that what they do is important, that it makes a difference whether even a child acts rightly or wrongly, that there is such a thing as right and wrong. What does a child see when he looks about him in today's world? He sees adults abdicating their responsibilities to him, perhaps with the best of intentions but often with the worst possible results. He sees parents who so misunderstand love as to think it can only find expression in the gift of a new whistle of some sort, or in the decision *not* to administer a well-deserved beating. Today's are parents who fail to realize that the sowing in a child of integrity and self-denial will reap rich harvest long after the sting of a good crack in the mouth has been forgotten. But we have denied our children the pleasures—for they are pleasures, finally—of receiving these gifts, and hence we have denied ourselves the perhaps equally great pleasures of bestowing them. For the parents of today, seeking to retain for themselves the careless freedoms of childhood as children to their children, have thereby forfeited the satisfactions of seeing their sons and daughters grow into real men and women, real mothers and fathers of whom they can be proud. It is the irony of today's parent, who believes that to make one's child happy one need only remain ever a child oneself, to have brought down upon the young people exactly that uncertainty, even panic perhaps, which was presumably to be avoided. Can we imagine a generation more filled with doubt than that growing up today? It looks to its elders for guidance and finds only a few more 'pals.' And if the parents don't care, or care only in the wrong way, where can the children turn? The church, all the churches—with variations according to the degree that fashion has replaced principle in one or another of them—have simply followed the prevailing winds. So from the pulpits come only talk and more talk about the latest miracles—of the cinema, that is—or of the trash which has most recently fought its way to the top of the best-seller lists. And *what of* the writers? *What of* the artists? Have they moved to fill the blank sheet of paper, the empty canvas which is conscience in our time? The answer is no. No, they have decided to go on painting and writing and filming only whatever is least worthwhile and filthiest. But what a moment for poets and painters, and especially for the motion picture colony, to disdain even one more tasteless fling in the hay in favor of reminding us of those values which we have so utterly forgotten, yet seem ever the more trying to forget: the sunset over Hawaii, a bear trapping salmon in our Pacific Northwest. Indeed, things are at such a pass that the moment has traveled through ripeness into urgency, the opportunity having grown into a responsibility. It is this kind of responsibility that I have felt as a teacher, and it is this sense of urgency that has compelled me to act as I have. I can only wish it felt by every child's hero who is tempted to throw the big ball game, by every hunter who decides on just one pheasant over the limit, by every bride and groom who might then feel each other's kisses not simply in a spirit of whoop-jamboreehoo, but thinking: 'Will tonight bring a child into the world?'"

And the next moment she knelt before God's throne.

Mr. Wadsworth hurried to her side, and knelt to take her pulse. "Miss Baylie!" he shouted.

"Will she be all right?" asked Mrs. Minor, thinking: She grew too fat.

"It's no use," Mr. Wadsworth said. When the ambulance arrived he told them, "There is nothing more to be done."

"Of course not," said a young doctor. "Not as far as the woman herself is concerned. But a good autopsy may teach us things that will help in the future, and not just in cases like hers. We learn a lot."

"I don't understand it," Mr. Wadsworth said. "She'd never missed even a day of work, and then this. And then this."

"Well, from what you've told me," said the doctor, "it certainly sounds like the big itch. And if, as I suspect it will, a talk with the family shows there to be a history, well . . ."

"I'm closing the school," said Mr. Wadsworth. "I have no stomach for any more school today."

The children filed into the assembly hall. They knew something was up.

They thought: This is a special assembly.

"No talking," said Miss Carter. "For the first one who talks there is the furnace. Who will that be?"

Mr. Wadsworth rose slowly, carrying his body like a piano. "There will be no more school today," he said. "You see, Miss Baylie has suddenly passed away. Now, I don't know if you can understand . . . but I want you to understand. Oh, she's dead, she's fallen down that elevator shaft! And the cables gave way one after the other, and we may wonder, many of us, 'Mightn't she have grabbed something on the way down? Aren't the springs down there?' But it only remains for us to stare down the hole." There was some noise. "Listen, she gave something to you. In ten years you'll know what it was. As for now . . . well, what does a fish know about the water?" He unbuttoned his coat. "You'll know what she gave you when you move into high school, and go on to college. She always gave one hundred and ten percent." Mr. Wadsworth rebuttoned his coat. That felt good. "She was always ready to lend a hand—be it in the lunch room, or on Work Day, or on Stupid Day, or for graduation: Miss Baylie." There was a quiet moment. "And now you may silently go. I expect the older ones to keep an eye on the younger ones."

The school opened like a can. It was near the end of May. Outside the children went to the park, hid in dark alleys, carried one another's books in kindness. Soon each would be in a different grade. One thought: Hooray. Boo-hoo, thought another. In the park many were attracted to the interesting flies eating a doodie. "That's human," they said. "There's no dog big enough to make that." "Of course there is," one said. Blocks away a big kid decided: I'll throw Kathleen's homework high in the air. "Awk!" said the girl. "Now I'm going to start kissing you," he said, thinking: This is Sergeant Rock, and we're moving into enemy territory. She thought, dreamland.

LESLIE GOTTESMAN

Racing to the Coast

The face fragments stumble past the sleep station
The children are stamping to get to the home station
We place the morning station
carefully in the locked Japanese hotel "collection"
machine station, it emerges in an instant
coffee station. The trance begs the window station
for a commercial. The baseball players are
involved in a revolution at the shaving station
You get up to leave the room station, I
believe, but disappear into the waiting station station
I am alone in the green station, it is the lamp
station to be broken. At the same time, the stations
whiz past the windows. There are some
stations to which we arrive, the arm station, the leg
station. I am making a station collection station
upon this small brown hill, behind the station, waiting
for your blue postcard from the foreign places station

We're Friends Again

"He will not dare to step with the divinely human
The unconsciously brief, the timesaving in general.
Idiocies? You notice I don't include neckties.
He was panting a lot. It was oddly diverting to see
The voice of a man who keeps calm under fire. I felt
About. The next-to-last poem is about a young married
Nose—to the point where a salt tablet might have
All but sang its way across the room to me.
Her husband's chuckle sounded again. 'What
Seat? I just meant that their apartment's so tiny, and
Apparently he was *at* their apartment when they—'
She sat down heavily on one of the twin beds.
I closed the door behind me. I began to open
More minutes, without drinking, and then I put it
A doll in the seat with her and turns its head around
The head. He had written, in letters that had not quite
Survivor's conceit, that he's the only one alive who knew
Simply because I was the owner of a pad and pencil, he
'Considerably' with age as our faces 'filled out,' I
This afternoon, stopped dead short in the middle of
The house, it's exactly two doors down from where Carole
Nominally ventilated, as I remember, abounded with M.P.s'
Presence in their apartment. Why, then, did I go on
Grounded everywhere, including, I'm sure, the middle
You would have been working on if you had known
Of performing circus people and performing, so to say
At this point, it doesn't seem to be merely chummy
Bull's-eye, poet's vocabulary, his non-stop talks, his
Suddenly appearing in your street in a canoe."

The New Left

There are no problems to solve:
The famine, like the blind men,
Has exploded.
But it's no joy ride:

Locusts of the world
Are focused straight into the silver
Scars running down it.

Penguins have a strange human
At the foot of the volcano.

Experts in the tropics
Accept their marigold garlands.

Then the rope tricks.
In the glare of floodlights
Their red petals, apples, petitions
Press together under the chin.
The dogs don't like to see any.

But don't blink your eyes or someone will
Come up with a cure
That's half again as big
As a seven-foot rich kid.

The Bad Seed

My second memory is
The new machine
They kept me in.

I have done something:
It's called a cat.

Our wings, you see, must have
New locking devices.

But suppose a gun would locate
A little playmate on the ship
With its stronger body.
He was a boy soprano.
He will die at sea.

Then there's the old man:
I painted him as a horse.

Among the flowers and leaves,
Temperatures and the price of gas,
Your plane approaches.

We weren't thinking of the child.
Our bunnies trampled the child.

Once it drowned six sheep.
Those sheep were very regular.

Poem

They broke into a flood of tears
I quickly undressed
All this is ancient history
He slammed the dick with his fist.

You risk nothing
A happier sex life
Till the flashes came
She could not go till the light came
It's part of being a woman
Cut it out.

Pedigree by Empire

I sing of America.
Up in New England
On some uneven starry night
Sis put Joe's thing in her mouth.
Later Joe put his thing in Sis' behind.

A little mouth, though,
Is full of dreams.
To miss America is to miss something
Large—the old South, the raw
West. The Indian cannot be
Overlooked. Look for a millionaire
Who thinks as you do.
Take the last look.
And that's physically impossible.

Hateful Positions

You do what everybody else wants if
I get hold of you during the day
On the beach for a few minutes
And the earth
Would pass into ecstasy.

I will do better
Out of the ocean
Will you come out
Woolly body dropped on the shore
Before going in the body to
Spots we fly to?

And those around her.
All year she turns to us
That ridiculous balloon
Gets lipstick on it.
She used both arms.

She brought back the white
Little daughter of yours
Then the cow and the flying
Horse
But you live a little
By banging them up again.

JOHNNY STANTON

from *Helping the Guy with the Prostitutes*

PART ONE:

Tank, Cells, "Clear the Alley!", Tommy, Red Pig,
The Mad Knife Fighter, My Arrest, and Oilcan Harry.

I put the bottle to my lips and drank down whole contents in
one gulp. I let out a scream and jumped off steel bed. I staggered
toward Tommy, clutching at my stomach, trying to rip it away.
I stared at Tommy twice over head to foot with wide open eyes. I
thought my veins were flying out of my head.

He zoomed away from me, he-hawing with insane glee, and
scooted out the door, but jumped back in because he heard someone yell:

"Clear the alley! Clear the alley!"

The automatic bangs on the cells and tank closed up tight. I
shut up, wouldn't vomit, too tough, didn't want to bring up pig
madness.

Tommy was rubbing his back against the cell bars. I backed up
to the wall and put my hands over my hearers.

A pig who's bald but sports long thick red sideburns smacked
his clipboard along the cell bars. He stopped by us and spit a
squirt of black tobacco juice at me.

"Hey Bush [that's Tommy's last name] what's doing with the
smart ass kid?"

"Just drank a little piss that's all. Ha, ha! Thought I was giving
him some warm orange soda. Ha, ha!"

The all powerful control mechanism slipped inside my head when red pig and Tommy laughed a long time very loud. I bull fought Tommy; he crashed down to concrete floor. Then pig guard put one of his paws through the bars and got me around the neck. He started in choking me. My mouth dropped open, my eyes widened. Finally I was able to push away his sweaty paw, ducked underneath, free, and spurted towards my steel bed.

"Well fuck my shit!"

"I'll be a suck egg mule!"

"Haw, haw, haw!"

The cowboys in the tank were watching, laughing, and commenting on all these goings-on. Somebody raised his leg sideways and exploded a fart.

"Pretty good," said the red pig, catching the joke and getting into its spirit. He sucked in deep some air, threw down his clipboard, slapped his knees, and jumped into the air. When he came down, he blew a fart so loud it echoed all the way back to the solitary cell where Crazy Pappie jawed on the bars and his tick mattress.

Tommy also watched these proceedings, hawing with everybody, not really any longer mad at bull-headed me. He started to jazz the red pig.

"You must be a farmboy r. p. to explode in such a vainglorious manner. You obviously spent your schooling years on a well-equipped farm."

"Yeah, Bush, I graduated from Parson's Farm, where you'll be going for twenty-five years. . . . That's the word I heard from down the judge's chamber."

Tommy spoke to the floor.

"Blow your brains out your asshole."

The red pig rearranged his boots and sideburns, then picked up his clipboard. He squirted more of his tobacco juice at the cowboys in the tank.

"Attention! Attention, you hard-ons!" he yelled, turning around in small circles very quickly. "Get ready to go to trial: Bush, Marx, Rechy, Redman, Duluoz, Stanton, and Webster."

My stomach pounded the floor, but there was no woodwork to walk into. I wanted to beat all the red pigs up. Red pig strolled out with a real god in his head, and the automatic bangs on the cells and tank opened up.

I was still blank when Tommy tried to run the togetherness routine on me. I shivered in the gray, damp cell. I told Bush to put his money into a carnival, while I thought back on my arrest. . . .

It was an L-shaped supermarket stick-up. There were private shotguns in an upper level all the time. It seemed that the store was in a busy corner of town. I had been a success in small cigar stores and delicatessens. I wanted big money to last me four weeks: no bother to run up and down the stairs eight times a day. I was sick of marshmallow cookies, cheese, and meat loaf.

I ate my Christmas dinner of dried turkey and a mound of stick'em potatoes down on Preston Street with the winos and the beat up roll-overs.

"Stop dead or I'll blast you," I heard as I walk away from cash register around six hundred dollars richer.

I dropped to the wooden floor and thought about whether I should be an epileptic or not.

I waited in a small room with three unshaven oldies and two negroes for the big truck with cops to come. Someone said that the truck came to the store everyday, except on Sunday of course. A small laugh about that. . . .

Crazy Pappie was muling with belly laughs in his solitary cell. Tommy was eartalking to the Mad Knife Fighter, a nineteen-year-old sex hoodlum, who had been lying in his bunk, combing his hair all the time. Something Tommy said tickled bushy hair's eyes. I knew it didn't concern me because I wasn't picking up the sidetrap, or watching myself turned loose in a pen with every red pig in the world.

The Mad Knife Fighter sat up and took off his shirt. He rubbed vaseline into his hairy chest. One of our fellow customers, an ex-seminarian, queer cowboy, asked the why's and wherefore's of this maneuver.

"I'll tell you now. . . ." said the Mad Knife Fighter, leaping off his bunk, then grabbing the squealing cowboy and pressing his cock and sticky chest against the queer's ass-hole and back.

Tommy seconded the Mad Knife Fighter's motion and ripped off the queer theologian's total outward cover. Tommy kept the top cover for himself, while the Mad Knife Fighter tossed the rest of the stitches to the multitude in the tank. The jesuit tiptoed through the tank inwardly joyous to have to recover his robes. The cowboys touched and bruised his skin until his little preacher stood up and was counted. Every one belly-shook with that. . . .

Tommy collected dust all the way up and down the alley. He'd pop in a head to spout something crude to numbers in every cell. He had to keep pushing his grease-gel hair off his forehead.

Three old cons in gray underwear sat playing dominoes in a cell: Limestone, an alkie who ached every minute with liver-rot, he drank sterno booze; Ray Moss, a cheap hustler, who considered himself a wealthy man because he had five gold choppers on his upper plate; and Oilcan Harry, a half-bred Mexican, whose hang-jawed, bony face concealed the best knowing mechanic mind in all Texas, he was doing time for stealing cars.

Tommy watched the game for a spell, probably spelling out in his head up-coming defense trial words. Also he poured out old Southern comfort jokes.

"Oilcan, how did a dumb-headed mother fucker like you get in jail with us smart crooks?"

Oilcan overflowed.

"My name is Oilcan Harry. I like to steal cars, wreck cars, fix cars, and even wash cars. I think everything's all right and difficult. When I feel dizzy weekday afternoons at three o'clock, I steal a car and drive fast through torn-down sections of town with high school pussy. Cops never seem to leave me alone. They don't like to see clouds in my head. They put me in jail. And I'm here, just sick and tired of all you hotheads."

It was ninety-eight degrees hot in sweating tank. My potent dream flood gate was wide open in the heat as I stretched out on my bunk, waiting for red pig to come back to bring me downstairs for trial.

I recalled university classrooms snapping shut into flying boxcars transported to building cluster of Houston County Jail. It was the first time I ate chili. I hated it, although I was mighty hungry. A kind prison pig had offered me some. Immediately I had to run through tank to back toilet to throw up. Tommy Bush had been first to shake his round soft belly. He was shitting in another toilet. He asked me if I had much schooling, and later on when I contradicted young tough kid, who fantastically claimed he busted out of El Paso Jail through its wallpaper, Tommy was the rescue siren of "Clear the alley! Clear the alley!" to stop rolling battle on the floor, which I thought I would've won. I was on top with a free leg and a head butt. . . .

I had quit school in New York for promise land trip—had stolen five hundred dollars which vanished in four weeks—hitchhiking criss-cross all America. I had hoped to feel togetherness with other school bums, but they weren't in the libraries of any big cities. I missed an afterwards great New York poet friend, Dick Gallup, in New Orleans by no letter writing to mutual friend, Harry Diakoff, back at Columbia University. Maybe I would've ended up in Tulsa, Oklahoma, not Houston County Jail, with Berrigan and the boys (*White Dove Review*), who a year later migrated to writing center point, New York City, but that's another story. . . .

Things weren't very pretty in my head because I couldn't sing at the top of my lungs. So instead I took out my book, VAL-MOUTH, sat up straight on steel bed, kind of worried about the future, and read until:

"Clear the alley! Clear the alley!"

PART TWO:

Letter to Girlfriend Back in New York

Houston County Jail
January 30

Dearest Alice,

Don't write to me in jail anymore because by the time you get this letter I'll be living back at the Brazos Hotel.

I went to trial this morning, and the lousy judge sentenced me to thirty days, the exact amount of time I spent waiting for trial. I was in the cop-out court. When the old judge peered down at me, he turned a little pale, I think. Maybe I kind of surprised him: he probably thought I was only fifteen years old.

Before the trial an assistant district attorney talked to me in the waiting-room cell. He told me that this particular court was geared to speed up the judiciary process. This means that everyone who comes before the judge here has to plead guilty, and then your sentence would be reduced accordingly. But the catch is that you have to plead guilty to a few more charges, so the police can clear up their books and have a good record. The lawyer also told me that if I was a wise guy and pleaded innocent to the charge, I would get six months to two years on a prison work farm, which is no laughing matter. He said that he hoped all this would be a lesson for me to remember in the future. It certainly will be! He said I looked like a smart boy. After I got out I ought to go home and get a steady job, and maybe even go back to school at night.

Speaking of schooling, last week I wrote letters to the Deans of Admissions at Columbia University and New York University. I've decided I want to go back to school in the worst way, unless I get some great paying job down here in Houston, which I kind of doubt will happen. But I definitely don't want to go back to Fordham. (By the way there's an ex-jesuit seminarian, who's in the same cell as me.) I put down your address as my return address on these two letters. Please send me their replies instantaneously.

Tommy Bush, that guy I told you about who let me read some of his books, and who is writing a novel, some of which I've corrected for spelling and grammatical mistakes, got twenty-five years for white slavery, assault and battery, rape, and sodomy. It was totally unfair. Tommy's a political prisoner! The District Attorney, who prosecuted him, and the judge, who sentenced him, were re-elected three months ago on a platform which assured the public that Tommy Bush would be put away for a long time.

Tommy used to run a long string of prostitutes; he even had a permanent house, where any kind of perversion was allowed. He told me that he had a very strong, intimate relationship with every prostitute he owned. If they did anything at all to displease him, especially if he suspected that they didn't "love" him any more, he would beat them senseless and leave them in the gutter outside the bus terminal in downtown Houston. He got away with all this stuff for a long time because he paid off big to the cops, the judges, and even a city councilman. But finally the papers played up the beatings so much that during the last election Tommy became a political issue. Therefore he had to go to jail.

Now the only way he might have a chance to get free is through appeal to higher courts, but he desperately needs money to get good lawyer. So he decided to write a book about his case, à la Caryl Chessman, emphasizing the filthy corruption in the city government of Houston. He told me that there's no Mafia-controlled operations like dope, loan-sharking, or organized prostitution in Houston because city officials run these shows, and they won't let the hoods take them over.

And to make matters worse for Tommy it's against regulations to write books in prison without the warden's permission, and Tommy's book, I'm sure, wouldn't be permitted, so he's going to have a hard time smuggling it out to a publisher. It'll have to be done bit by bit.

One of the books Tommy let me read was called VAL-MOUTH, by Ronald Firbank. It's pretty funny and English, and maybe I'll like him better than Jack Kerouac, but I'm not sure about that—Kerouac's really great—until I read the rest of Firbank's novels.

I hope that when I get back to the Brazos Hotel all my things are still there. Like a stupid ass I gave this shyster power-of-attorney. After that I didn't see him again, not even at my trial. Some of the guys here told me that this lawyer will take anything he can hock. I hope not, but we'll see.

I can just picture socialist-radical you reading this letter saying to yourself: why is Johnny so frivolous. (I'm not really. . . .) Why doesn't he write about how it really feels like to be incarcerated. What is jail food like; are there special places to wash up; how many are supposed to be in a tank, and how many are; where do the women prisoners stay; how do the guards treat the prisoners; is there much brutality; are there any murders; is the jail segre-

gated; what do the prisoners think about freedom, justice, and
equality; do they talk much about women and their past experiences; write out some short character portraits of your fellow cell-
mates; is there any homosexual promiscuity in jail; etc.; etc. . . .

What you really want me to do is write a novel. But I'll have to
wait quite a few years to digest all these new adventure experiences. Also the prison authorities make you sign a statement which
states that you won't write anything bad about the prison or its
personnel for at least three years after you leave here. That's
crazy!

As soon as I get back to the Brazos (by the way I hope that
Mexican homosexual I told you about a few letters back isn't still
living there), I'll write you a long rambling letter à la Dean
Moriarty answering all your questions. It will be shocking, you
can bet on that. Maybe you can get it published in some Socialist
paper, or maybe even the *Catholic Worker*.

Well so long! Write soon.

All my Love,

Johnny

P.S. There's a guy here whose real name is Oilcan Harry. Imagine
that!

PART THREE:

Madness of Insanity, Cowboy Fight, Arm Stump, Crazy
Pappie, Parson's Farm, Lake Jigaboo, Drainpipe, Vomit
Flame of Anger, New Question, Fucking, Life Force and
Death, Helping the Guy with the Prostitutes.

I put the bottle to my lips and drank down whole contents in
one gulp. I let out a scream and jumped off steel bed. I staggered

toward Tommy, clutching at my stomach, trying to rip it away. I stared at him twice over head to foot with wide open eyes. But Tommy didn't move or even roll his belly. He just crossed his legs and kept his head low. He wasn't moved by my stale play-act of good Southern comfort joke. And of course I gulped down real orange soda not piss this time. I had just written a letter to my girlfriend back in New York and I was feeling okay, but Tommy was holstering an I'm-the-only-guy-here-to-do-twenty-five-years frame of mind. His thoughts dissolved then solidified into rotten prison farm work system.

Meanwhile the Mad Knife Fighter was doing his favorite James Dean rebel without a cause act on some old worn down con man in the corner of our cell. He blew his nose on his knife-spoon and made the oldie swallow the snot down like medicine.

A lean, wiry but solid packed cowboy in the tank for armed robbery didn't enjoy this natural wit to its fullest extent. Not that the sad, dark-haired Texas tough guy was a brother to this old dusty con man. He just hated the Mad Knife Fighter to bottom depth. So the cowboy only needed little excuse, such as joy antics, to try to tear out Knife Fighter's guts.

The cowboy tore off all his clothes. I knew his mind swelled to a peak when he saw snot slobber down the old man's chin. I jumped into my new mind crystal ball to know what would happen. I was waiting to feel big joy in man to man fight with all its swinging back and forth naturalness, and its moving realism.

The whole Houston County Jail gave an ear to the whooping, full jet running cowboy, whose words echoed and vibrated in a misty vision of intensity built up since childhood, and with a swirling, completely naked madness of insanity.

"HEY YOU KNIFE FIGHTER I'M AFTER YOU. I'M GOING TO STRING YOUR BRAINS AROUND THE TANK, FLATTEN YOUR PRICK INTO A PANCAKE, SHOOT MY POWERFUL TEXAS FIST UP YOUR NOSE,

AND SPREAD OUT YOUR ASSHOLE IN CIRCLES LIKE
A GREAT WHITE NIGHT AMERICAN EAGLE, THEN
SHIP YOU BACK TO PUERTO RICO WHERE YOU BE-
LONG, YOU SPIC MOTHERFUCKER."

He was jumping up and down in alley right in front of our
cell, when the automatic cell-tank bangs shot closed tight, catching his right arm up to his elbow. Split it right off! His half right
arm did the hysterical shakes in the middle of our cell floor. The
dusty con man heaved out his guts, splat! covering the dancing
arm.

The cowboy spun around hoping to dash back to tank, then
stopped dead. With full knowledge awake he spotted his right
half arm stump of blood, muscles, and bone marrow waving
circles senselessly in the air. His inside throat voice tried to find
full release in wide open mouth scream as loud and piercing as
shelter sirens, but he was too struck dumb in his eyes to give wild,
ten volume sound.

The tank-cell block door opened fast and red pig leading four
other guard pigs winded in breathing heavy and armed to the
teeth. Red pig banged the cowboy upside his head five or six
times before the pig woke up in knowledge and sight of cowboy's half arm stump. He put his eyes top speed in and out of
cells and tank to make sure our reactions to light were dim. Then
everyone pretended not to watch.

"Clear the alley! Clear the alley!" rasped one of the guard pigs.

Four of them stretched out the cowboy and carried him away,
one at each leg, arm, and stump. The Mad Knife Fighter rolled
into his bunk around a laughing gas fit. The cowboy was to be
carted away to meat choppers in jail hospital, never to be seen
again.

The pigs left. The automatic cell-tank bangs opened up. Red
pig leaned against thick iron door outside cell block. He was wait-

ing. I closed my eyes for a few seconds and coughed slightly. A hornets' nest buzzed into the tank. Cowboys pissed on their mattresses and filled their heads with air.

The Mad Knife Fighter got up lazily from his bunk, thanked me kindly because he knew I had been ready to plaster cowboy from behind in hairpin style if he had roared into our cell, and, still in laughing rage fit plus belches and farts, he ambulated slowly down the alley arm in arm with the cowboy's left behind arm stump, and banging it against cell bars like he was red pig with clipboard.

He rapped on the tank block door with the stump, and jazzed to r. p. that the medics forgot something. Then the Mad Knife Fighter yelled the "Clear the alley!" signal, and in came the slow stately red pig with a billy club over his head and his gun drawn.

He told the Knife Fighter to sack the cowboy's half arm against the wall in the corridor. The Mad Knife Fighter walked back in still smiling and farting. He lifted his leg sideways when he passed red pig, who became violently angry. The pig wheeled his club into the backs of the Mad Knife Fighter's knees. He sank into a heap on the floor. Everything flashed red, and he whistled and screamed as though he had a built in squad car siren in his throat.

Some of the cowboys in the tank were all smiles, as the automatic cell-tank bangs opened up again. They wanted to go out and beat up on the helpless Knife Fighter, but Tommy put a quick end stop to this when he brought out of hiding a sharp, real long inch blade and stood nearby the Mad Knife Fighter.

Everything settled back to normal cell-tank paces. The old con man wiped our cell floor clean, and the Mad Knife Fighter stretched out on bunk for restful nap. . . .

I followed Tommy to the back of the alley near Crazy Pappie's solitary confinement cell. Tommy conversed with Pappie about his long prison farm sentence. He suddenly roared out with a baby-like wave of his bulky hands.

"Awwhhh, fuck that wheelchair judge! Imagine," Tommy said to his waving right hand, "that old bastard lectured me on morals for the benefit of the working press. Now he's the only pimp in Houston to run a permanent, high class whore house. What am I going to do, Pappie? What am I going to do?"

The old jail bird started to talk about what he liked and disliked. He told Tommy about the Normandy Beach Invasion, which he was in on, and how much he really liked a long stay on top a French whore.

Then he bent his jaws closer to the end of his solitary cell to pass on information in a whisper.

"Tommy, when you're first kicked over up at the farm, after around two months, and you're next to the ground picking cotton in the southwest field, break out for the trees. The farm pigs won't see you from where they plant their asses, and they only take a head count before noon and in the evening.

"Head south through the trees until you come to a small stream. Walk downstream. It'll flow into a pool, where you can even see the bottom the water's so clear. The pool's thirty feet wide. To the left you'll see, you can't miss it, what looks like a giant sewer drainpipe. It goes underground for at least three quarters of a mile to Lake Jigaboo. You could ride a motorcycle or one of those small cars through it, or even a speed boat, if there was more water.

"A crazy preacher politician had it built back in the early thirties. He was going to have the land cleared from way past Parson's Farm back down to Lake Jigaboo, all in all around five hundred square miles, and then he'd put all the Texas nigras on it. They could farm it, live well, and be away from us white folks. Haww! what a mess he started. Only this tunnel got built before he resigned his office. But the way I heard tell, lots of people, especially the rich bastards, went out after his ass shooting. And even the state police weren't too happy, they didn't try very hard to protect the old preacher. Five or six times he came close to dying, if you know what I mean, Tommy. . . .

"Well anyway, you go down that drain stack, boy, and don't worry because it's total black darkness inside, you just walk in the trickle of water and keep your hands over your head. You'll touch a rope as you go deeper into the tunnel, then another rope, and another, and another. Just pull them down and hold on to them. Don't let them ropes scare you, I know who put them there and why.

"I was doing time in Parson's Farm for manslaughter back in the thirties. My best buddy's name was Leroy L. Singer, he was there for life. One day out in the fields three of the guard pigs beat him up real bad. That night when we came back in he didn't go to the infirmary because he had no belief in doctors, thought they were all con-men playing around with knives and axes. So the next day he died picking strawberries in the hot fields. I was right next to him when he fell over. Before he gave up his god forsaken soul he told me that the foreman on the tunnel construction job was his brother, then he whispered to me the plan they schemed up for his escape. I didn't follow Leroy's escape route like he told me to do, Tommy, because I was due to get out legally in four months. It didn't seem worth it. But you use it, Tommy, you can use it.

"Now listen carefully, when you get to the fifth rope in the dark with your hands over your head, stop, it's the last one. You climb up that rope, and when you're up there, push on the tunnel wall around half an arm's length to your right. There's a trap door there. It'll lead you into a bunker Leroy's brother made. You search around, and you'll find a light generator. I don't see any reason why it shouldn't work after all these years. You'll find some clothes and new shoes, and maybe ten rolls of quarters too. You're bound to see the other tunnel, it goes straight up from the bunker, it's only big enough for one guy. And remember, before you go up, pull in the last rope, leave it with the others, and turn off the light. The bunker tunnel will leave you out behind a clump of bushes next to State Highway 78, which runs along side Lake Jigaboo. My advice to you, Tommy, is to hitchhike back to Houston. Hide in Houston, Tommy, they'll never find you here."

Tommy stood there without any noise, just nodding, with his hands in his pockets, but then he blasted out a deep laugh, rolling against the tank, and spitting every which way. I ducked my head to avoid his dribble. His fists started to collide with the steel bars. He screamed in mad rage and vomited into his hands.

Crazy Pappie didn't say a word.

After a while Tommy's energy waves of hate subsided, his great red flame of anger burned slower, he sucked in deep gulps of air, redirecting it through his veins until he had totally calmed himself down.

He whispered into the air in front of the solitary confinement cell.

"I'm going to clean out your bad shit, Pappie, and kill such a lying bastard as you dead."

Then Tommy raced his body motor in a flash down the alley to his cell.

Several minutes later I trotted back to the cell, but before I sprinted in I blew some blood and snot out of my nose much to everyone's delight, especially the Mad Knife Fighter who awoke pleasingly refreshed from his nap.

He smiled his usual mad, fiendish grin, pulled down his pants, displayed his prick to each of his friends for three or four minutes, then took careful aim and pissed on Oilcan Harry, who happened at that moment to pass by in the alley. But no fights occurred, Oilcan's head was smaller than his neck, so he couldn't decide about underneath toughness of Mad Knife Fighter. Also Oilcan was a good sport about piss, didn't mind it at all, had sinus trouble since he was young kid.

All this piss pleased Tommy to no end.

He started to jabber about the time he and two girlfriends transported six squalling babies from Houston to San Antonio in back of horse trailer with fake horse's ass and tail sticking out. He also told us about this big deal politician who likes to drink scotch and water mixed with little lumps of shit. Tommy imitated ward boss lift glass of scotch and shit water two or three feet over his head and then letting brownish liquid fall into his gaping mouth.

Tommy got up from his bunk and bumped heads with Mad Knife Fighter. They whooped it up together with old fashion joy and exuberance. I too felt amazingly good, forgetting all my sad endeavors, leaving them unconnected in the alley or under my steel bed. I watched everything like an idiot, and sat on my hands because they were buzzing, and throbbing too much with life.

Tommy and the Mad Knife Figher suddenly stopped shooting around their whole bag of tricks. They turned towards me in a serious moment. The Mad Knife Fighter slapped on his dark glasses, and Tommy flipped his hands up to his armpits, pretending he had big milk titties under there, but I already knew that he had lost his sense of smell a year and a half ago.

Tommy's eyes were shining with a new idea: he held on to things of the mind with waves of power and subtle logic in full release. He bent over me to ask:

"Johnny, tell your good brother Tommy the facts, have you ever in your young life experienced the old pushy-pushy?"

At the same time he made the appropriate automatic gesture with his hands.

"Maybe, Brother Tom, you'd better rearrange the words through your teeth," rasped the Mad Knife Fighter, while he cleaned his nails with the teeth of his comb. "Johnny boy here seems to be only smart enough to walk back and forth from a lamp to a desk."

Tommy fired a big glob of throat phlegm into my right ear.

"Wash out your ears, boy," he said, "and then maybe you'll understand the words I'm spitting out to you."

I went into the tank, took a shower, dried myself off very carefully, came back into the cell, sat down, and asked Tommy to shit out his mouth and fuck up his ass.

Tommy roared with bestial lust and almost swallowed his thumb as he signaled to me his pleasure and approval.

"Pipe down!" he said as he whipped his hand to below his stomach. "Ouch!"

Then the Mad Knife Fighter scrambled over to his bunk, and took from under his pillow a reddish brown, almost rotten apple with a glass tube sticking out at two ends. He whipped out his prick, stuck it into one end of the glass tube, and rocked back and forth singing hillbilly songs until his body shuddered and shook and his come dripped out other end of tube.

Tommy pointed his finger to this drama and asked me:

"Now Johnny, don't be shy, tell me whether you ever did that before?"

I confessed to youthful masturbation, but not in such an imaginative way.

Tommy put one of his smelly fingers up my nose. He said:

"Now think this over very carefully son. Did you ever do that sort of thing, just demonstrated so masterfully by our esteemed colleague, up a real live wet charged pussy vagina tube, boy?"

I had to stand up to answer that question.

"Not exactly," I stammered, but didn't continue to explain because my nose exploded in four sneezes, sending Tommy's fingers flying back to his hip.

Tommy patted me on the back, also wiping my snot juice off his fingers, and said:

"Well, well, well, I know exactly what you mean, boy. I'm sure a little experienced pussy would do you a world of good."

I said:

"What do you mean, man?"

"I'm not going to scrub you down prematurely, but do you think you can handle a little pussy pimping?"

"Of course," I said.

"I knew a whore once," yelled the Mad Knife Fighter, "my first fuck, whose pussy was as strong as a pair of pliers. For a joke and a little extra moola she'd duck waddle across a bar snapping up all the loose change. I think she could even suck off all the foam on a full glass of beer."

"Never mind that horseshit now," Tommy shook his head, and continued, "listen to me, boy, you told me that you lived in the Brazos Hotel, right?"

"Right, Tommy!"

"Well, you know that tall, real bony looking colored guy, who sometimes runs the elevator?"

I nodded very seriously that I did in my hopeful job important manner. The Mad Knife Fighter started to laugh his ass off.

"His name is Jesse Sims," Tommy went on. "He pimps for a string of hot tamales he transports illegally from Mexico, changing most of them every few months. Jesse used to be in my employ. I paid him pretty good, and he set up his own bunch of girls, who reside and work for a living on the top floors of the Brazos Hotel."

Before I was bounced into jail I lived four or five months at the Brazos, never once suspecting or for that matter ever seeing through my own dark-shaded four eyes any pussy of young Mexican shape, except real oldies with several thousand face wrinkles of age.

"Jesse is good tight-lipped fellow of class," Tommy said. "He owes me many favors from way back. He has only a small operation, but that's okay because he's very quiet with the cops and there's no trouble. You go up to him, boy, and mention old Tommy Bush's name, and Jesse will lay the pussy out for you. You'll work with him, helping him sell or rent out all his Mexican boxies, and Jesse'll pay you good money."

"Not Confederate money, either," said the Mad Knife Fighter, as he rolled over and over in his bunk, holding his stomach from pains of laughter, then grabbing between his legs and pulling furiously up and down. "Haw, haw! Helping the guy with the prostitutes."

Was I feeling good all over? Yes I was! All my mind-body apparati blew up in me towards anticipated pleasure of shaking the bedboard screws loose. I danced through buttonholes, my head spinning in crotch blood and pussy fluid. Massive thighs heaved out my mouth of molten lava. And in the pit of my heavy vitals I banged frantically in a beating, whapping roar, sideways clutching my dick of enormous dimensions, lifting the rim of universe in night fireworks of carnival wheel, and blasting, flogging, ripping through a hundred naked bodies of life force and death.

Delirious and breathless in exhaustion I flopped down on my steel bed. Meanwhile Tommy and Mad Knife Fighter greedily swallowed up all my juice, and both farted with joy of renewed strength and satisfaction.

For the next ten minutes or so I lay quietly on my bed, with little smoking bubbles of blood bursting in my head.

Just to make sure of my dreams of girl work I asked Tommy in my best voice of business to write a short introduction note to Jesse for me, explaining all the facts.

Tommy, infinitely happy, said sure and started to write with his pencil. While I watched him or eye checked the Mad Knife Fighter, who was still slobbering in a heap at the rear of our cell, the space reserved in my back brain for mind image dream life death work force exploded. I had a beautiful idea. I'm sure I was

responding to inner voice urging me to be future great intellect
and writer.

I slapped old Tommy on the back. This he did not appreciate
too much because he was bending intently over his pencil when
I put on him in exuberance my friendly whap. He was about to
say something, just opening his mouth, when the pencil shot up
his throat as his head snapped down. The pencil wobbled there
for long moments as he stuttered, then choked, and finally it
sailed out in cascade of vomit and tiny clumps of blood.

"What's the big idea?" Tommy sputtered.

"It's this. Listen!" I said in enthusiastic jolly conversation tone.
"Why don't you copy out ten pages of your writing work. I'll
hide them in my shoes and underwear, and when I get out
I'll send them to *Evergreen Review*, a world famous literary
magazine."

"As famous as *Harper's* or *Atlantic Monthly?*"

"Better even . . . much better as a matter of fact. I think I'll
also send a letter to the magazine editor explaining your horrible
situation. Maybe he'll want to get together a world wide petition
protesting the injustice done to you, signed by all the famous in-
tellectuals and writers, who will immediately admire your work."

"Yeah!" said Tommy.

He wrote feverishly in a great heat since there was so little
time. . . .

I finished hiding the pages and introduction note to Jesse in my
shoes and underwear, when someone yelled:

"Clear the alley! Clear the alley!"

From Here to Eternity

Me? I ain't no hippie. I'm better than that. I'm a full red-blooded American.

I help people out.

I don't know what the social dealers or the street guards would do without me.

There are eighty-five, hairy, dirty, low-grade hippies on this Block. And how could they ever all be fed if I wasn't around.

I like to feed hippies. They don't give me any trouble, no sireee!

They can't. Something's wrong with their heads, and with most of their arms and legs. They don't talk much. Little Groovy and about four or five others have never even mumbled a single solitary word.

And they're all very dirty.

Heard tell their folks fought on the wrong side of the Race War. They sided with the niggers, and look what happened to them.

My grandparents and my mom and dad were on the right side. I'm their living proof of that. I can walk, talk, take a bath, shit in a toilet, and do lots of other things.

You know, you got to be careful with hippies. You can't feed them too fast, or they'll choke. FM-22-5, a sergeant in the street guards, says I'm an expert.

Whenever a new social dealer comes to our block I show him how to feed the hippies. It's part of my job. It's funny to watch one of those dealers with a real fat pot belly hanging over his belt trying to feed a hippie. He goes at it so slow and careful that suppertime's around before he's finished shoving down breakfast.

The only thing that kind of dealer is interested in is not getting his suit all dirtied up, but it always does.

I always have to show him how to do it because I'm an expert.

A hippie can eat twice as fast as you might think, if you know how to make him do it.

My name's Robert E. Lee Prewitt. I'm thirty-two years old. Everybody knows me on the Block. This Block is only one of hundreds the State of New York uses to keep the race loonies in.

Race War's been over a long time. The niggers were beaten senseless. When the hippies finally joined in, men and women of sense everywhere really let out and gave it to them all.

Everybody in the countryside was given machine guns and madness grenades. That sure did the trick, but all the cities were smashed up. Life's not like it used to be. But let's not talk about that stuff, that was before my time.

I've lived on this Block a good bit of years now. I like it here. I don't care much for the countryside and those two-bit small towns with nothing to do at night, and I ain't so good-looking.

But everybody here trusts me.

I haven't seen many of the big buildings, only once really and that wasn't half enough.

They're falling down. A street guard told me he saw an airplane building crash.

I don't get around much because I'm too busy with the hippies. I like hippies. It makes me think how lucky I am that I ain't no hippie.

You see those two run-down buildings across the street behind the busted street lamp. The uppity niggers live there.

They think they're big shots because they talk to themselves about race relationships. A lot of good it does them.

They always laugh at me when they ain't too busy dancing, hollering, or climbing up lamp posts.

But I never have to be scared of falling down or having my head busted in. Sometimes the uppity niggers run around in circles trying to find a place to hide, only they don't.

You see, you never can tell when they might start in shooting off their heads, you know, go down plum crazy and act like they're blackfaces in the movies we see every Sunday.

I don't like going off my head like that. You never know what they'll do next. I'm glad I ain't no uppity nigger.

Let me tell you something funny about the hippies.

There's about ten hippie girls, some of them not bad-looking either, who set up tables in the street for supper every night.

Sometimes when they're done ahead of time, they all sit down cross-legged in a circle and talk. I sneak up behind them and listen.

Do you want to know what they talk about? It's like this.

They don't say a word for a long time. Then one of them says, "Thank God, I'm not a hippie." Imagine that. And all the rest of them nod their heads and look happy.

Nobody says anything for a while. And then the next girl in the circle says, "Thank God, I'm not a hippie," and they all nod their heads all over again. And it goes on around the whole circle, and they never say anything else.

But I know they're real genuine hippies. Or they wouldn't be here. Boy, thank God, I'm not one of them. . . .

You know I play in a band and can even read music. Most of the guys in the band are street guards except the leader. He's crazy. We all know it, but we never talk about it except among ourselves. We don't want him to lose his job.

I play the drums. . . .

No one can get along without me on this Block. I was sick once, so I know. It's a wonder all the hippies didn't die while I was two weeks on the Chopping Block.

I could go back to the countryside if I wanted to. But I don't want to. I'm having a good time here. And besides, everything would run down if I went away. I know the countryside and I don't like it. This Block is fine enough for me.

Mr. Pole, a social dealer, once asked me why I didn't write a book about hippies. I was telling him what was wrong with Little Groovy. He's a hippie, you know, and I can always tell what's the matter with him by the way he twists his right eye.

I was explaining this to Mr. Pole, and because he didn't know anything about it, he got so all-fire mad.

But someday, maybe, I'll write that book. Only it's too much trouble. Besides, I think I've forgotten how to write words down, and, anyways, I can talk better. . . .

Sometimes when I'm feeling downright lazy, or a street guard or a social dealer is mad at me, I wish I'd be a hippie with nothing to do all day and somebody to feed me.

But on second thought, I guess I'd sooner be what I am than be a hippie.

You know, only yesterday, Doctor Jew, the Block Head Chief, said to me, "Prewitt," he said, "I just don't know what I'd do without you."

And he ought to know, seeing as he's had the bossing of hundreds of hippies for going on two years now.

I've been living on this Block for fifteen years. I've got no complaints. But this Block could be run better.

The real deep-down trouble is that the social dealers have to keep their jobs through politics run from the countryside.

Just look at Mr. Wopp. He's ugly and tired all the time, but he knows his job. Of all the dealers he's been here the longest, four years, and he's learned a lot.

But one day politics will come along and throw him out and send in a new dealer who doesn't know anything about the hippies. . . .

Would you have ever guessed that I was in love once.

Yes, my friend, I certainly was. She was a woman street guard. Man, wasn't she big and so mean. The uppity niggers had to jump into the street when they saw her coming down the Block. And still she'd shoot their tails off.

I won't tell you her name. I never really knew it. But she had green eyes, and short black hair, and a tough foul mouth, and she liked me. She told me so. And she always told me to be a good boy.

And I was until afterwards, when I went adventuring into the deserted parts of the city with two uppity niggers. I did that because, you see, she went off and got married, and she didn't even tell me about it.

I've seen a lot in my time. . . .

.Once three years ago during the summer I got a job in the countryside working for a Frenchie and his wife. They owned a farm.

I went away on the railroad that comes and goes in and out of the city every two days. I rode over thirty miles, and it only took me five hours.

But I soon made up my mind that a farm was no place for me. Mrs. Frenchie was scared to death of me. Maybe she thought I was a city slicker or something.

She wouldn't even let me put my arm around her when her old man was out working in the fields. The street guards had told me I'd be able to do that right away.

I had to get up at five o'clock. I never had any fun. And I never had no time to make any new friends.

Let me tell you one thing. I'd sooner feed mush and milk to hippies all day than milk cows in the early morning dawn.

One bad morning I forgot to board up an old well in the north pasture. A neighbor's pretty new calf wandered by, fell in, and got drowned.

I saw it all happen.

Then I walked down to the railway station like anyone else, bought a ticket, and rode on the train back to the city. Lucky for me the train was just leaving.

I was really glad to get back on the Block.

Now you better believe all my hippies were mad with joy to
see me back. . . .

There was a new social dealer feeding Little Groovy. "Hold it,
my friend," I said. "That ain't no way to do it. You some kind of
animal with no brain. Don't you see how he's twisting his eye?
Come here, I'll show you."

He gave me the spoon, and I guess I filled Little Groovy up
with the most comfortable meal he had since I went away.

Hippies ain't that bad when you understand them. I heard
Mr. Wopp tell that new social dealer that I had an amazing gift
in handling hippies. . . .

Now I'll tell you about the time I went exploring the city. I
had no idea to do such a thing. It was Slackwater and Webster
who put me up to it, although they didn't have to twist my arm
very hard. They're uppity niggers, you know.

I was walking down the Block, on my way to deliver a message
for a dealer, when I saw Slackwater and Webster hiding behind a
traffic light and making signs at me.

I went over to them.

"How you doin', boy," squeaked Slackwater. "How's your
hippies?"

Webster started laughing to himself.

"Doin' fine, nigger," I said. "You been shot at lately?"

"Yeah, man!" They both nodded and looked down at their
shuffling feet and didn't say a goddam word more.

I felt good then so I tried to cheer them up with an old-fashioned comfort joke.

"Come on, boys," I said, "Don't be down in the dirt. Tell your
brother here when you goin' to wash that mud off your bodies."

That joke didn't set on them straight, it made them mad, and I
was walking on, when Slackwater said out of the clear blue,
"We're leavin' the Block to go uptown. Come on with us."

"What for?" I said.

"We're goin' up top a big building," drawled Slackwater, his head bobbing up and down like crazy.

"And find us a store to rob," whispered Webster looking all around him.

"But the white folks have all moved out to the countryside . . . long before the Race War even started. Only street guards left and a few poor lost souls."

"That ain't the way I heard tell," shouted Webster with that hungry eagerness that only uppity niggers still have left. "The rich white folks are movin' back in."

They both jumped up and down like monkeys so I believed them.

"All right," I said. "I'm goin'. Let's go!"

We sneaked down to the corner. We looked around, didn't see nobody, then left the Block.

Maybe we walked along for about thirty minutes, when I stopped up short.

"What's wrong with you," asked Webster. "Let's keep goin'."

"Wait," I said. "I gotta go back."

"What for, godalmighty," yelled Slackwater at the top of his black lungs. He was so nervous he kept on scratching himself.

"I wanna go get Little Groovy," I said.

That blew their minds, but I didn't care. I knew they'd wait for me.

You see, uppity niggers can't leave the Block without a street guard and extra-special permission.

So I went back and got Little Groovy.

He can't walk or talk, or do anything except maybe play his jew harp every once in a great while.

I had to carry him in my arms.

I found Slackwater and Webster in a jittery fit, crouching down behind a broken wall.

We continued uptown.

We climbed up the first big building we came to. It was dusty and broken down. Some top floors had fallen off. Probably no one been in it for years and years, but you never can be too sure.

Rats were all over the place, and we didn't find any store to rob. It was a real bad place. The stairs were steep and slippery with busted wires, bits of glass, and plaster. And if you slipped through the bannister you'd fall a thousand feet or maybe a hundred.

When we got to the top, Webster starting shivering with fright. He went off his head. All uppity niggers do sooner or later.

I never look at one without thinking he's going to shoot off his head.

You know, it's a rough life for them. . . .

But I talked to Webster soft and kind. That's the right way to handle them when they get high strung.

If you get mad and frighten them, they get worse. I ought to know, even I'm that way myself sometimes.

We left that useless building after Webster calmed down.

It was getting along in the afternoon.

We kept on threading our way uptown. It was quite a job with all those piles of rubble. Buildings fell down in the distance. There was a strong smell of shit in the air.

Up ahead we saw the biggest building in the world. It was tough. It had held out not bad against time, while all the other really huge buildings fell into the crap heap of the city.

We were going to rob a store in that building.

But first we needed to cross a gaping hole. We couldn't figure out how to get around it. It was just there like so many other holes in the city.

I was the only one thinking.

I found a long board nearby, and I put it across the deep space of the pit.

I went across first, carrying Groovy.

Webster came next. But Slackwater got scared under his skin right in the middle and stretched himself out on the board.

"I'm goin' off my head, man," he yelled.

"No you ain't, brother," screamed Webster. "Every fool knows you gotta be standin' up to go off your head."

Slackwater started to cry.

He was shaking like a leaf.

You know, there's nothing more sorrowful than a crying and shaking uppity nigger.

The sad twilight of the city was creeping up on us. And I knew we had to be on our way, if we wanted to see what we were robbing in that giant building.

So I said to Webster:

"Stop your mouth runnin' off, boy, and take a hold of Groovy. I'll go fix Slackwater."

And I did, too, but he was so scared shitless and dizzy from thinking about going off his head that he had to crawl along on his hands and knees while I kept giving him a push.

When I got Slackwater across and took Groovy back in my arms, I heard someone laugh and I turned my whole head around as fast as I could.

A street guard was standing there mighty tall with his arm around a naked woman. He was staring straight at us.

They walked out a doorway of a two storey house that didn't look bad at all considering the way the rest of the city looked.

The street guard had his gun in his holster. And it was his woman who was doing most of the laughing.

"We're really gonna get it now," said Webster over and over again and getting into a sweat.

His nappy hair stood on end.

His bulging eyes almost popped out of their sockets as he hopelessly shook his head back and forth while taking a fast looksee at that big lady.

"For chrissakes, watch where you're bending your eyes, boy," I whispered as hard as I could under my breath and kept my eyes on the ground.

"Hey you, boys," shouted the street guard. "What you doin' uptown here?"

He lifted up the brim of his hat and was scratching his head. Then his hand slipped down and rested on his gun.

"We wanna look at the big buildings close up, that's all," I said.

And he said, "You shouldn't be here and I oughta shoot you up or run you back downtown, but you can see with your own eyes I'm pretty busy. So just be sure and get back before dark."

"We're not goin' back til we rob ourselves a store," said Webster proudly.

The street guard and his big woman shook their bellies brimful with laughing.

"All right," he said with a bad smile. "But you better watch out for yourselves or the packs of wild dogs will get you when it turns dark."

Then they walked back into the house arm in arm, joking with each other real pleasant like, but I wished he hadn't said that about the wild dogs.

We started off again and we went much faster.

Slackwater was okay, and so was Webster. They didn't seem like they were going to shoot off their heads. As a matter of fact they began rubbing their hands together and talking about the store they were going to rob.

The biggest trouble was with Little Groovy.

You see, he was almost as big as me. All the time I was calling him Little Groovy, he was growing up.

He was so heavy to carry that I couldn't keep up with Slackwater and Webster. I was all out of breath.

So I told them they'd have to take turns with me carrying Little Groovy.

They said they wouldn't do it. They didn't want him along from the very beginning.

Then I was pissed off with rage and told them I'd leave them right there and they'd never find a good store to rob, and the wild dogs or maybe the giant rats would come out and eat them up.

Slackwater looked like he was going to shoot off his head that very minute, but he didn't.

Webster was breathing heavy and snorting out his nose, but at last he said, "Give'm here to me."

And after that we took turns carrying Little Groovy. . . .

We finally made it to the mile-high building.

When we stood at the bottom and bent our heads back to look up, it was so tall we couldn't see the top.

I gazed at the sky.

Dreadful darkness was approaching. . . .

We began climbing up the stairs and searching for that big store to rob. There were wide holes in the walls of the building. It sure did look better on the outside than it did on the inside.

Also it turned cold and a chill wind blew right through us.

By and by it got real black all of a sudden, and we were dizzy with hunger, and we couldn't start a fire.

You see, I forgot my matches, and they don't let uppity niggers carry matches—it's against the law.

All we could do was shiver.

And we never thought about being hungry. You know, on the Block you never have to make your own food. It's always ready for you at the right time.

Worse than everything else was the quiet. And there was only one thing worse than that, and that was the noises.

There were all kinds of noises with quiet spells in between. I reckon they were rats, but I always heard things coming up the stairs after us . . . the wild dogs—you know, thump, thump, bump, crackle, crackle, just like that.

Slackwater went off his head even before we reached halfway up that building.

We never reached the top.

Then Webster was yelling and hollering and jumping up and down.

You listen to me, and never go robbing stores with uppity niggers.

I never had such an awful night.

It was miserable out. For a few hours it rained like hell, and the wind blew in through the yawning holes in the walls, and soaked us all the way through.

We sat on the stairs, crying, with shivering bodies and chattering teeth, and huddled in each other's arms.

I shivered so hard I thought my body was going to shake loose from me.

And Little Groovy, with nothing to eat, just goaned and shivered all night. Why I never seen him so bad as that before. He twisted that right eye of his until it ought to have dropped out.

And every once in a while he let out something like a mad howl of fear whenever he opened his eyes real wide and stared at the black darkness outside.

It was the closest Groovy ever came to talking.

When he howled at those dark shadows it made my hair stand on end, but finally I starting thinking that he was just trying to cry out his sorrow to the uncomforting sky.

How we made it through that night I'll never know, but we didn't die, and next morning we went right back the way we came.

I was never more happy to be back on the Block. Groovy got to be awful heavy. The Head Block Chief was mad as can be.

He said that I was out of bounds, and it's against the law to take uppity niggers out of bounds. But also he said he'd let it go this time, but don't let it happen again, or I'd be back out to pasture.

I knew what he meant.

Other people were glad to see me.

Mr. Greenhorn, a new social dealer, who had to feed the hippies three meals while I was away, put his arms around me and laughed til he almost near cried, he was that happy I got back.

Lots of hippies rolled down the street, smiling and trying to clap their hands.

I fed them right away, and then fell straight into bed and slept heavy as a log. I should've helped the plumber, who had come in from the countryside to fix the gutterpipes on the street guard barrack, but I was just strung-out, goddam tired from my night out with the boys.

And you know what, Groovy didn't even twist his eye for two days, it was that tired.

You know, the next time I go big adventuring to rob stores, I'm going all the way up top that giant building.

But I'm going to leave early in the morning and come back before it turns dark. And I ain't going to take no uppity niggers along.

They're crazy and shoot off their heads too much. But I'll take Little Groovy along. Somehow I can't get along without him.

And anyway, I ain't going to run away. Living on the Block is a hell of a lot easier than robbing stores, you can bet on that.

Besides, Little Groovy is bigger than I am now. And I could never carry him up the top of any building.

And he's growing bigger every day. Some street guards even call him Pig Pen.

You know, it's amazing. It's just fantastic. . . .

The End

LAURANCE WIEDER

The Doctrine and Discipline of Remorse

I've been staying inside a lot lately.
Walking around it seems I don't know anybody

Or sometimes it seems that I know everybody
Which I guess is an example of the alienation

Of modern youth in an urban environment, or
Is it (this feeling) caused by merely living in
The way that traffic deaths are caused by inattention?

Frequently our lines of cleavage fail, I submit
Because like Leonardo's Flying Machine it

Doesn't work, which means all categories now exist
And have themselves exhausted interest since

It's hard to fall, and harder still to be original
My life turns against me like the famous monster
Turned against the well-intentioned doctor, his father.

Once I traded friendliness for honesty because
I was afraid of being left alone and now I am

Left only with facility and no ideas on anything.
These flyers. These pamphlets on child rearing.

It was a quiet planting. I could feel
The seeds splashing into the yellow dirt
And I finished with my original selection.

O Wind, I could have chosen from a dozen occupations:
Bank clerk, professor, scientist, physician, union

Leader, President of the United States, Secretary-General of the
    United Nations.
But no, every Fall my brain refuses work

And I find I have to say I'm sorry
To the educators, administrators, and the parents
Who expect only the best from me.

TOM VEITCH

Beads of Brains
from "The Luis Armed Story"

The black farmer stands in the baking sun sweat-soaked jeans and underwear. The gracious women approach, cautiously at first, ask him the time of day. . . . Around these women a cool cloud of breezes and incense and sweet perfumes of Persia and the ancient Orient . . . boat along the Nile. . . .

My digestion improves. Sweet bells in my ears, my dying ears! What value to place on the weight of these sentences, if that is what you call them. . . .

In the night window is a hairy monster with beads of brains in his forehead and small jewels glistening in his palms. . . . The trees unfold, to announce his arrival. Gracefully, ever so gracefully, we bow to him and take his hand, kiss his hand. . . . He is very alive, bless him! He strengthens us in our moment of doubt. . . .

True enough, we are in doubt. Horrible scary structures of "reality" bind us down, fetter us in, scare away the seeds of wisdom from our hungry eyes. . . . Oh love, where are you? I so want to hold you in my arms! I so want to arrive at last at the crystal moment. . . .

We dream of this moment. In our windy streets of dusty doubt we dream of green fronds wet with water and swaying in the gull-swept afternoon. . . . A lilac tree grows behind my house. I listen to its lovely breath! So innocent, it disappears at night, then reappears to make my breakfast. . . . I love you lovely lilac tree!

The whole world may chew on these cadavers—words! Dead moments of mind bliss preserved in crystal to activate the receptive vacuum tube. . . . Click, click—buzz, buzz! Awaken dusty radio, from your sleep of twelve centuries. . . . Your cynicism is dead!

Yes, it happened once, in a post-modern age, when once an electric storm sent a current into this "thing" in our attic, this box of wires, tubes, glass, strange filaments began to glow. . . . Pa brought the candle. "What's this!" he yelled. Little Susan came running behind and me and Jeff pushed her out of the way so's we could see. . . .

"It's the radio, Pa!"

"I know it's the radio, dang it. Been in our family for a hundred generations. Relic of a thousand years. Worth a goodly fortune. But anybody can tell ya a radio ain't spoke since the Day of the Bomb . . . and this one is makin' an awful racket!"

Sure enough. He turned the yellow knob and scissors and wedges of dayshine came out of the radio and we all turned big eyes to each other as a voice said

"Lovely bodies of light, come forth
and shine on me. . . ."

I was down on the beach, looking for the colored sea shells my sister liked to collect. When I went back up to the house Robert was waiting for me on the porch and his face was white as a sheet.

"Hey man, N.Y. has just been *blown off the map—!*"

"What? Are you serious?" I knew he was serious. We went inside and listened to the radio for two hours hearing the reports from helicopters circling the crater which was filling up rapidly with the ocean, and listening to the President and various historical people weeping and telling us to have courage

and pray for the eight million souls—

and meanwhile our own men in bombers are working overtime to assure that the *necessary retaliation* is released upon the back of the million-headed Chinese dragon. . . .

After we were sick with the craziness of the radio I went outside and I walked in the garden for half an hour, looking at the tomatoes. A big green worm was crawling on the juiciest tomato. Eat, big green worm, for tomorrow you may never eat again. . . .

Looking up I saw Our Lord was walking in the garden!! and His Face was the face of Truth, more beautiful than any face I had ever seen!—My flesh fell to the ground naked and burning. . . . I was stripped by lightning! I awoke from life's sleep! Oh! Imperishable moment! Oh! Truth! Truth! The Divine Body shining on my life, radiant in my dismal mind room, the gray dead sit up on their couches, astonished—

Oh! Forgive me! I grovel! I worship!

I am close tender a word springs open now to you almost seeing each other, eyes pull you and you sit inside me laughing a nod a nod a beauty drawn singing yowl gas! Away flight across the landscape float down off the mountains in the wind settle gently in the bright green sea . . . to create a hole, an outline for you to rise white dove to dwell in, a spout of flesh graceful in the rain, for your presence to illumine all body dog thought yes it can be done many spots of matter have yes many times yes it was done any other reason for walking shoulders high across the landscape—

—a load of milk heavy in my lungs—anyone who believes in everything who is born of earth, sad mother come and speak now above my bed your son lies crushed wound he is bleeding pig . . .

. . . and lo there is an electric cackle of sound and a brilliant explosion of light from the center of the church. I can see the figure of the Virgen. I can see her feet and her blue gown which falls loose about her feet—someone is standing so I cannot see the face. . . . A thought in my head: someone here is to be exalted now. . . . "I have come for you."

And woo it is me rising in the air, above the heads, into the dome of the church, and my mind is laughing awake suddenly in focus my whole body alive with some new chemical, some holy electricity burning and laughing in every part of me . . .

. . . the thought within breaks—like this—and I become the

biggest empty space in the cosmos—no floor, no chore, no shore, float up the beach eating apples and spice die laughing in the morning wind float down off the coast carrying pollen dust from meadows high in the coast range. . . .

"Stand up Luis."

He was smiling. Under the twisted mask of life flows our life, and nothing can ever put it out. He touched me.

Death copyright 1967 by Time Inc. Dimly now, my external awareness receding, I saw the Doctor probing for a vein in my left arm. . . . At that moment there was no pulse, no blood pressure, everything had come to a stop.

Suddenly I knew.

"Am I dying, Doctor? Is it now?"

No reply. I heard no reply.

Sensation had slipped out. I heard nothing, saw nothing, felt nothing. To Doctor eyes I had reached point absolute, i.e. clinical death. "He's dead."

But inside there was a sudden surge of sensation—magnified, finely focused brilliant! Exquisitely I saw and felt my toes die, then the feet, cell by cell, death waves washing the sands clean . . . up the legs coming, cells winking out, night descending on the flesh. . . . Closer now to me, vision growing sharp and clear . . . hands, arms, abdomen, chest, each cell flaring in heat of nova— then gone. . . . Systematically I die. This is my death. The brain shall be last, knowing all until the end. . . .

Now the neck. The lower jaw. The teeth. A world dying, winking out. How strange to feel one's teeth die, one by one, cell igniting cell, galaxies of cells in dying brilliance. . . . Now I grope for this other thing. . . . There is *something* else, something behind me, at the last instant. What is it?

I know it well. It is familiar, opening before me, something more beautiful, more gentle, more loving than the mind or imagination of living creature could ever conceive. . . .

"Go to them, Luis. Go to the East and help them. There will be many dying of radiation burns and radiation fever. Cure them and show them the life to come."

I nodded. We embraced, and he left me.

Rosa, my sister, I wake up dreaming of you, and in this dream I touched you and you were healed and became very happy. It made us so happy to see you so happy, like a little girl you seemed to us then.

Luis came home once, after three days in jail for hurting his friend Donaldo. Our father, Fernando, was standing in the kitchen and our mother, Teresa, was yelling at our father in the way that she used to, when she was crazy with the whiskey and with the sex. . . .

Papa looked at Luis as he walked through the door, and his eyes asked Luis to please help him, for her voice strikes the root of his mind he can not speak a word nor utter a sound.

Luis looked at Mama. She had not seen him come in. He walked straight over to her and slapped her very hard on the face, so that there was a red mark when he took his hand away.

"Luis!" Rosa screamed, from behind the yellow table.

Mama: "Ohhhh! Nobody loves me, not even my own son! My own Luis who beats his mother. . . . What am I good for? Why don't I kill myself and then you will be free of me!" She ran into the bedroom and fell on the bed, sobbing and talking crazy lonely talk that scared us little ones into tears of our own. . . .

"Luis, why did you hit her?" Papa took Luis by the arm.

"Papa, that was nothing. Watch me now!" And Luis walked into the bedroom with very big steps. Rosa screamed.

"Luis! Don't touch her again, don't touch her you crazy kid, I swear I'll kill you Luis! Luis, don't touch her!"

We all sucked our breath in, expecting the worst. But all he did was go up to her and touch her with his hand. In that instant there was light around his hand and Mama became suddenly as a little girl, three, maybe four years old, smiling and laughing.

"Luis—we didn't know!"

ALAN SENAUKE

Attacks on Cabbies Have Dropped

These things that
violence calls
hard
are the nails and
screws of nature.

How can we walk
or dodge the
knives of displeasure
without an
interest in
flames and
bottles?

If then
not
or parts
of lights have
a separate
"Whose is it,
Whose is it!?"
Under the glass
they phone out.

I don't want to
star. A
cabbie is great.
Falling from shade
wheels is excessive.

Fall's Bullets

for Jay Cantor

Through the green brakes came
California. California, California—the
present is so kind to you. Oh New York!
You always live a little in the past.
You have only a reputation and some
mannerisms. Where is your once vigorous
personality? What can I do?

Oh, I must walk
through "dog-fields" of heart. You are
walking there too. Softly! The papery leaves
have fallen into the afternoon yellow of the earth.
A mother is speaking to her son.
She says, "Do not be afraid. What I give
is love. The price I ask is love also.
I don't *want* you." You are walking by, like
silent racers on the asphalt track.

The banjo sounds in every house. Its
driving music leads the citizens to saner
life. Cezanne has done his best. In return
the world has given him a reputation. But
how little of his vision remains with us.
Art should be like the fingers of the hand.
The cigar is lit by the roadway, in the canal,
the tunnel, the byway, the freeway,
the turnpike, the boulevards. Thick blue
ash covers the land. I call it art because
of the way it transforms the humdrum life

of objects. Everything becomes something
new—a thing covered with blue ash. At last!
Poseidon, if just once
you could see beyond yourself.
Your ponds and streams are
unfathomable. Shifting blue waters cover
your breast of incivility. Mrs. Verloc
took another bite and spoke some more. "This
throat sandwich is wet, consisting of tongue."

The law of September dawns on us. We aren't
the "children of light" any more. Not when
life is ending. I feel the way it is when
hurricane winds fall off. Still, October
is beautiful. The boys carry guitars through
all the streets. They look keenly for the ones
to serenade. It is February. Snow in the
gutter is as grey as dishwater. I am so
cold. And the youths have not yet played
their tender song.

My ships are dispatched in every direction.
Oceans burn beneath my inquiring
vessels. There is a finger on the
spine of the sea always.
Dan came in with Janet. "Everybody's
waiting for me to tell them what they
know," he complained. The waitress
interrupted. "Coffee's a dime!"

Zazen

"Dogen's way is continued practice."
I have placed these words above my sitting place,
Three feet above the top of my Zafu.
In my private Zendo, I meditate, Shikan Taza,
Seven hours each day.
Shi means a stopping of the mind,
As a truck rams a warehouse wall.
Kan is the view,
What the teamster sees during the crash.
Taza is sitting.

I must sit . . . sit.
The walls step back and lie down
When I sit.
The roof flies up and shines—a new star in the firmament.
The kitchen is a festival of dancing knives.
This all happens as I sit, but I am
Not led from our Way by three delusions.
"Mayka!" the master shouts.
"Do not believe mind-pictures!" he warns.
So, sitting in the sixth hour,
Dusk climbing from gray holes
In the mountain,
I will see the first star
On the other side of a clear brown eye.

Air

The water is leaving the water.
Air has left the air,
And travels as a harmless gas.
But to think twice of this air
Could make me faint.
Even as the air is charged with electric bolts
It becomes water.
If, however, water is leaving water
Then it must revert to its elements—
H plus O. And if air has dropped its veil
How can I feel its presence?
I see a cloud hanging in a valley—Air?
I hear a gale blast pushing against every window.
Is this the lost air?
If so, I don't expect its menacing beat to last.

My Name Is

My name is Alan
                    And if it's not Alan
It's Donald.
                              Donald has
                         Five rings in my mind
                    To do the things
                    I must get done.
                              I clatter down

An icy runway
     Chasing the fighter who
  Copped my guitar.
Circle #1 encounters
          RESISTANCE
          From mental force which
                    Alan thought dead.
       This resistance is fear of falling
          From heights
To drop—a blur along the meadow's edge.
Circle #2 embraces
          These flaccid thoughts
             But Donald can only
                    Depict the struggle
  By writing our name in big letters—
             A L A N
I have often thought that the wood
             Of my chair
                Was more attractive varnished
                Than natural.
       So seeing a mahogany forest
       And feeling mind gears slip into
Circle #3
             I was surprised
  And felt stomach rise to top inside of skull.
  Feelings of unity and aesthetic unity
             Are the realm
                Of Circle Three.
                    Alan is a musician
       In the State Orchestra.
                    Donald sits brooding
                    Near a saxophone
       But not near enough to coax notes.

A dollar fluttered to the purple evening
Earth.
Donald calculated he has
Six dollars left.
Circle #4 had been employed
Circle #5 is
Special function zone.
I feel it once when saw
A man eat the head of a live chicken.
Great blood fountains
Covered his face.
And he cried in joy.
I feel sometimes I might want that
Or things like that.
Alan is tired of in-bed out of bed in-bed
Donald is curious about seeing the addition
Of all his
KARMA.
No good I tell him
But Donald is unapproachable
On the subject.
I see at least two things
For each he sees.
I
Could have twice his Karma.

Poem

Sit down and listen!
I have a thrill to communicate.
Have you ever felt foolish
as you walked down the street
and saw small spikes
break through the pavement
to suck away all the fresh air?
Have you smelled the foul gas they replaced it with
and were you overcome?
While peering into a shop
have you heard the abuse heaped upon you?

I have just found out
we are not alone.
If you know what I am speaking of
you will rejoice.
I am with you.
I love you and touch you
with my soothing fingers
as Autumn breeze caresses each leaf
before gently urging it
to hurl itself lightly to the ground.

I feel what you feel.
With these words before you
I am revealing *our* life.
For you I would do anything.
I cry like a saxophone,
adding my primitive tones
to the song until it resonates

in your soul
like a tuning fork.

Take my hand.
Stand up now
and listen to me a last time.
I am trying,
I am trying.

Your attentive souls will help me.
This is the thrill I mentioned.
Help me and you help yourself
to squeeze the trigger of desire,
to be like a raindrop
falling through a mile of cloud
into the embrace of its original lover,
Father Earth.

Forget About It

Every tortured being
Possesses an infinite ability
        To be wrong.

The morning star
Has nothing but contempt
        For the wind.

But the wind
Doesn't care.
        He blows.

CHARLES LINDHOLM

A California Novel

I

The trip came to an end in Fresno. It was dinnertime. John leaned over his chicken leg and smiled evilly. "These are my innermost thoughts," he said. "The day has finally come for the parting of the ways, that is to say, it's about the end of the trail for us."

Hakamine lifted his eyes from his plate. "What are you saying?" he asked, clutching at his fork. He knew it was the end. It had been coming for a long time, ever since John had seduced Hakamine's beautiful fifteen-year-old sister named Deborah. She was a cheerleader with red pom poms. Her hair was reddish black, the color of darkened mountains looming close at sunset. John had looked at her over his nose. "Want some candy little girl? Get into the car." He had looked at her over his big nose. Actually nothing happened then, since John really didn't have a car and in fact did not know how to drive, but later on, he took her out in the woods and she returned with grass on her back. "Your sister is a good lay," John told Hakamine. Hakamine was overcome with jealousy and later slapped his sister and left a red palm print on the side of her face.

So Hakamine sat clutching his fork and looking at his fried chicken. "I've been like a father to you guys," he protested.

"You think you've been like a father to us because you drive us around in your lousy station wagon," John replied. "Really you're nothing but a dirty Nip, a slimy little yellow bastard." John put down the chicken leg, afraid that Hakamine might leap across the table, spilling dishes and chicken and french fries and coke and hit him in the face and give him a bloody nose. I looked very seriously at Hakamine, who was turning a jaundiced yellow. He had large scars on his face, but never mentioned where they came from. He clenched his teeth and looked for the waitress. "Give us the check," he ordered.

Hakamine knew he was Japanese, but he was sensitive about it. He was afraid girls didn't like him because they were prejudiced. This was true. He tried to make being Japanese into a beautiful heroic thing and therefore he had a samurai sword, which he showed me. He cut a chair in half with it and told me a story. "Once upon a time," he said, smiling at me, "there was a famous Japanese samurai who went to the court in England. Everyone laughed at him and made sport of him, but he didn't care because he was proud and brave and strong and handsome. The Duke of York had a large sword cast from the finest steel and he took his sword and chopped a huge block of wood in half with it. But the samurai threw a piece of silk in the air, and when it landed on his sword, it was sliced in two." Hakamine seemed very impressed by this story, which he had just made up. "I also have some fine Japanese prints and silk screens," he told me. There was nothing to say to that. This had happened months ago, before I had even introduced him to John.

The night Hakamine met John was the night we graduated from high school. John had dropped out of school two years earlier. "I make my own way henceforth," he wrote in the school literary magazine, which he ran. "I break asunder the bonds which encompass my mind," he went on. "I free myself to create, to think, to be as a free and limitless organism." He went on and on, until the whole school was bored. The principal talked to his mother, who was seventy years old and a drummer in an old lady's band. After he dropped out, John slept fifteen hours a day. He played pool and preyed on high school sophomore girls, who gave him money. John looked like Mick Jagger and often pretended to be English for purposes of impressing girls. He was ugly. His parents said "John is the last of a long series of miscarriages." His father was a member of the Ku Klux Klan in the thirties. "We didn't have nothing against the niggers," he told me in a moment of confidence. "We were out to get the dirty Wop bootleggers." He kept a gun under his pillow in hopes that someone would try to break in. He hated people of every nationality.

"I've never met anyone like you," Hakamine told John. He admired John because John could walk over to a girl and talk to her and smile and pretend to be English and brush back his hair and leer. John did this as often as possible, because he had just broken up with his girl friend. Her name was Sterile Cheryl. John told me the story. "When Sterile Cheryl was just a little girl," he said, looking at me over his nose and smirking, "an evil, evil old Negro wino followed her home and in the heated dark of the moist Denver night he took advantage of her. He ripped her from stem to stern and, due to the unseemly largeness of his organ, he left her, so to speak, sterile." The rape traumatized her. John knew it. He liked to rub it in. "Cheryl's a nymphomaniac," he told everyone. John claimed his cock had grown three inches since he had been going out with Cheryl. That was a lie. Really it had only grown about an inch. John used to screw Cheryl every night in the back of someone's car. Guys used to double date with John and Cheryl just to watch them in the rear view mirror. John knew it. He enjoyed it.

But now Cheryl had broken up with him. She used to come over to my house to listen to her Bob Dylan records. She was beautiful. Boys ran after as she bicycled past, her long blonde hair streaming out. Everybody's tongue hung out while she was around. I wanted to screw her silently in the basement while my mother was fixing dinner with Bob Dylan playing in the background. I asked her why she had broken up with John. "Because he's rotten and lousy," she told me, putting on her lipstick. "Any-

way, he wouldn't marry me and settle down in Utah." Cheryl was
a Mormon.

I never saw her after that.

Hakamine thought John was magnificent. It didn't matter that
every time John walked over to a girl and talked to her and
leered and brushed back his hair she would tell him to get lost.
"John has a fantastic approach," Hakamine told me the next day.
John liked to ask girls if their bunny was making money. He
said, "Sit on my lap and we'll discuss the first thing that comes
up." Sometimes he would say, "Hi, say haven't we met somewhere before? Wait, don't tell me, let me guess." Once a girl
rolled her electric car window up on his arm. He was drunk at
the time. "You don't know what you're missing," he said. He
thought he was Frank Sinatra. In fact, he used to practice looking
like Sinatra in front of a mirror. Mainly he practiced throwing
his coat over his shoulder and dangling a cigarette. He didn't fool
anybody. He used to mimic all of Sinatra's songs. "It's the timing
that's important," he told me. He liked to get girls drunk and sing
to them. He would sing and smirk to me over their heads. Then
he would take them into somebody's parked car and screw them
and make a mess. He always tried to get the girls to give him
their panties, but they hardly ever did. He wanted to hang them
up on his wall. His wall was presently covered with rejection
slips from Playboy and the New Yorker. They said, "Dear Mr.
Barton, Thank you very much for your manuscript. Unfortunately your story is not quite suited to the format of our magazine."
John thought this was encouraging. "I've just got to find the right
format," he said, showing me his last rejection slip. He thought
the panties on the wall would be more affirmative than rejection
slips. Actually, there wouldn't have been that many. John was
getting too old for the high school girls. They had heard about
him, and after Cheryl left him and came over to my house he
had a hard time finding a girl. "Maybe I should have married

that bitch and settled down in Utah," he told me, biting his fingernails.

II

When Hakamine drove he wore a hat that looked like it once belonged to midget marine drill instructor. It was too small for him, and sat on the top of his head. Hakamine claimed it was a Japanese boy scout cap. He also smoked a corn cob pipe he had bought for twenty cents. I was with him when he got it. "I've always wanted a corn cob pipe," he said happily. He made a point of smoking the worst tobacco he could find.

The year after he dropped out of school, John got involved with a girl named Rosemary. I never met her, but he told me she was a pig. One day her old boyfriend called John up. "You aren't fit for her," he told John. "I'm doing her a favor going out with her after she's been seen with you," John replied. He said some other things too. He had been thinking about insults and had some funny ones ready. The boyfriend, who was named Ralph, challenged John to a fight in the high school parking lot.

John claimed that 300 people turned up to watch the fight. He invited his evilest friends to come and watch. One was Bruce Hubly, who was famous for stomping three kids from West High at the south side MacDonald's. Austin Yearling, John's neighbor who had bitten off someone's ear in a fight, was also there, and so was Bob Pinetta who had knocked out three of the wrestling coach's teeth during practice and had been dropped from the squad. Anyway, Ralph hit John in the chest and collapsed his lung so that he had to spend two weeks in an oxygen tent. After that John had trouble breathing and Hakamine's pipe smoke always made him cough. This was a good way for Hakamine to show his superiority. He never coughed. He could even inhale the smoke and blow it out at John's face. It was Mad Dave who taught Hakamine this trick. "Simple Yoga," he explained to us much later.

"My good health is due to clean living," Hakamine told us. He flexed his muscles. "Good food and plenty of exercise, that's the ticket," he said, walking on his hands around the swimming pool. "Friends, the body is not just a place for your brain to rest. A sound mind in a sound body." He pushed John back into the beach chair. He thought this would humiliate John and make him doubt his virility. "Real men are strong and tough," Hakamine confided to me, knowing that I lifted weights. I had to agree. I gave Hakamine my weight lifting instructions and went away.

John already doubted his virility. "My cock is longer than the cock of any other man. All I have to do is display it to a female and she is immediately passionately desirous of me," he said. In actual fact, guys were more attracted to him. This was a source of embarrassment. "I hate fags!" he used to yell at old drunks on Larimer street.

John thought that Hakamine's hat was a personal phallic symbol. He figured it out according to Freud. "You see, the hat is essentially in the form of a penis. It is like Hakamine's own phallus in that it is yellow and too small. As a consequence of these painful deficiencies, he tries to compensate by constant exposure, to show that he is unashamed of the shameful reality. And that's why he wears that stupid hat all the time."

Hakamine had a story about his hat. He told it to me while we were staying in Los Angeles. We were sleeping in an unfurnished apartment some of Hakamine's friends were letting us use. It was beautiful to be in Los Angeles. John and I looked out the window at the new city. The air smelled different than Denver air. It was salty. We found roaches in the sink. They were the first roaches we had ever seen. Hakamine wasn't impressed. He had been in Los Angeles before. That night he told me the story of his hat. John was asleep. "This hat," he said, "is a memento of my trip to

Japan." He got a dreamy look in his eyes. I wished he would go to sleep. After a minute he started again. "In Japan all the rivers cut little paths through the countryside, which is green. There are bridges with pointed tops, and pagodas and forests. The girls are sweet and the sky is always blue. Colors are prettier there. They live in paper houses. A girl gave me a bath there once and it was beautiful. It was a steamy room, and I could hardly see her. I got this hat in Japan. It's a Japanese boy scout hat. I know it's too small." He was in a nostalgic mood. I told John about this the next day. "Apparently when he wears the hat he is able to recapture the mood of some prepubescent sexual experience," he said. "Obviously he's regressing because of his inability to cope with the present. All those Nips are the same." John had a theory that the Japanese had been our enemies in the Second World War and should therefore be exterminated. "Look what they did to William Holden," he said.

Hakamine told me about his mission before we left on the trip. We were at John's house listening to the Old Lady's Band. They were playing "I Want To Hold Your Hand," and John's mother kept dropping the drumsticks. Hakamine leaned over to me. "I am really going on this trip as a mission," he said. I didn't take him seriously until we got to Las Vegas. It was night, and Hakamine and I were buying double ice cream splits at an ice cream stand. Locusts were smashing themselves against the shiny walls of the stand. Hakamine pulled a switchblade out of his boot and flipped it open. "There will be blood on this knife," he said, looking at the moon. I smiled at him. Mad Dave told me that Hakamine had a permanent callus along his ankle from keeping the knife in his boot.

Mad Dave loved the grunion runs. John and I went with him to a run after we had left Hakamine in Fresno. The silver grunion are about four inches long, and they mate and drop their eggs on shore once a year. Millions of wriggling grunion covered the beach, glittering in moonlight and Mad Dave ran insanely over the sand, throwing the fish in his green duffle bag. "Mad Dave strikes the fucking grunion!" he shouted, knocking down the other grunion hunters who were walking bent-legged across the beach. "I like to get them just as they're dropping their eggs," he said, showing us his slimy hands. John and I joined the hunt, and afterwards we built a bonfire and cooked the fish on spits. Mad Dave pulled out his vodka bottle. The next day, while John and I were lying hung over on the sand, Mad Dave raced around smashing crabs with his shovel. The beach was covered with dead fish. He told us what he knew about Hakamine. "I've known him since I was four," he said. "We used to call him Kamakaze." He thought Hakamine was in trouble. "He's headed for certain death," Mad Dave said, smiling.

We had left Hakamine in Fresno when John had leaned across the table and had told Hakamine that he was a slimy little yellow bastard. We had just come back from San Francisco, where Hakamine had spent a week searching for his enemy, Krazy Kato. "It will be a fight to the death when I find him," Hakamine said. "Hakamine is completely insane," John told me. "Whoever heard of someone named Krazy Kato?" It was Mad Dave who had first sent us to San Francisco. He appeared in the night, wearing his leather jacket and smiling. He put a cigarette out on his tongue. He took a Coke bottle cap out of his pocket and bent it in half. "You try it," he said to me. It was impossible. He took another bottle cap and put it on the inside of his elbow joint. He bent it by flexing his biceps and gritting his teeth. "My name is Mad Dave," he said, shaking hands with John and me. We were still living in the unfurnished Los Angeles apartment at the time. Hakamine was out driving around the station wagon, using up all the gasoline. Mad Dave took out a bottle of vodka and we sat around and drank it all. "I'm the speaker for the Hollywood Slicers," Dave told us. "It's the meanest gang in L.A. Old ladies tremble at our passing, grown men faint at our breath, cops shit in their pants when they see our jackets. Young girls come when we look at them. We are the evilest, the meanest, and the toughest. Our power is more than your mind can understand." He laughed, and blew smoke out of his nose. "Tell Hakamine that Krazy Kato has skipped town to San Francisco," he said, leaving. John threw up on the wall-to-wall carpet. "My ulcer," he explained.

Later on, in Fresno, John threw up again, this time during a lawn party held by Hakamine's friends. This was before we left him. We ate steak in teriyaki sauce. "Delicious!" John said, grimacing. He threw up in the swimming pool. Hakamine was furious. "Can't you behave like a human being?" he whispered, shaking John by the collar. "My ulcer," John explained. We slept in the local Fresno high school that night. The halls in the high schools are open because the climate is so mild. The janitors came in at six in the morning and woke us up. "Get the hell out, you bastards," the janitors yelled, brandishing their dustpans. Hakamine's feelings were hurt. "The Japanese people are always being thrown out of everyplace," he told me. "Look at the California concentration camps in World War II. Even those niggers think they can tell me where to get off." Mad Dave had a plan to deal with the Negro problem. "What we do is take all the niggers and put them in Arizona. Then we build a wall a thousand feet high and five hundred feet thick around them. Then we drop atom bombs. Later we can cut a gate through the wall and make the place into a national monument." Hakamine told us how Mad Dave got his name. "At first his name was Jerry, but they call him Mad Dave because he is crazy. When Mad Dave was fourteen he went into a sailor's bar and called everybody fags. That's why they call him Mad Dave. Really, he's very weak. The reason he can bend bottle caps is that he has been biting his forefinger for years to get a callus on it." Hakamine took the cap from a Bubble Up

bottle and bent it. It cut all the way into his finger and made him
bleed. "No callus," he said, looking tough.

Before Mad Dave appeared out of the Los Angeles night to
tell us about Krazy Kato, Hakamine, John and I had spent two
weeks in the city, living in the unfurnished apartment with wall-
to-wall carpets. L.A. was big and sprawling, with no downtown,
and there was a bus strike while we were there. The cars lined up
like buffalos standing silently, covering the roads for miles. Everyone wore sunglasses and short sleeve shirts, and all the buildings
were brand new. "A city of the blind," John said, stealing a line
from Frank Lloyd Wright. It was very different from the emptiness of the prairie we had driven through from Denver. The
country had been flat as an open book and we were all alone on
the road, seeing only an occasional Indian wrapped in blankets.
It was 105 degrees, and we were very quiet. Hakamine leaned
over the steering wheel like a racing driver. He smoked his pipe
and wore his hat all the time. He drove like a madman, winding
the old wagon up to 90 miles an hour. John sat clutching the door
handles. We left Las Vegas after only one day. "Think of the
dissipation we're missing," John said, but Hakamine didn't care.
"I have a man to meet," he said enigmatically. That was before I
knew about his knife.

While we were still in Denver, Hakamine had shown John a
picture of a girl. "A nice piece of tail," John commented, making
mental plans to seduce this Japanese girl. "She's in Los Angeles,"
Hakamine said. "If you ever come near her, I'll kill you." John
started to laugh. "Why Hakamine, your friends are my friends.
Share and share alike." Hakamine turned pale and walked away.
Later he showed me the same picture. "The most beautiful girl
in the world," he said defensively, looking at me. She was OK.

It was this girl, according to Mad Dave, who was the cause of
Hakamine's search for Krazy Kato. Dave told us about it while

we were sitting on the beach with the dead grunion. "Diane is Hakamine's great all-time chick," Dave explained. "Everytime he thinks of her, he gets a hard-on. But, she loves Kato's cock and follows him everywhere he goes. Hakamine thinks that if he beats Kato, who is the King of the Yellow Peril gang on the east side, Diane will give him a big kiss." He started to laugh. We sat around the dead ashes of the fire, thinking about Hakamine. Talking about girls made John horny.

HILTON OBENZINGER

Four Poems

1

I will move
you should have curtains
above
my lungs
where will it be Havana, Pittsburgh
whose
recommendation
are you anyway
I could choose
without decisiveness a rug
we have more fun
today
in the factory
you know by name
or I will move the chair
your hair
is so kinky like the world
whose intricate
lassos
and the delicate
you take oboe
players into the snow
bank
my back
I am an antelope

the radiator
before
I move the soap

2

Its own
this
watch the boulevard
the blue of
work societies
I feel sad
all right I understand
now
you think news is
something you should
shower in the middle
of curtains
perhaps amputate
the clear
because the woods are you
warmer
we judge juice
only by the content
honors
if I could be a cantaloupe
am I silly
to say such things
against the warehouse
this radium
without the door there is
no rose
as if Demeter

3

And if
the tree
an unmarked bus
are you
down in my last quarter
who is
this
with
the welding system
the lip
is a muscle
I see
the black Archway cookie
the barge wavers
as if the theory of life insurance
my stomach
why should things
happen
this pocket is so smooth
with
the wish
as if are you
in the cow
the auction
I take each plate

4

That
in the package
comeback

he is before
debate
as an old custom
you design
you look in the daylight
the community
which grows
how petition
grains arrive to begin
this is probably wrong
we'll die
the ring
never leaves
the rare movie
together
I'll remember this anyway when
the loaves
you blouse
is such nice material between
the latch
which
way in the book
as if ginger ale
the will
to distract
and the embassy where

Prologue to My Brains

Ah well, I walk out into the road all fancied up.
I must admit I feel fine. But, you see,
A statement of this sort is misleading.
To say, "I feel fine" is to assume
That a missing link looms in that feeling.
Ideally, one should liquidate that missing link.
I went by the white picket fence. Less
Than a day in Paradise. Already I feel
The common light of the celestials around me.
I asked an angel, the prettiest that ever wore
Blonde hair, "Is there a cafe nearby, my Angel?"
He answered, "Down the road two miles.
The waitress there, I know her. She is very sweet.
I am sure she will want to take
A photograph of you. You are probably
The first boy with long hair she's ever seen."
In the restaurant, listening to *C. C. Rider*
On the juke box, I remembered that it was
Exactly two years previous that I wrote the song.
The prim waitress squeezed the shutter,
And my first impulse was to cover up what
I was thinking about. The Bighorn Mountains
Came up on the clouds. What fresh Wyoming air!
But let me return to what I was discussing earlier.
Too many people in the world fill up their time
Doing evil things. When I write
Sometimes I find it hard to assume their roles.
Surely I am an evildoer too. Where did I spend
Those 7 hours? I spent them in
Hollywood with you. Then I climbed
Up with my friends the breezy California coast.

"Mrs. Bodampa, tell your child to play
By his own house." How many times have you
Heard that when you were a child?
How tedious that type of thinking is, after all.
We are all evildoers. It is unreasonable
And proper to hate each other.
And we should, if that's what we really do.
I would like to sit awhile, looking at you,
And talk about all the tiresome things we do.
Well, that is what we heard on top of the cliff.
Alan furiously began taking the hill apart.
He threw chunks into the raging Pacific waters.
His curly black hair made sparks rubbing against
His anger as he threw them. But I don't mean
That anything disturbing was meant by this gesture.
I am sure Alan felt the friendship we all had right there.
And how it would last for years.
He was moving with the rocks and the trees
And the daffodil under the rock.
We all picked up rocks and threw them overboard
Until we disappeared on top of our rock.
Precious minutes and we would be gone!
And we should, if that's what we really do.

The Dry Saint

Today he sleeps in a large bed,
A fresh-air sleeper winter and summer.

There is also a nice moment
When he meets his all-female family-to-be.

Yes, you have a very white hand
Under his chin, the sunken part of Europe.

Then he hails a taxi
In order to touch Europe with water.

He went in on both sides,
Too stung with men who don't change.

The Dick

Pick up your dick:
The dick.
Look at the dick: he has a skin.
The dick: what is he doing, that he does not die?
What is he waiting for, that he does not die?
How few of us are left, how few.
Even the dick,
Wistfully hoping, who is it?
The dick is a human being.

Bright Lights! Big City!

Every animalcule of the sun
In the fields and plantations
Of Mind lights our body wheels;
The broken glass
Hammered by Aeolian spikes
As well glances back
At the Zoo of Light
And trumpets forth
Melodious steaks
To the lions and bears.
Industry rushes
Like a Traveler
Late to the airport,
Disintegrating as he nears.
This Traveler too
Illumines the Flesh
And with his fingers
Turns the switch which turns
His Hammock of Night
Into the Dynamo.
Such did the Atoms
Distil on his Head
The Light from the open window.
And to their tasks
Enchanted Millions
Trudge onto the Floor
Of the Airy Tent
And there dissolve.
      Oh, Impenetrable Wanderer, stay!

Hoo-Kah

I done di
and I done da
I done jist about everytin
and when I got a ding

to do

I do is must thinkin about what you do
and da is no yoke, baby
Mehly a expression of lotsa hate
put aboard a boat for de banana o Panama

what dey brings back whay's up yo sleeve
Putting dem airs on, natcha?

DAVID ANDERSON

The Oil Murders

I dreamed at night I would love the Oil Lady, a dream returning often enough that she seemed at last to have a familiar character. Her skin was black so that the shapes of her body were
visible only reflected out of the light of the moon. Her skin was
slippery and in the morning I would wash it off my hands, when
it always reminded me of crime. Her blackness, which was like
liquidity in the dark, made her confidence more possessed than
that of the real visitors I might be sleeping beside at that moment
(or they might be gone). She signaled by a movement in the
area near her curving arm. I understood that the window was
to remain open, as though when we were finished she would not
have the strength to open it herself. When she was ready she
pulled her lips back from her black teeth: they always confused
me. She always spoke to me although I never heard what she
said. Her hair pooled in the lower part of the bed.

Real women became confused with the Lady in my dreams,
or I felt I owed them less, so that when I woke up (the phone was
ringing), it was morning and I was too dazed to answer. The
woman's stains were still damp. They flowed toward borders.
I got over them and went outside, and followed her footprints
until they left the angle of the house—probably less than an hour
before. They stepped off toward the dunes: I had imagined that
the Oil Lady lived someplace distinct.

I rang my knuckle against a beam: then eased my shoulder
into it. The sun had begun to free the sand and a haze of them
stirred against what was still visible of the Eastern main. The
pipe was eroded and broken, its opening appeared to my view

as the emptiness of a ragged vessel, as if the pipe had been completed then attacked along its extension through the city. Irregular
cylinders rolled and *gnawed* against each other, in the wind
across the city, pushed away from their joints by the men and
the stiffening automobiles and the time since the pipe had been
promising: each section having two mouths foundering in the
street drawing their own peculiar shadows from the sun. But this
opening, a hundred feet from the westernmost beam of my house,
was the end of the pipe, as near as it had gotten to its connector
in Central City.

The phone was ringing.

I lifted my hands to feel the air around my nostrils, and went
inside to pick up the phone. Harriman told me that there had
been a murder.

"Hello?"

"Work. Do you suppose you could answer the phone more
lively?"

"Yes?"

Harriman's voice seemed to be separate from the receiver.

"A murder, the photographs are here. I don't know."

"I'll be down," I told him.

On the floor, alongside the bed, a reproduction of the window
seemed to be made of smoke. A breeze came from the desert
through the window and vanished into the dimensions of the
room: I looked at the opposite wall for traces of it. Papers pasted
on this wall hung in the air.

The city had been collected on the surface of the desert. Its
position looked arbitrary in the distances of sand. It seemed that
any wind would scatter the city from its place.

The air was drawn up through the atmosphere by the sunrise.
The buildings hung from their wires. Men had come to the desert
to mine the oil that had been discovered there: an emergency in
warfare had made oil valuable. They had dug wells and laid

out pipes along trenches dug in the most efficient directions. The entire area from the edge of the forest to the dunes two miles north was punctured and shifting over scattered equipment and metal huts of the searching crews. Then, at night, the searchers returned to find that the city was larger.

The original buildings in the city were one-story structures because it was impossible to make foundations in the sand. Planks were gathered in the forests and nailed together along the lengths of the main pipelines. The buildings were arrayed beside the pipes.

Since the men came from the West, the pipes were closer to the western side of the forming street.

When a second deposit of oil was discovered in the dunes the people became more willful. Additional stories were balanced on the *wood*. It was difficult to realize their size because of the purity of the sky. Messengers were sent away.

We lost touch with the government. Someone killed the men in the hills when they fell out of sight. The women were sent into the desert because of the danger. No one had ever documented the mysterious killers.

I remembered waiting for my first visit.

I thought that there were always two women, who left before dawn. One left signs: stains and tracks. The other was more immediate, I awaited her when I was awake, she had *disappeared*. I expected to see her behind the city as I drove through.

The crews went to the forest for wood to repair the buildings. Sometimes they stole in the dunes the women kept, had forbidden to us, for intricate webs of house support like mirages to be exposed across the desert. There was often the scrape and sharp sound of a building falling. If I wanted to commit a murder I would be simple, call my victim into one of the buildings the maintenance crews hadn't reached and pray for wind. But it was hot, I prayed Wind often enough anyway, and sometimes it arrived.

The main and its subsidiaries stretched into the distance: they gave the illusion of wholeness. Men bent under the clarity of the buildings.

Harriman was behind his desk watching the desert through the window. The panes cast an incoherent pattern onto the texture of his face. He held a thick photograph diagonally below the shaft of the incoming rays. These rays seemed to expose the air of the room. Harriman turned to me a moment after I had come in.

"Well," he said. "Here it is."

I accepted the first photograph: pure gray, grained, with one dark spot stained in the center: sand with some wet shape soaked into it.

"What is it? Blood?"

Harriman slipped the other pictures to the desk top and sat down. The surface of the desk was intricate but well defined. The reflection of the sunlight was like a layer inside the photographs. It seemed to have been revealed.

"They're labeled," Harriman said. "Chops and pieces, a rag of flesh folded into its insides here. Whatever women's parts are named."

The photographs were not in order. The murderer had either surprised his victim outside of her door or pulled her out: there were no traces inside the hut. He had gutted her six feet from the door and *borne* what had not dropped there thirty paces to drop into a well. In some pictures, the dust had already shifted into something. The room inside the hut was a single woman's, a border of wild food and old iron of the well diggers around a circle for sleeping. Her moving in sleep had dried and twisted off layers of the dust, in the circle, so that pale colors of it floated over paler, like dreams.

A white childish puff in the upper left hand corner seemed to be an imperfection in the print.

It wasn't our mystery.

"A woman," I repeated.

"I don't know, it's hard. One of the crews found her."

"They'll be angry," I said. "We can't touch this."

Harriman said nothing. His lips were deeply embedded in his face. Harriman's features seemed to be covered by an overflow of skin downwards from his forehead. He pressed his index finger to the corner of his eye and it closed.

"Why shouldn't she be recognized?" I asked.

There seemed to be no reason for anyone in the city to want to kill a woman. They came too suddenly and left secretly, there was no place for *motivation*. Because of the privacy the women maintained, I didn't think a man could locate his victim among them. In any case, the mutilation would have been unnecessary if it had been intended to hide the woman's identity from us.

It occurred to me that the woman was made singular only by her involvement in the construction of our case. Still, they watched their land, so that even a random killing would be difficult.

I wanted to discourage Harriman.

Harriman said: "It was done to keep the women from recognizing her, or else it was insane. The murderer might have been afraid that the other women could connect him with her. That would mean a motive too, whatever. Still, it was more likely another woman: they might have been bitter, the personalities distinguishable by the group. What do they do?"

The savagery of the killing suggested that the murderer might have been mad and thus our guesses, which were all attempts to duplicate the murderer's choices, beside the point. This was why we didn't immediately discard the idea of the murderer's having been a citizen.

"All right," I said. "We weren't supposed to find her."

"What do we do?" Harriman asked.

"Up to you," I said. "I was once offered your job."

As Harriman turned around in front of the window different parts of his clothing flashed. A ruler waved in one hand in and out of the light.

"The problem is, should we solve it? If it is a woman, and if we can. How can we approach them, what'll they do? If they find out we were there."

I watched him over the broken clock atop his desk.

"All right," he resigned toward the window. "First round the doctors. See if you can find out anything about the woman who lived in that hut. Find out if, just by chance, she wasn't known with a citizen. If that doesn't work, we'll figure. That's it."

I smiled again and stood up angry.

The doctors stood in front of their records shaking their heads. There were five doctors in the city. Besides having their private practices, they were paid by the City Fund to treat the women in the duncs: we accused them of claiming payments for more treatments than they had actually given. We had misrepresented our purposes to them in order to gain access to their records, so they *distrusted* us.

Our convictions, without the corroboration of the women, were always equivocal.

Some of the doctors collected souvenirs from the earlier days of the city. Others underwrote life insurance.

A swath of the old man's bone had appeared through the skin of the old man's nostril. He sat in front of his safety box.

It wasn't worth breaking open the *steel*.

"No," he said. "I haven't made any calls to that location. Not recently. They move around so much, maybe a year ago would do you no good."

I advanced my chair until my arm was lying next to the silver on the table.

"A year?" I repeated.

"At least," he replied. He waved his head in the air. "It won't do you any good. I'm being honest."

Outside, I took the medallioned coin from my pocket. It was old, government issued, stamped over with the name "Groves." I let it drop through the sunlight and the shadow of the house into the darker sand beneath the beams.

Interviewing the doctors was hopeless, it was a stall. Harriman seemed to be hoping that, by a lucky chance, we would be able to solve the murder without going to the women. The murderer would have to be a citizen. Since there were no clues in the photographs which would implicate a man, and since we could not return to the woman's hut without the risk of being discovered there, the man would have to confess. I was wasting gasoline.

I thought of the killer burying his clothes and his bloodied weapon under some unclear place in the desert.

Harriman was afraid that if he went to the women he would arouse them. The women's civilization existed only in the line separating them from ours. At the same time, I knew that Harriman wanted to see them. He wanted to extend the range of the city's justice so that it would include the women. Harriman imagined himself breaking into history.

Harriman thought of the situation as an opportunity to display bravery. He would have to tell the women that the work crews had trespassed in their sanctuary: he would probably have to tell them that it was done often. The situation had never happened before. It was subtle. *We didn't know what the women felt after we fell asleep.* They might want revenge: it was possible that the murder we were investigating had been committed popularly by the women.

So I was angry when I arrived at the last doctor's house at dusk.

The colors of the sun intruded upon the city as its heat withdrew through the shadows of the sun's dust. Houses seemed to transform after the day, they filled up their colors and traded with the softer air. Two automobiles had been abandoned behind the house.

The house was expensively kept. The splinters on the door had been varnished into a new surface. When no one answered my knock, I went inside.

Thomas was one of the doctors who sold insurance.

For a moment the room was very cool to me. I surmised that the curtains over the western windows had been open for the morning and closed after noon, when the eastern curtains had been opened to admit what light was least directly connected with heat. A desk in the center of the living room was brown wood topped with glass. All the drawers were locked.

The other rooms were more elementally arranged. There was a sense of establishment of space.

I went back to the living room. Each line of the walls was emphasized with a device. A stethoscope was suspended from a hook at the junction of the north and east walls. It seemed to radiate the sun and the blue of the walls from its shine. I unscrewed the two halves of the stainless disc of the stethoscope and removed the diaphragm from between them.

A brilliant cylinder mounted between two windows of the eastern wall paralleled the horizontal of the ceiling.

I fussed with the desk locks for a while and then took a meal from the kitchen and sat down to wait. The doctor returned after the room had stopped gleaming: my eyes had grown sensitive in the dark. I watched him as he stepped to his desk and pulled the lamp toward him. I thought he scraped his foot against one of the desk drawers. The flash of his match blinded me momentarily, when I regained my sight he was grinning at me.

The light from the lamp seemed to be adhering to the walls.

Doctor Thomas flattened one palm on top of the desk and leaned away from it.

"Are you a thief?" he asked. He nodded toward the knife and fork which converged on my plate.

Doctor Thomas seemed to me to be too big: I had imagined public servants to be small men. It seemed that if he moved his body the room would retreat from it. I watched his palms cast over half the desk. In that light, they seemed to have no veins. His hair was a fringe of light; it was gray and white.

I picked up the fork and spun it in front of my eyes.

"There's been a murder committed," I told him.

"Every day, I suppose." He seemed to be speaking from far behind his face and controlling his expression mechanically. He pulled his hands back off the desk and fed them out toward the drawers.

"Put it this way, then. Have you done anything wrong?"

"Certainly," he said. As he spoke he *tested* the drawers.

"Where were you last night?"

"Here," he said.

"Alone?"

I was irritated by the doctor's distraction. He seemed to be listening to the grains of sand falling from the ceiling.

"No," he said. "There was a woman. Name? Name? I don't know, they come and they go. They seem always to be stealing something. My imagination has always been: outside—the desert —the woman squatting to extract the mucous for something private."

"Let me describe the murder to you," I said. I stood up. "The murderer was waiting for the woman to return. He was watching with one eye and one was in the shade of her hut's arch. His stomach was unsettled because he confused it with the woman's. The horizon was clear so that he knew that sounds would still exist behind it if he wasn't careful to stop her scream. She came fast. The murderer leaped out, dizzy, with his left arm straight out in front to push into her mouth while with his right he pushed the point of the iron into her stomach. She didn't scream but he wasn't surprised. But there was a scraping sound when her weight shifted around the axis of the iron. Then he lost his head."

Thomas's mouth moved oddly past his words. "A woman was murdered," he said. "I suppose you know what you're doing."

I understood how Thomas could sell insurance. The arrangement of his house and the settlement of age behind his features indicated that he was prepared for a *future calamity*. He seemed to be concealing it in his eyes.

Men bought insurance because they thought it committed events during which they might be unconscious without loss. It extended their dreams.

Thomas went to the door and opened it.

My car stalled on the way back to my house; I had to get out and twist the engine before it would start again. There was no one in the street. Those who weren't with the crews were waiting for the women. Breezes blew through their windows.

I stopped at the gas station to fill up for the next day. The station itself seemed to be very stark, so that the stars were points far away from it. The support beams touched the ground without pressing on it. They were geometric collisions crowded between the box and the plane. Between the building and the stars was a third gold plane.

The pumps were fifteen feet in front of the glowing face of the building. Each jagged metal edge had been polished, so that the attendant might cut himself on them if he was inattentive. He came from the door and moved through the air between these silver edges and the mysterious building.

When I got home, I threw the diaphragm away. It disappeared a couple of feet above the ground.

I dialed Harriman and waited some time for him to answer.

"What did you expect?" I told him.

I heard his breath.

"Forget it," I told him.

"I can't," he replied. "It's murder."

"Stop," I said. "It's not your problem. It's outside the city, it's their problem. You don't have any authority—you don't even have a *right* to go in. Look, if you don't leave alone someday we might not be so glad to see the women coming. Brave man."

"Listen," he said. "If you thought you could have done my job better, you should have taken it when it was offered."

There was a howl in the connection: I wondered about the unknown place gathered around the distance between speakers.

"All right," he said. "If the killer was a man, he's ours. It won't make much difference. We turn him out to the forest and they get him anyway. So I'll admit it won't make much difference. If it was a woman, you're right, there's not much. But suppose nobody gets him. *They might not even know about it.* If we don't talk to the women now—it can happen again and again. We're exposed."

"Go to the directors," I warned him. "I'm tired of your hobby."

"If they find her they'll know we were there," Harriman said. "It's too late."

I broke the call. I watched the redness expand behind my wrist as I opened the north window. The directions between my pores momentarily interested me.

I always imagined the mysterious killers and the women lying down with open mouth, so that images of the moon's circle stayed in their throats, was in my dream when the woman came to wake me. The room was vibrating, swelling, and I didn't want to go.

She retreated to the window and shivered across her body.

I noticed the form of the hand which rested on her skin then rose: she touched her lips, came toward the bed, she whispered over my head. Her shoulder slipped from my wrist. I fell asleep.

When I woke up again there were two women in the room walking in a dance. I realized that both of them might have been there before, although I had identified only one. I couldn't understand what they were doing. One woman stepped forward and asked me clearly to go with her.

"All right."

Two of us went through the window. One woman remained in the house.

I went because I thought I was still asleep.

The desert was clean, its dust settled by the exhalation of the moon. Its texture stretched over its depth. All of the shapes of the horizon were visible, the sky continued below them. There was no tension in the sky: it seemed to fit exactly over the area of the world.

When I looked back, I could see straight across the city. The buildings seemed to be standing up.

The woman was ten yards ahead, waiting on the top of a dune, and when I reached her I saw the other women seated on the ground. There was nothing to do.

Twenty paces behind and to the left of the seated women was a metal hut with a semicircular roof: its shadow distended toward us. A small window was like a hole in the front of it. The face of the hut and its shadow, together, looked like a jaw. Over the seated women I saw two more women, each one holding the hand of a young boy. They seemed to be harder. There was an imperfection in the ground behind and to the right of the group of women. I knew that this was the well into which the murdered woman had been thrown.

When the women stood up their limbs flashed over each other upwards like birds. I counted seventeen individuals. They began to walk toward the hut.

The simplicity of the area defined by the two groups of women and the hut and well, gave me a sense of *scene*.

The woman's face was sharp so that when she spoke her skin seemed to be deflected by her bones. The crescents of her cheeks repeated the crescents of her eyes.

"One of our women has been killed," she said.

The first two women came out of the hut. One was carrying a metal rod and the other a hairbrush. The others were entering the hut, bringing things out and across the square to where they cast them in the well.

All of the women had red hair.

"Do you know what her name was?" I asked.

The woman shrugged. Skin funneled from her shoulders running into the fall between her breasts.

"What can you tell about her?"

For a moment I saw her as a profile against the sky. She stretched her fingers apart to place a tip on each nipple. "Nothing," she said. "We watched the police. That's all we know."

I wanted to ask more.

A woman came out of the hut with her hands empty.

One of the women opposite us began to walk her child toward the hut. The women who had stepped away dropped their arms. They seemed to be *expressionless*. Flames appeared inside the hut and the woman came out. She walked to the center of the field and knelt. The second boy raised an arm, shadows raced across his fingers. The light twisted on his face.

"You burn our sons," I said.

The woman shook her head and gestured toward the struggling boy. She tucked three fingers into her crotch and laughed. A drop of sweat spun out of her mouth.

I turned to the fire: it attracted things to itself: and turned away again. All of the women seemed to be sliding under redness. For the first time, I noticed how the desert had opened up the woman's face.

"Why?" I asked.

"We need your help."

I thought she was bleeding.

She sent me back alone, directing me over the flatlands which moved under my feet as the sun rose. The visit had made me aware of the end of the city. Once I noticed the gauze on the buildings. The distant levels of the desert lost their texture, they seemed to be feeding light to the sky. A wind blew down between the earth and the sky.

The other woman had left my house. When I looked back to the dunes, the heat had already pulled them above the horizon. I fell asleep.

When I woke up the wind had settled. The phone was ringing. I imagined the phone to be a dead bulk.

Harriman was calling. He named an address in the center of the city and I dressed and went outside. I wetted my hands before I touched the car door. My shirt filled up with water.

Once while driving into the city, I was afraid that if I hit a dry weed it would capture the engine.

From the opening of the street I could see the interval through which the gas station had collapsed. I let my eyes race through it. A bright shield shimmered into the space. As I drew closer, the site was momentarily concealed behind the surrounding buildings.

Three men were climbing over a pile of nails and timber. They bent down, scraping their palms through the material. The planks seemed to have been suddenly discovered there: they seemed to be independent. I walked around the heap, trying to gauge its height. I tried to position my arm so that it was parallel to the ground.

On the beams a base of red gave into a lighter brown crusted with black circles erupting through gold.

Harriman was behind the pile, holding an iron box in front of his stomach.

"Harriman," I said. "I see you have something to occupy you now."

"What," he said.

"Did you go to the directors?"

I didn't want Harriman to go to the dunes because I felt that I had been chosen by the women.

"They said to wait," Harriman complained. "Now it looks like I go again. I told you so. We might have stopped this."

"They told you not to go," I said. "I don't understand."

The iron box dropped out of my sight. The weight of it, when Harriman relaxed his arm, pulled his arm through an arc suggested by his shoulder. Harriman's eyebrows ran across his eyes. I thought he was puzzled. He *took in* my expression.

"The beams were dug away, and the wind: the house fell in—"

"I saw," I told him.

"Did you know anything about the attendant?" Harriman asked. "Gordon."

"He was quiet," I said. "He seemed to guard his door."

"Did you know he had a boy here?"

I realized that Gordon's silence had reflected his pride.

"Small things," Harriman said. "Gordon might have killed the woman. Perhaps the child was his son. They took it back and they killed him. Apparently the child was here for a long time."

Harriman waited for something from me.

"Fine," I said. "Full circle."

"Sure," said Harriman. "If the women are satisfied we certainly ought to be. But what if they're not? Where are the other boys?"

"I understand that the women didn't do it," I told him.

Harriman shrugged. "Good. If you think you can solve it some other way: I'd be impressed. Without going to the women. I think I'd have to surrender my job, to the better man who could do that."

"What else do you know?" I asked.

"The man was ordinary," Harriman said. "He worked his pumps and cheated on his budget. He was insured."

"Who insured him?" I asked.

"Thomas, the doctor."

He grinned.

"All right," I said. "I have to do it."

Harriman moved his leg in the direction of the pumps. It was getting later, the sun glorified his chest. I expected to see past his throat.

"I'm going to the directors tonight," he said. "Before then, fine. We'll find the neighbors, check on the insurance."

"I'll see Thomas," I said. "Let me. *Can I do it?*"

"Until tonight," Harriman said. "I'm sorry. But we have to get them to tell us things. Things aren't going to get any more dangerous than they are now. Because if the women did this, they already know."

"All right," I said.

Harriman tapped his chest. "Be careful," he said.

My car had faded from the street.

I went to Groves first. He told me that he had treated the woman against measles a year before. He went out of the room. My hand was touching a device.

The bronze cylinder fit into my palm. Chevrons alternated around the circumference at the bottom and just beneath the silver disc mounted on top: its side etched completely around with lines parallel to the height of the cylinder. A group of parts, wheel, a tip of string standing out of a hollow silver mound, were arranged on the disc. A silver hood closed over them.

"Put it down," Groves said. "I've got a revolver."

I set it down and turned to face him. My hands were in the open.

"Why?" I asked.

I thought that Thomas had committed both murders. Having noticed on a visit to the dunes that "Jane" was pregnant and living separate from the other women, he had later returned to kidnap the child from her: every man wanted a son. Thomas entrusted the stolen child to Gordon in return for insuring him, because he thought himself to be too likely a suspect to the women. Perhaps she had not reported the kidnapping to the other women because the loss represented a failure in her responsibilities as guardian. Ashamed, she had searched by herself. Two nights before she had found her son at Gordon's house. Gordon had seen her and reported to Thomas, who killed her that night when she returned to the dunes. He had mutilated her body because he didn't know that she had not told the other women about the kidnapping: perhaps he felt he had a right to the child. My visit the next day had frightened him because he didn't think the police would become involved. He had lost his nerve and killed Gordon, who was the only other witness in the city. Perhaps he thought the women would never find out. Or, perhaps they would think that Gordon had taken the child and died by accident.

It seemed to me ironic that Gordon had been killed by the man who insured him.

I realized that it would be difficult to prove a case against Thomas if I was correct. I would have, instead, to use what evidence I could gather to goad him to an *overt act.*

I left Groves and drove to Thomas' house. The city was tumbling into evening, the evening seemed fat.

Thomas opened the door. His features were ready to attach themselves to his face. They were poised to express motion. Four fingers were secured on the corner of the door.

I went in. The walls seemed to be held without gravity, the body of the furniture had gone into the surfaces. The tension of gravity had been replaced by some softer exchange between the objects. Next to the chair I had sat in the night before were my knife and fork. I put them into my pocket.

Thomas was foreshortened behind the desk. He looked like a construction of varicolored parts.

"Do you know a woman named 'Jane'?" I asked.

"Ridiculous," he said.

I smiled. "How's your insurance?"

Expressions replaced each other on the front of the doctor's face.

"I'm not insured," he said.

"I mean the business," I told him.

Thomas bent down behind his desk. All of the light that came into the window went into a few things: distances were uneven. The lines of things flashed between each other. I remembered the shape of the fork in order to grasp it in my pocket. Thomas passed a folded paper to me, Gordon's insurance policy. He brought up a revolver and set it on the glass.

"It lapsed last month," he said. "On the margin."

"It looks forged."

The doctor's mouth stretched. "It is," he said.

Thomas dipped a nail behind the shadow of the revolver. The gun was like a splendid machine on the desk.

Thomas held up his arms. "I stayed here," he said. "After you left."

"All right," I said. I left him alone.

I imagined the city flooded with oil. A wave of black jolted the buildings. There were bulges in the surface contracting over the city. It became a mirage at night. Fixtures on the ceiling became coated with oil. It lingered off the front of buildings like tassels. I tossed the knife and fork into it.

I met Harriman in the restaurant. He was telling me that a woman had been seen outside the gas station two nights before, but that Gordon had not opened for the women for a year. No one had seen the child.

I imagined the confused infant spreading his arms in the desert.

Harriman stopped. "It's nothing," he said. "It's lousy, I know."

"Fine," I told him.

A strange look came to Harriman's face from *somewhere else.* "I can't help it," he explained.

He pressed his index finger to the corner of his eye and it closed.

Harriman seemed to be pleased when I said something.

From far off the woman and I seemed to be two figures standing apart. She shed some of her paleness down from the air. The woman told me about Jane. She had not told the women about her child.

I loved the woman. Her legs like round swells of sand fell under my hips.

When I looked back the woman was standing alone in the center of my vision.

When I got back to Thomas' house it was empty. I walked through it without molesting its precision. I climbed out the west window: it took no effort. Sixty feet away there was an oil drum.

A bullet went into the wall of the house. I realized that I had heard a shot.

There were no *signs* in the sand around me.

"What did you find out?" Thomas shouted.

I had found out enough. He had stolen the son and given it to Gordon. The woman had found it, he had gone to the woman's ground and killed her. He had lost his nerve and killed Gordon.

I told him: he fired again.

I fired three bullets into the drum. I fancied that I could see the bullets. Flames exploded and fell back to the drum. I had a momentary sensation of depth. Thomas didn't reappear.

I hated that bastard.

DAVID LEHMAN

Watermelon Season

Today I'm in Paris
        and believe in the sky of Paris
                the rows of organized flowers
I will buy your face in a store
        and believe in it
My soul is a happy clown, eating dinner
                        I believe in dinner
The earth is paper
        I believe in the earth
                I believe in my hands
They are crayons
                and because of the sun
    They are drunk
                        driving into Barbizon, France
As the rest of me tries to escape my feet
        which always manage to follow
Hello! I'm lost, suddenly, unquestionably
And it's no different from London or New York
                I do believe that
                        after all
Today is just like any other day
        only not the same, says Heraclitus
You don't walk into the same day twice
    you can push against it
                be very deliberate, stay in one
                    mediocre place for hours
    your feet as swift as a tree, a poplar even

but you don't stay back
           you survive
What Peter Kennard calls "the fun city survival kit"
             your body, two flowers,
                 a big "hello!" and some orange juice
           you survive
You don't walk into the same day twice
               the syntax is impossible
And besides it just won't work
                   I've tried
Even the clouds are blue in Paris
   and the airplanes, they can't do it
This couch is as bloody as the sky
           is drunk with you on it
              and none of you can do it
And your blanket is on the floor, on the street
   even the streets are drunk in Paris—
                    I believe it—
       but even so they can't do it
I will paint them green like snow
             and a whole icebox of colors
Where Millet and Corot lived
           they couldn't do it

A Journey to the Vital Center

That morning I forgot the American language
(Quite different, you know, from the English of England)
And Europe was flying to meet me, you were leaving
The plane was crashing—O
The misery is so perfect that I could die now! I said

Willingly, but reconsidering, realized at once
The unalterable truth: that though perhaps allergic to reality
I am in really no mood to give up the ghost.
And then I did.
  In a rush, descending into the depths
Of the wild chocolate unknown. I never liked chocolate much,
And it was hell flying around that mess. For a while
I was the lone survivor of thermonuclear war,
When Americans no longer had the luxuries
Of a washing machine. There was nothing to be
President of anymore, not much sense
In protest either. Time was quickly abolished
Since there was no one to be measured against.
The sunset was violet as the night, because
I called it that.
  What was yellow?
Orange and green mixed together, like the achievement
Of buttercups and the sun, all in one. Not bad.
Not like a kid who was yellow as a banana if he was afraid.
Bellies had been yellow then, as were chickens, but no more.

There was one subway left
Between Grenoble, France and the first of the Swiss alps
And I rode it often—
I never walked on this particular land because suddenly
I considered it a temple
For all I knew it may have been Friday the 13th,
1968 and now I'm not superstitious or anything
But what with fallout, dust, garbage cans,
Dead bodies, lack of paper and writing utensils
And all the other symptoms of this new reality
I think I will pray now, I thought
For you, subject of this poem, Jeannie, heaven, and sleep

In a way this was the beginning of religion
I was proud of my invention, but where were you?
I'd always thought of you God as a white rock
In the picture of spring, and then
You'd be gone.
      Now and always.
In my heart I wanted to converse with you at leisure
I wanted you to point out the Vietnamese War
Dead to me and show how they differed
From the older dead of World War II
Perhaps they'd have marks on their forehead
I wanted you to point to the floating heads
Of hell, I was sure I'd find Richard Nixon
There, and the cop who beat me last spring at Columbia
Oh, definitely, you'd be there Mrs. Curoti
For throwing us out of our hotel room in London, and
I anticipated weeping at seeing the killers of Socrates
And Robert F. Kennedy, the moustache of Adolf Hitler
Which I was sure would be pasted against the craggy toilet
Wall, maybe General Motors Dow Chemical
The war in Vietnam Mayor Daley the idea of slush
On the city's snow streets anti-Semitism sadness
The blight of the neighborhoods newspaper scandals racism
And the bad films of Hollywood would all be lying there,
Carrion men groaning for burial!
      But all was silent.
The only rumble was the rumble of the earth
As I crawled on it, and up the ladder, on the highway
Of the dark machine, and on, climbing
The spiral staircase to heaven, passing purgatory on the way.
A disturbed soul finally got friendly, and called to me.
He was blonde haired but wore a black moustache.
He spoke in confidential terms and we smoked a cigarette

In silent camaraderie. All we had left was a willingness to die,
He said, and you still have yours. Hold onto it.
Just that moment, before another word could be said
A casual group filed past on a Cook's tour,
Their ruddy faces cheery with excitement,
Their loud shirts and focused cameras impervious
To the distracting moans. This was promising:
I left my unfortunate soul, and tagged along.
In the distance a neon sign seemed to welcome
Our coming. "Good God," I said, hoping
"Have I made it there at last?" But it was only Dante.
He and Virgil were propping the sign on Beatrice's shoulders.
"Beware the bomb," it said. "It ends all, it begins all."
"What bomb?" I asked myself, grinning
When in came the wind. "The black bomb," he answered,
And walked away.   The angelic orders were next.
The black angel was an American. He had been to hell
Many times, he said. His girl was just coming down
On an LSD trip. "I'm discovering the life of words,"
She said. "Rimbaud, he was right.
The alphabet is a stock market of colors.
But I know more. Apples, you see, are breasts . . ."
And she gave me a great idea for a poem.
I was exalted, predicting what a fine poem
There would be: The Life of Words.
"This is truly heaven," I told the angel
Who had wrestled with Jacob. But he rested his hand
Sadly on my shoulder. "Don't get married," he advised.
"I wouldn't advise it."
                    But for this fatherly note
I was waiting for you, God. I was waiting for the heroism
Of your somber note. I was waiting, earnestly I was

For you to point to the ocean in the fine faraway night
To paint a new ocean, if need be, and say—
                    "The vineyard is wailing.
                    Look at the wailing vineyard."
If I had my way, and enough paper, time, and pencil
You'd create the greatest verse of the new universe
I am about to construct, and your instructive discourses
Would be most inspiring.
                              But where were you?
Hanging at the edge of that craggy rock,
I stared; a note of urgency crept into my throat
And out into the world:

                    Listen God, I love you (I screamed)
                    You're a great guy and all that stuff
                    But I just wish you'd explain one thing to me,
                    Just one—
                              Why do sinners' ways prosper?
And why does disappointment all my pious endeavors
At finding you end?
                    Oh, I know that only Moses knew you
Face-to-face, but your back, your feet, anything,
A word would be more than sufficient—

And a shot of light shook the cavern
To its deepest foundations. I got up
And wiped the dust off my brown baggy suit.

    He said, "Shalom," which I remembered from Hebrew School
    To mean "hello," "peace," and "goodbye."
        And then he was gone again.

All evening long I'd been tracing your shadow
Behind my door and down the hallway
And then deeper, past smaller houses, then larger ones

Into lazy pockets of earth
Halfway down this corridor of night, past countries
In chains, on trains, just to reach conclusions
About its possible owner, you, dark gypsy shadow
In this harbor
Of sudden light.
        And here, who knows with whom I was talking.

Back again. And so, minus one ghost, I keep on going
I'll just have to do without you ghost, I decided,
Not that I have eight more left, but—who knows?

And the sun welcomes me back with smoke
Narcissus S. Grant welcomes me with the mirror of the military
        past
The "well" of the night has been completed with "come" as
New York gives me a welcome farewell from the myths of reality
Ed Goltz smiles "you're welcome" for the clever thanks
        I planted in his beer and
There is a welcome sigh of relief on this airplane
        from Philadelphia to Cleveland
        which has finally begun to move
Thus dispelling the welcome sign my brain had implied
        to the fantasy of air crash
Where oxygen masks would be most welcome
My radio alarm is about to welcome my presence into
        its next musical day
And though I've recently found it almost impossible to breathe
I've always saved my last welcome for you, air

Welcome! Welcome night! Welcome stars!
Welcome tears! Return, O eyes, and soak in the milky stars!

There were bears, buckets, a nest of kisses, lions, and twins,
        up in the stars.

PAUL SPIKE

The Diary of Noel Wells

(Noel Wells wrote this section of her diary while living as a guest in the mansion of fabulous capitalist Thaddeus Mace, whose son Philip she had recently agreed to marry. The Mace estate is the largest private estate in the Bahamas. Thaddeus Mace, and recently his son Philip, have in addition to their great financial holdings long been noted for their selfless service in behalf of the United States Government.)

Depressed, depressed, depressed. I've been down in the dumps ever since Philip left for Africa. The life around here is really stagnant. Philip arranged for me to have my own car and driver on call at all times so I wouldn't have to deal with the whale, which is what I call his mother. She is really too much. She is a member of about fifteen million clubs and spends all her time talking to various club members on the phone. These are clubs in New York and San Francisco and Washington and long distance calls.

Philip wouldn't tell me exactly what kind of oil deal he was going to make in Africa, in fact he didn't even mention oil but I imagine that is what the deal is about because before he left his father kept briefing him on all these different men who operated in the oil "game" as Mr. Mace calls it. He was going to the Congo and on his way back he says he will probably have to stop in both Miami and La Paz, Bolivia. He said he might not be back for six weeks.

Have I explained to you about Philip's guns? He wears these two pistols in holsters under his suit jacket. They are very dark blue and in the sun they are enormously impressive. He wears

them because he is very rich and says that many people are jealous
of his position and might try and take revenge on him for being
richer than they are. I guess that's a pretty good reason. I know
that I feel safer being with him because he has the guns. I asked
him if he had ever killed anybody and he said he had killed seven
men. I asked him who and he said that they had all been maniacs
out to hurt either him or his father. I guess life as a Mace will be
very exciting if not always typical.

I don't do much of anything. I am starting to write poetry after
having talked so much about it with Manda. I showed her this
poem I wrote about a scene I saw when Chris and I visited Guate-
mala last month. It was pretty short:

> The horses run rakes in long fields
> Of night here in Guatemala, the girls
> Dance on the seeds hoping for yields
> And after dark the boys caress their curls
>
> Peasant father and peasant mother
> How glad to finish the days trip
> Their faces are like voyages to another
> Time to healthy appetite and tight grip
>
> Lizards creep out of the barns
> The ox is off in heavenly sleep
> While grandma the socks darns
> And the dog brings home the sheep.

I guess it isn't exactly great but Manda seemed to really like it.
The title is "Lizards Creep Out." Philip thinks it is really silly
writing poetry because nobody buys it anymore. He said that if I
wanted to write he could get me a job writing the news scripts

for the local Nassau television station which is part of Mace Com-
munications. There is one guy here, his name is Wally Norton,
and he is the main news broadcaster. In fact, he is the second best
in the country after Durlon Dean who is the stateside commenta-
tor at 7 o'clock. They keep Wally Norton here because he is
Thaddeus Mace's favorite broadcaster and the only television
show that he will watch is Wally Norton's Scoop On the World
which is on at six thirty here.

I've begun to worry about what ever became of Alex Washer,
the boy who I went with all through Jefferson. Alex had the
blondest hair I've ever seen on a boy and big blue eyes and a tiny
perked up nose that was adorable. He had a blue T-bird that was
blown and stroked and with tons of chrome. I mean, it was all so
high school. But you know I get these nostalgia rushes. I just
lay down for hours and start to go back over things that happened
years ago and it's really beautiful, like actually living your youth
over again. I mean, at least we can never have them take our
memories away from us even if we have to get old and lose the
freedom of high school.

Alex was the first boy I ever slept with. He was also the second
boy I ever kissed with tongue and mouth open. We really grew
up a lot together, educated each other. I was remembering the
Prom, the Junior, the other night and how it had been with Doris
Taylor and her date Paul Imperiales and me and Alex all at the
same table. The theme was "Wild West" and the gym looked
just like that show Comanche Trail that is now off the air I
think. Paul and Doris brought this bottle of gin in Doris's raincoat. That was strictly not allowed. We would have been expelled
from Jefferson if they had caught us with that. Now, it's really
funny how you get when you're in your twenties, I'm already
twenty-four, it's like a dream. But it just occurred to me how
stupid we have been to have taken those chances just for a little
thrill. I didn't even like to drink and I don't think Alex really did

or the others. But I mean we just had to be so impressive and big for the others, you know. It's funny, the teachers were right not to trust us. We were irresponsible kids. That night I made the Court, as one of the Prom Queen's torch guardians and I was really happy even though I expected to. I knew I would make at least that but not the Queen itself. I was not that popular and Cathy Flinch was sure to take it. From what I understand, that night she really took it because her date got sick and puked all over her dress which had cost something like a hundred and fifty dollars in Boston. She deserved it actually, her and her Cape Cod "cocktail parties" all summer, to hear her tell it.

Alex, Alex I wonder where you are tonight. Out there in the darkness of this night. My memories take control of me for a moment and I imagine once more being back with you in the car out on the Bluff. I miss you and wonder where you are.

The whale just came through and said that Mr. Mace had told her that he might have some word from Philip tonight at dinner. I hope so. I guess I can bear another silent dinner here even though lately I've begun taking them downtown or out at Cole's Island with Manda or some of the other people out there.

Alex once took me to this motel in Connecticut for two nights and all we did was make love and I peeled these green grapes, huge juicies, and then put them in my mouth and kissed him and transferred the grape into his mouth by squirting. He thought it was really erotic! I loved to do that. Maybe when Philip gets back I'll do that with him.

Mr. Mace has heard from Philip and said that all was well in the Congo and that he might be able to stop back over here for a quick visit before going on to Bolivia in three weeks or so.

Today I got up early and ran downstairs and it was a beautiful day so I called up this girl named Melonie Warburton and asked her if she wanted to go sailing and we agreed to meet at the club in an hour. So we got there and the first five minutes out of the dock a storm came up and we sat on the island for the entire day. I had to spend the rest of the day and night reading.

Manda and I had lunch at Pinochio's and then went to the little "scotch" beach. We were sunning and talking about art and also rock music when these two men appeared out of nowhere. One was Swedish and the other was from Finland. The Swedish man was not what you would expect. He had dark hair and skin and was sort of hairy and chunky, not at all a Viking type. But he explained that he was part of the Swedish people descended from invasion of Serbian or Slovakian or something! type of people. He was very nice though and his name was Rudy. We talked, the four of us, for a long time about the Island's particular style of living and the foreigners' impressions of it. Then, Manda and the Finnish man, who was very tan and tall, went for a long swim.

Rudy and I lay there on the beach and watched them. And we kept talking about things like his country and New York and topless bathing suits. And then we entered into this sort of up-tight phase, a thing in which you sort of run out of words and just lay there and stare at your toes. This phase, in my experience, usually means you're both thinking about S—E—X, invariably. I knew that I would have to tell Rudy when the time came if it did, that I was engaged and not interested in any little extracurricular fun and games. I was thinking this when suddenly Rudy just as naturally, as matter of factly, as if there was nothing at all out of the ordinary in his actions, reached with his left hand right on my crotch. And he squeezed really gently and said, "This feels good and soft, I like to touch you there. You don't mind?" and then he kissed me and I was really surprised to find that I liked it. Anyway, he got his hand all the way into my pants and was really going at it and I kept thinking, Why don't you stop him? Yet I knew I really didn't want to. I mean, I sort of did not like it and found it very scary but more of me seemed to just melt

under his fingers and I almost passed out there. My head went
back on the spread and I had this image of his dark fingers going
in and out of my hole and felt them curl down and then up into
the muscle of my womb. Oh, Philip I probably could never explain to you how I felt, how confused I was.

Fortunately, Manda and the Finnish man came back from their
swim afterwards. He had tried to pull my pants off altogether but
at this point I absolutely refused. My God, I was so embarrassed.
Manda acted as if she knew nothing at all but I was sure she
knew exactly what had been going on. After all, the beach in that
hot sun is not exactly a place to hide something, I mean a normal
lover's lane or anything. Rudy acted quite relaxed as if nothing
had happened and I am afraid I must have been blushing something awful. Well, we stayed and talked about little things for
another hour though my heart wasn't in it at all. I was terribly
confused about what had happened. I mean, Philip so far away
in such an unpleasant place as Africa and me his fiancée not even
able to be faithful to him for a whole month. I kept thinking that
maybe Chris had been right when he once called me a "mature
baby" and said that I had a lot of growing to do yet even if I already knew a lot of things. To allow Rudy to paw me out in
public like that had been absolutely immature. Thank God when
Manda said she had to get to her painting lesson so we could
leave the beach and part with these Nordic men. As I left Rudy
I gave him a friendly good-bye though I must say not a very
enthusiastic one and he grabbed my arm and held it. I tried to
pull away but he wouldn't let go and Manda and Lars were up
ahead already saying goodbye so they didn't see how rude he was.
He said, "You'll see me again won't you." It wasn't even a
question!

I told him to please let go of my arm and that I regretted very
much what had happened on the beach because I was engaged
already to someone else and very much in love. I asked him to

respect my reputation and try not and brag about what he had gotten down on the beach from me. He still had a hold on my right forearm. So I tried to rip my arm free and then he let go and he laughed and said, "Being engaged is nothing. I'll see you soon." And then he winked and tried to kiss my cheek. I almost broke into tears because I had no effect on him, he was determined to try and see me again.

When I asked Manda if she had seen what had happened on the beach between Rudy and myself she said of course, and she said, "You're lucky. He's quite a hulk isn't he." I was shocked by her total amorality as she knew I was engaged to Philip. But then I realized that she played around so much that she probably expected everybody else to be just like her. Manda is getting old, at least she has to put on a lot of make-up and liner and I feel she is just as hostile to me as she is friendly because of my younger complexion. At first I thought she was really exciting but now I find I cannot respect her. At least, not as much as at first.

When I got home I felt so bad I slept through dinner and then Ramon one of the Mace servants came up with a nice tray of fruit compote and sherbet. After I ate this I went back to sleep. The next day I got up early and decided to take a hike out on the Mace ranchero, which is what they call this peninsula of the island that they own and which is used half as a vegetable farm and half as a radar tracking station and a small base of soldiers which is mostly underground. It is a great place for a hike since they have marked out special hiking trails for the Mace guests to follow and every mile there is a little pavilion rest area with a water fountain and picnic table. Also the trees are labeled like in botanical gardens and sometimes ponds have little markers that tell you what the various kinds of birds around the water are and the water bugs and the lilies. I set out with Carol, a secretary to the Mace family and a friendly companion. Mrs. Mace never lets me do anything alone. If I'm not going to be with friends she makes sure one of the secretaries goes with me. This can be a big pain but I was glad on that day because I really didn't feel like being alone. The thing with Rudy had gotten to me.

In any case, we hiked and then had a picnic down by a completely deserted beach which was lovely. You would have never known that there was civilization near by except that this Army helicopter kept hovering around at all times. They keep the peninsula very well guarded. Carol started talking about this yacht trip she had taken all over the Bahamas a few summers before and it was very interesting because she had been with this Venezuelan businessman and his party and they had thrown the wealthiest parties she had ever been to. She had had an affair with one of this businessman's sons, a boy named Enrique. He had been sort of crazy and kept talking of philosophy of science and something else which I forget which completely impressed Carol. She kept saying, "He knew all about the philosophy of science. The philosophy of science." He had been a student at some college in New York State, a Catholic school. Anyway, Carol told me this long story of the trip including how Enrique got drunk and wanted to fight a duel with the captain of the boat who was named Captain Page but how the Captain had been forced to go chicken in fear of Enrique's father's money. And then this boy Enrique had claimed that the man had lost all his honor so he was now the captain of the ship. Then the captain got angry and was going to fight the duel and then Enrique's father got angry, he was very drunk, and pulled out his wallet and offered Page one hundred thousand dollars for his ship and Page had to accept because the ship was only worth about seventy thousand. And then when he had accepted the money the father punched him very hard and knocked him out and then they all went back below while somebody carried the Captain to his cabin. After that, Enrique was in charge and he got them lost and they had to call the Coast Guard to come and tow them into Miami.

We got back from the hike around four and I took a nap.

I was walking into this dress shop downtown when I felt this tap on the back of my neck and I turned around and almost jumped a mile. It was Rudy. He was wearing these short shorts and blue sneakers and this red and white striped polo shirt which I thought was extremely loud. He kissed me on the cheek before I could duck and then asked me to come to lunch. It was three days since the "episode."

I should have slapped him. I guess I didn't because I felt so embarrassed at seeing him. I could still feel his rough fingers on my vagina.

I absolutely refused to have lunch with him. So then he insisted that I go for a drink with him. I told him absolutely N—O! Then he said he was not going to leave me until I accepted his offer. I said he had better or else I would call the police. He laughed. Anyway, I went into the shop to try and avoid him but he waited outside even after an hour of trying on dresses. Then I went to the Hotel Creole Victorian and tried to escape him by having a facial but there was a long line and then I tried calling a friend who had a suite in the hotel but she wasn't in. And then I tried walking down Mace Street but he wouldn't give up, all the while he was right at my side with this confidence that you wouldn't believe! So finally, I guess it was inevitable really, I had to give in and go for one drink in order to ditch him. He took me to this place called the Maserati Pit. It was this little bar in a wood building that was frequented by racing fans and owned by an ex-race car driver. He ordered me a banana daiquiri without even asking me and a Gin Rickey for himself. I asked him why he was so rude as to order me a drink without even asking me what my preference was. He said that banana daiquiris were his little aphrodisiac and I ought to at least allow him a fighting chance in his struggle with my virginity. I laughed and said that my "virginity" was not really very important anymore but that my honor was and that I was engaged and that just by sitting in a bar alone with him I was disgracing myself and my fiancée. He was really conceited and paid absolutely no attention.

He had this way of smiling that was so goddamned self-confident I felt like kicking him.

Anyway, eventually I decided my best strategy was to keep absolutely quiet and pay no attention to him. But then he started talking about his childhood in Sweden and about how in the winters they had gone on these skiing trips all over Sweden, Norway and Finland. He described these trips as very gay times with boys and girls sleeping together and switching partners every night and pranks like playing naked soccer in the snow on some hilltop north of the Arctic Circle. And then he started telling me about how he had once been engaged. She had been an orphan from Stockholm, he was from a small town in the middle of Sweden and they had gone together for three years. And then she had died of cancer. It had been cancer of the liver, something really rare. He told me about his fiancée as if he was just telling any old story, almost as if he had a philosophy that when things went wrong you should try and bury your feelings in action, that feelings and action were not the same thing at all. So I asked him if weeping wasn't both a feeling and an action and he said that it was usually just a surrender to emotion and not a real action. So then I asked him what kind of action he had taken when his fiancée had died. He smiled very slightly but didn't say anything. I pressed him on it and he said that I would probably be shocked. I asked him why, if he had gone out and slept with another girl right away or what. Then he said that no, he had gone homosexual for two years. I'll say he shocked me! Not that I have anything against homosexuals at all but this Rudy certainly hadn't been acting like one with me down on the beach or then this afternoon. He said that he had fallen in love with another man and that for two years they had lived together and then one day he had decided that he wanted to end the affair. Then he had gone back to being a heterosexual. I asked him if he ever thought of going back to homosexual sex and he said no.

So this bit of surprise had the effect of opening me up to a conversation with him. Before I had always thought of this man as part of the incident on the beach and suddenly I was listening to his most intimate secrets. It was funny because now that I think of it I realize what a good technique Rudy had in making me receptive to his seductions. By telling me intimate secrets he made me unconsciously start telling him some of my own inner thoughts. Like suddenly I was talking to him at that stupid bar about things that Philip and I had never discussed and probably never would because they just were not the kind of things we would ever discuss. For instance, I started in telling this stranger all about my thing with Chris from the very beginning up to the punch that he gave Philip. And I guess that was a real mistake. Rudy was a very good listener. Actually, he was enormously polite, the first real European man I had ever had anything to do with. It was strange. About forty minutes before I really hated him and suddenly here I was finding him a better conversationalist than the man I was going to marry. I really felt confused.

We talked a lot about my problems then after his confession. Rudy talked about Chris a little and thought that he sounded like an extremely selfish person. I realized that that was it. Chris was so selfish that he could only look on me as an object, he wanted nothing but "success." By success I mean he wanted to get in with the kind of people that I was now in with: Manda and the Maces. He just wanted me as a kind of plaything. That was why I had rejected him in the first place. I must have sensed that long ago but didn't finally realize it until Philip met me at the Thousand Faces reception in the spring. And then when he had asked me to be his guest down here, I understood how little my engagement to Chris meant. Chris was nothing like what I really needed. Rudy was right that afternoon when he said that it sounded like a life with Chris would have been very boring.

I had to leave but then ended up staying and talking to Rudy for about two hours longer than I had expected. So when I went to finally take a cab back to the Maces and he said that he wanted to see me again, I found it impossible to refuse. After all, I had led him on at this point and just couldn't cut him off so cruelly without explaining to him exactly why I felt it was wrong to even have just a talking relationship with another man. I agreed to meet him at this place, the Club Jailai, on Thursday night for a drink.

Carol and I spent the day out on Munson's Isle which is very close to this one. We had lunch at a fantastic luxury hotel there owned by the Maces and then went water skiing in this perfectly smooth lagoon. The water was so blue, it was unbelievably blue and clear and I told the man who took us skiing that I wanted to come back in a few days and try the skin diving there. He had recommended this to us.

The number of rich people there was absolutely amazing. When I say rich I mean really rich—oil millionaires and British people of the aristocracy with titles.

I had this dream about Chris last night that was really weird. I dreamed that I was in this room and wearing my Junior Prom dress which was all white and frilly. Then suddenly, I don't remember what exactly I had been doing but it was something like wringing out a washrag or a towel or something, I looked up from my seat at the window. Chris was standing in the window with his arms straight out at either side and his legs straight and together. It was like he was the crossed panes which separate windows into four smaller squares. I thought this was very interesting and I got up to look closer at him. Then he laughed at me and I asked him why. "Because I'm the window pane and that's symbolic like the pickle dish." Now I remember that the pickle dish was some kind of symbol I studied in high school somewhere in one of my classes. It's funny. Anyway, that was the end of my dream because I remember as I was waking up that I felt glad that he was the window because it might rain in on me and soak my new dress and he was protecting me.

Dreams are funny. I spent the day with Manda, but I didn't tell her about my date with Rudy. I've got to get ready for that now.

Sometimes it is even hard to write something because you are afraid that you will read it later and realize how stupid what you wrote was compared to what really happened. I'm not sure that makes much sense but it doesn't matter I suppose. I guess I should feel ashamed. But what good would that do? One part of me wants to confess everything to somebody here and then get out and go back to New York. Another part of me is perfectly content to repeat what happened all over again. And then another part of me just wishes Philip would hurry up and get home.

I saw Rudy this afternoon and he wants me to meet him at the club which Cole owns. I am not sure if I did the right thing but I said yes and planned on standing him up. Which is what I am going to do. He looked so goddamned smug and confident.

Yet, that's not fair either because he was so gentle and sensitive. In fact, I have never known a man who depended so much on how the woman felt not just on how he was feeling. I think European men are very very different from Americans.

Decided to go to the great lagoon on Munson's Isle again with Carol and do the skin diving which the man promised us was so great there. I did not meet Rudy at El Gitano so imagine that's that. And that is definitely for the best. Ramon drove us to the airport so we could take a helicopter to the island rather than the speed boat. I think Ramon is about the most handsome man on the island. He is very brown but it is a chocolate brown and not dark bittersweet-chocolate type. He says he is married and has five children which is amazing as he looks about twenty-five years old.

Skin diving was lovely. Except for all the water I kept swallowing. It is impossible to describe what it is like underwater in words. I mean, it is like entering another world. There was one really frightening thing which was this fish with a gigantic mouth which was all brown and huge, HUGE! it must have weighed five hundred pounds. This I found extremely frightening because I have never been close to another living creature so much bigger than myself unless it was at the zoo where the animals are kept behind bars, naturally. Also especially interesting were these fish colored a beautiful blue, royal blue. They kept whizzing along the reef at steady paces as if they were on rails or something. I think they are called parrot fish. I was glad no sharks came around. Ha!

Later, on the beach, Carol and I had this argument with a Spanish count about which was better athletically, the U.S.A. or Europe. It was really hysterical because neither Carol and I knew too much about any sports and we had to defend stuff like American football, which is I think soccer. He did admit though that Americans were the best basketball players in the world but claimed that this was because no other countries played basketball. I knew this was absolutely untrue. They had the greatest drinks at this cafe there, the bartender invents a new kind of cooler or punch just about once a week. Carol told me he was world-famous and had been featured in an advertisement in many magazines for some kind of whiskey. I had not seen it.

Got back to the house and took a long hot bath and then had a

drink on the terrace. Mrs. Mace came up and invited me to go to
the casino with Mr. Mace and these guests who own some kind
of company that manufactures liquid transistors or something. I
agreed to go. This really surprised Mrs. Mace because I usually
refuse these invitations. But tonight I felt in an especially cheerful
mood. We had dinner which was very good—roast turtle, my first
taste of that delicacy imported from the Yucatan. There is an
island there which Mr. Mace owns, though it is unofficial. He
keeps these giant pens of sea turtles there and a breeding station.
It is one of the few islands, according to him, where sea turtles
will lay their eggs.

After dinner Mr. Mace was feeling especially good so he decided to drive to the Casino in the horse carriage which is très
elégant. He has these two big white coach horses to pull it and
they are kept in a special barn out in back. They have a lot of
saddle horses, used I guess for the annual hunt of the Nassau
Hunt Club, but they are kept out on the peninsula where the
radar station and the vegetable farm is.

The Casino was fun for about three minutes. I was given about
two hundred dollars by Mrs. Mace to play with. She wanted me
to play roulette but I hate that game because you lose so fast. So
I played blackjack and found myself winning a little and then
losing a little. It was like that all night. I think I ended up with
about five or six dollars profit when I finally decided to quit.
Mr. Mace and his guest, a Mr. Calliano, went to a private room
for some kind of big money card game or something. Mrs. Mace
lost some money at roulette and then went into the night club
section to watch the show with Mrs. Calliano. I was really bored
and should never have gone.

The next day I decided to write a letter to Mom. I haven't
written to her in two months and am sure she wonders what has
happened to her "little girl Noel."

Today I realized how gigantically bored I am. Have been ever since Philip left for the Congo. Oh, Philip I wish you would hurry back. It's not fair to leave me like this during our "courtship" or whatever it is officially.

I think I am really mad at Philip. Went golfing with Carol and a guy named Mory Welt-Cottingham the Third. Get that. He is a fantastic golfer and a snob. Who wouldn't be with that name. At night we took motorbikes around the island; Carol, Mory, me and a fellow named Randy Hoff.

Mrs. Mace says she is worried about me because I seemed bored. She told me she is going to tell Mr. Mace to tell Philip he had better return soon. Otherwise, she said, I may become so unhappy I'll start taking a "lover." I cringed when I thought of Rudy. Thank God that's done. I am a silly idiot and more immature than Chris realized.

I have been thinking about a funny idea which occurred to me. It's about making decisions. I mean I realized how important it is to make decisions and not delay them. This has always been my biggest problem because I just let things slide but never come to a conclusion about my real feelings. For example, with Chris I went with him for over a year even though I didn't really love him that much. I just refused to make the decision not to see him anymore. It took Philip's invitation to his home to make me make a decision. Now that sounds complicated maybe, but I think it's a piece of real personal philosophy. It's the problem which has gotten me into the most trouble I think. Today I went skin diving again. I really like it underwater, it's so soothing because it's such another world. So silent.

Mrs. Mace thinks she may have to have an operation. She is flying to Boston to have tests.

At breakfast, I was reading the paper when Mr. Mace came

in. He never has breakfast with me because he always is up by at least five-thirty in the morning to have his own breakfast, do laps in the pool and begin work. I think he is a good friend of the President. I heard Ramon say that to one of his friends in Spanish the other day on the way downtown.

Anyway, he stopped and told me that he might have a surprise for me soon. I hope that means Philip.

Today it was overcast so I read and then went for a drive, then called a friend in New York. The Maces don't mind my making long-distance calls I found out. Finally I had to resort to watching television and went to bed early.

Carol and I went to a flamenco show downtown tonight. It was all right but the most interesting thing was this couple I saw. The girl was very tall and beautiful, she was Japanese. Her eyelashes were incredibly long and I don't think they were fake. The man was like a Viking god: tall, blonde, with a great build. He was wearing a white shirt, ordinary, and a pair of black leather jeans which were skin tight. She had on a dress that you could see right through, think she must have been wearing a body stocking.

Have been trying the new policy of making all my decisions right away and not putting them off. Like I told Manda immediately that I did not want to go to a party with her tonight whereas before I probably would have said, "I'll call you back later." Then ended up going even though I felt like going to this Spanish thing.

Mrs. Mace is in Boston.

Saw the couple, the Japanese and the Viking, out at Cole's Island. I don't know why they fascinate me so but they really do.

Mrs. Mace called and said that I was to use her appointment at the beauty parlor if I wanted it. I think I will because it is fantastic and I haven't been to one in years. Wait till Philip sees me

with a new hair-do. I hope he'll like it—though I don't know if
I'll even like it. Brenda Esterbank is having a party tonight.

Mrs. Mace arrived back today and said she was going to have
the operation in the fall. It's some weird thing to do with her
glands in her neck. I think it's her weight. It must be, she is such
a whale.

Philip came back at noon! I am so HAPPY! He's going to be
here for only two nights before going on to South America for a
week and then home for good. But two nights is enough!

We took the cabin cruiser out alone for the night. It was so
beautiful out there on the Caribbean. Philip is a fantastic captain.
In the afternoon he showed me how to deep-sea fish but I didn't
catch a thing. He caught two sharks. Yuk.

I can't tell you how romantic it is to be on your own yacht,
with champagne on ice and steaks and a good sailor and a good
lover. Because Philip is the greatest lover anyone could ever ask
for. Anyone, anywhere. I know it.

In the morning we went swimming and then sailed back. It
was really memorable—something words won't do any justice
to. I am sad now though because in about ten minutes I'll have
to go downstairs and drive Philip off to the airport. I wish he
didn't have to go. I don't know if I can stand another miserable
week alone after such a great two nights and the boat trip.

Today I did nothing but swim and read. I miss Philip. A lot.
I am also mad at him. Very mad.

One thing I don't understand. Last night as we were driving
to the airport he said something strange. He said, "By the way,
the grabby guy is dead." I asked him what he meant. The second
he said it I thought of Rudy because of the way he had grabbed
me. I asked him what he meant but he wouldn't say anything

else. Maybe he meant Chris. I don't know what he meant. I
started wondering and I think I'm going to ask him when he
gets back if he has killed anybody else since he told me he had
killed seven men. That would be terrible, it would be murder
if he had killed Rudy. He didn't deserve to die because of what
he did to me. Though maybe he just died.

Carol and I went to a party at some new discotheque tonight
and it was pretty bad. The food was good though. They had the
best canapes I've ever seen and they tasted as good as they looked.

I got a letter from my mother. She had nothing to say. Just a
bunch of news about a lot of people she thinks I remember but
I don't. Oh, she enclosed some notice of engagement from a girl
who was in my class: Cassie Evans. She is engaged to some guy
from New Haven.

It was a beautiful day so I went to the beach with Manda. We
met some interesting people from Mexico. The guys were awfully
pushy though. As usual, Manda went off with one of them for a
swim and I was left with this other eager playboy type. However,
I used my new policy of making decisions right away.

This evening, I read and then watched television. I miss Philip
a lot. Mr. Mace is in Washington. Mrs. Mace is worried about the
operation.

Facts About the Authors

DAVID ANDERSON was born in Schenectady, New York in 1947 and graduated Columbia College in 1969. He was associate editor of the *Review*. Police have repeatedly reorganized his face in the course of class war.

TED BERRIGAN was born in 1934 in Providence, Rhode Island, received in 1959 a B.A. from University of Tulsa. He edits *C Magazine*. His books include *The Sonnets, Many Happy Returns,* and *Bean Spasms,* collaborations with Ron Padgett.

Artist JOE BRAINARD has had three shows at the Landau-Alan gallery in New York. He is editor of *C Comics* and publisher of Boke Press books.

KEITH COHEN was born in Quantico, Virginia in 1945. He graduated Columbia College in 1967, was a Woodrow Wilson fellow, 1967-1968, and is presently a graduate student in comparative literature at Princeton. His works have appeared in *Art and Literature, Paris Review,* and an anthology, *The Young American Writers.*

JONATHAN COTT is 26 and lives in London completing a Fulbright fellowship. He was an editor of *Review*, 1962-1963. His essays have appeared in *The Young American Writers* and *On Contemporary Literature,* and his poems in many magazines and the anthology *Young American Poets.* He writes for *Rolling Stone* magazine.

ARNOLD EGGERS, born in San Francisco in 1945, received his B.A. from Columbia in 1967, is currently a student at Columbia's College of Physicians and Surgeons.

ALAN FELDMAN, 24, is presently a graduate student in American literature at Columbia. He was *Review* editor in 1964-1965, and was awarded a *Saturday Review*-National Students Association prize for the best short story in a college literary magazine in 1965. He was a teacher. He is married.

AARON FOGEL, *Review* editor in his junior year, graduated Columbia in 1967. A Kellet fellowship sent him to Cambridge, England. His works have appeared in *First Issue, Art and Literature,* and *The Young American Writers* anthology.

Born July 3, 1941 in Massachusetts, DICK GALLUP attended Columbia's School of General Studies. He has published *Hinges,* a book of poems, and *The Bingo,* a play, and his works have appeared in *C Magazine, Poetry, Mother, Paris Review,* and other magazines. He is married and has two kids.

LESLIE GOTTESMAN, 24, born in Portland, Oregon, graduated Columbia College in 1968 and received his M.A. the following year. Big fucking deal. He was editor of the *Review*, 1967-1968. His works have appeared in *C Magazine* and *The World*.

DAVID LEHMAN was born in New York in 1948. Educated at Yeshiva and Stuyvesant High School. Currently a Columbia senior and poetry editor of *Review*: His poems have appeared in *Paris Review*, *Poetry*, *Bones*, and the *Yale Literary Magazine*.

"Free lance derelict, song-writer, and jet set bohemian" CHARLES LINDHOLM graduated Columbia in 1968. He received an Evans fellowship to travel. Is traveling. For years he worked at WBAI writing news.

PHILLIP LOPATE graduated in 1964. He has worked for the poverty program, edited poetry anthologies, and ghost-written for famous stupid people. He was chairman of Alumni for a New Columbia. Philip Llopate is 26.

HILTON OBENZINGER graduated in 1969. With Alan Senauke he edited *Review*, 1968-1969. He has had one poem in *Paris Review*. One.

RON PADGETT was born in Tulsa, Oklahoma in 1942 and graduated Columbia College in 1964. He was associate editor of the *Review*. He won the Gotham Book Mart's avant-garde poetry award in 1964 and a Fulbright to Paris, 1965-1966. He has published *Bean Spasms*, collaborations with Ted Berrigan; *The Poet Assassinated*, a translation of Apollinaire's novel; *In Advance of the Broken Arm* and *Great Balls of Fire*, poems; and an anthology of New York poets, edited with David Shapiro. He is married and has one kid.

Born in Brooklyn, New York in 1945, EUGENE SCHWARTZ received a B.A. from Columbia in 1967. He lives in a log cabin in Colorado, teaches at Colorado State. He is married.

1968-1969 *Review* editor ALAN SENAUKE now plays lead guitar for the Montgomeries. His poems have appeared in *The World* and *Sundial*. He is 21.

Two books of DAVID SHAPIRO's poems have appeared, *January* and *Poems from Deal*. He was associate editor of *Review*, graduated in 1968, and is a Kellet fellow at Cambridge University.

MITCHELL SISSKIND is a football coach in Chicago. He graduated from Columbia in 1968. His stories have appeared in *Tri-Quarterly*, *Art and Literature*, *Paris Review*, and *The Young American Writers* anthology.

PAUL SPIKE has published articles and stories in the *Paris Review*, *Village Voice*, *Evergreen Review*, and *Penthouse Magazine*. He was a member of the Danforth Foundation's seminar "The Identity of Higher Education," 1968-1969 and is currently editor of the *Review*.

JOHNNY STANTON is superintendent of his building in New York City, is married, has two sons. His stories have appeared in *The World, C Magazine,* and numerous other magazines. Angel Hair Books published his novel, *Slip of the Tongue.*

CHARLES STEIN was born in 1944 in New York City, graduated Columbia in 1966, did graduate work at New York University and Hunter College. He is author of *Provisional Measures* and *The Virgo Poem.* His poetry reviews have appeared in *The Nation.*

TOM VEITCH: "Born in Tulsa, Oklahoma, 1941. Attended Columbia College for a year and a half, became disillusioned with that, moved on to hand-to-hand combat with the world. Still engaged in that struggle and winning. Spent two years in a Benedictine monastery. My favorite color is green. I like to play chess and the ponies. My father was an international drug merchant who was strangled to death last summer by the mafia, or possibly the CIA. Working on an imaginary biography of Grayson Kirk." Veitch's works have appeared in *C Magazine, Lines, Fuck You, Kulchur, Art and Literature, Paris Review, Spice, Adventures in Poetry, Angel Hair, The World, Reindeer, San Francisco Earthquake, The Young American Writers* anthology, *The World Anthology,* and *Acid,* an anthology in German.

LARRY WIEDER graduated Columbia in 1968, spent time in Jamaica, and is currently a creative writing student at Cornell University, where he also teaches. His poems have appeared in the *Paris Review.*

BRITT WILKIE: "Codes modulated—collective blips—movie director—general attempts to organize form / in such a way / as to prevent the familiar pulse show from dissolving in flack of heat and light / other interests like flowers, lapels, old furniture—indefinite affect charge—variable symbol." Wilkie did covers for 1968-1969 *Reviews* and for this book.